BLAKE AND YEATS: THE CONTRARY VISION

Blake and Yeats: The Contrary Vision

HAZARD ADAMS

NEW YORK / RUSSELL & RUSSELL

CORNELL STUDIES IN ENGLISH

VOLUME XL

To E. E. Bostetter

who pushed and pulled

Preface to the Second Printing

It is perhaps best for the author to leave completely alone a book published over thirteen years before. Doubtless many of his ideas have changed, and his whole approach to the subject would be different were he to write the book again. In my case the situation is complicated, because in the thirteen years since *Blake and Yeats* appeared I have published several articles on Yeats and a large book on Blake. I discover that in these later efforts I have managed to present more clearly, at least to myself, a number of matters dealt with in *Blake and Yeats*. For example, I have extended the remarks about *A Vision* (Chapter VII) into an essay considering Yeats's relation to neo-Kantian literary theory. It is called "Symbolism and Yeats's *A Vision*" and may be found in the *Journal of Aesthetics and Art Criticism*, xxii, 4 (Summer 1964), pp. 423-436. Since publishing *Blake and Yeats* I have been particularly concerned with certain dominant modern movements in literary theory and how Blake and Yeats are related to them. The first chapter of this book touches upon this matter when it raises the problem of symbolic forms with respect to Cassirer and Langer, but at the time of writing I was not fully prepared to treat my whole discussion of Blake and Yeats in terms of an identifiable development in critical theory from, say, Kant to Northrop Frye. If I were to begin again, the development of the principle of symbolic forms would be more at the center of my discussion than it was in 1955, when it was lurking on the edges.

Two essays appearing this year provide the theoretical structure that the book doesn't fully express. The first, "Blake and the Postmodern," appears in the festschrift for the distinguished Blake scholar S. Foster Damon. The second, "Yeats, Dialectic and Criticism," appeared in *Criticism* (Summer 1968). The latter essay begins again with the two poems I discuss on pages 141-145 of this book and considers Yeats's debt to a Blakean dialectic and his relation to the dialectic of science and art suggested by Cassirer's *Essay on Man*.

In the meantime my book *William Blake: A Reading of the Shorter Poems* (Seattle: University of Washington Press, 1963) has provided a clarification of Blake's treatment of time as well as extended discussions of Blake's lyrics. I would call the reader's attention particularly to the chapter on "The Tyger," which develops at considerable length the brief discussion on pages 237-241 here, and my long chapter on "The Mental Traveller," which is discussed briefly here on pages 241-243. Two other essays, published elsewhere, are worth mention because they emphasize the Yeatsian dialectic. My "Yeatsian Art and Mathematic Form" (*Centennial Review* IV, 1 (Winter 1960), 70-78) concerns itself with Yeats and symbolic systems or forms, and I mention it even though I am less sure of a part of my reading of "The Statues" than I was when it was published. The other essay is "Some Yeatsian Versions of Comedy" in the Yeats centenary volume *In Excited Reverie* (London: Macmillan, 1965). It deals with matters that are related particularly to the section on gaiety in Chapter IX.

I have mentioned Blake's treatment of time, and it is here that I must offer some remarks clarifying, if possible, a matter that could have been handled in this book in more consistent language than it is. Some of my discussion of Blake and time now seems to me misleading: I speak on page 4 of the possibility for Blake of a "total configuration in time which out of time may be a unity," on page 5 of the idea of the cessation of time, and on page 16 of Los's "apocalyptic vision of a timeless reality." Remarks like this suggest a sort of Platonic timeless reality in Blake where the famous Blakean contraries are resolved or transcended. This now seems to me wrong, though we can easily be misled by Blake's own language on the same point, as in Night the Ninth of the *Four Zoas* where Urizen cries out "Times are ended." Blake's quarrel is not with time (there is really no time that the imagination doesn't somehow make) but with the Urizenic mind that limits time to linear measurement and negates the existence of time lived. Generally when I speak of time in this book one may substitute "measurable time" and read on without confusion. In Blake's apocalypse only the denial or *negation* of lived time ceases to exist; things move back into prolific contrariety: there is "war and hunting in Heaven." My remark on page 40 about harmony in Eden is true only if we know that we are not talking about harmony of stasis but a harmony of contrariety, like the tensions in a work of art.

Blake, then, does not really conceive of the sort of nontemporal, nonspatial superreality of which Yeats seems often, albeit ever so tentatively, to speak. Blake conceives of ultimate reality as ultimate creativity, activity rather than stasis. Instead of working *in* time man makes time work. So Blake does not really make a distinction between time and timelessness, but between a time we struggle in, an enclosure such as Urizen reasons into existence, a spatialized or measurable time, and a time created and converted immediately by work into eternal living truths or imaginative forms. This time is capable of being always "present" to us, as Blake saw Jesus present in the imaginative work of the Bible and we now see Yeats's Crazy Jane present in *Words for Music Perhaps*. If we try to substitute for Jesus some historical Jesus we create what Blake would think of as Antichrist, the Christ contained in linear time rather than the Jesus who makes time meaningful. The same occurs if we evolve Crazy Jane from Yeats's Steinach operation.

Perhaps a useful way to distinguish between Blake and Yeats is by reference to a third position, Kant's. Blake would reject the existence of the unknowable Kantian "things in themselves," not merely our inability to know them. Everything that exists is knowable, vision can be total. Yeats's position is not the same: The Kantian "things in themselves" are apparently not knowable, but Yeats seems to insist that man nevertheless strives to know or formulate them imaginatively, and he fails. Man's problem is that, convinced he is a rational animal, he is constantly smitten by suspicion that the world is irrational. He therefore comes to formulate his reality from contraries: "I cannot discover truth by logic unless that logic serve passion, and only then if the logic be ready to cut its own throat, tear out its own eyes." Blake carries contrariety right into the forms of reality, which are created by man. Adopting a more ironic perspective, Yeats dramatizes man having to accept contrariety in a universe not quite of his making, grudgingly uncertain that it is the real shape of reality, and equally uncertain that it is not. It is from this situation that Yeats spins both tragedy and his peculiar comedy.

This difference between Blake and Yeats suggests that a greater burden of history presses upon Yeats's imagination than upon Blake's. Yeats sees himself in history and struggling to dominate it. He makes of this burden some of his finest poetry and prose. He is not afraid to think himself a child of his times, struggling to dominate history. We do not sense the pressure as strongly in Blake, who casts himself more in the role of the orderer of time and events or the voice through whom these events are divinely arranged. This difference, which must not be thought absolute—it is too roughly put for that—I have sought to express in a number of ways in this book; but fundamentally it is an epistemological difference which Yeats sees as having cultural and historical causes.

Some reviewers of this book argued that I emphasized all the differences at the expense of Yeats and somehow was implying that Yeats failed at Blake's game. (One reviewer, of course, claimed the opposite.) This was certainly not my intention. It would have been, if true, a little like saying that Shakespeare failed because he created so many heroes who failed. Blake and Yeats play out their dramas on different stages: "One law for the lion and the ox is oppression." I was trying to explain a difference of tone and strategy. These two poets do see the world differently, but their visions each have their own integrity and elegance. My intention was to write a book in which, as Blake remarks of Beulah, "contrarieties are equally true."

Finally, a couple of obvious errors ought to be corrected. First, David Erdman's researches show pretty conclusively that the historical allegory in *Europe* can't be referring to the "glorious revolution" in England, as I try to make it on page 80. I do not believe that the error harms the general drift of the argument, however. Second, on pages 61-63 the argument may sometimes mislead. For instance, where I am talking about contrariety of vision I seem to be saying that one side of this doubleness brings truth, the other error. For Blake truth simply isn't achieved except through opposition. If one side completely dominates, then you have a negation rather than a contrariety. Los is, of course, Blake's hero and he is contrary to Urizen. Even though Urizen wishes to negate him, he cannot negate Urizen, because if he does he will negate his own contrariety and bring error out of his own imaginative endeavor. This is why I should not even have intimated on page 63 that the clash of good and evil keeps things going. To label something as evil is always to negate it. Historically good and evil are debased contraries, but, so designated, they cannot be prolific. Reason and energy are the prolific contraries from which the negations good and evil seem to have fallen.

HAZARD ADAMS

Irvine, California
1968

Preface

MY major aim in this book is to bring together and compare Blake's and Yeats's symbolism. After completing the book, I see that it is really only one link in what might be a study of symbolism in the poetry written in English, and perhaps the book can be thought of in this way, though it emphasizes the particular symbolisms of two poets without overtly placing them in a tradition. References to a tradition of poetic language or symbolism are generally those of Blake and Yeats themselves.

The book is not primarily about Blake's influence upon Yeats, though throughout I have mentioned the question of influence and have tried to suggest where influence clearly exists. My attitude toward the question of Blake's influence upon Yeats is, first, that it is not the most important question in a comparison of the two poets and, second, that in many cases Blake's influence can never be sorted out from the influences which played upon both Blake and Yeats.

Yet because the similarities between Blake and Yeats, and Yeats's echoes of Blake, are so striking, I have begun the book with a chapter discussing the obvious relationships and the question of influence. From this chapter I turn to a consideration of Blake's aesthetic theory and to Yeats's interpretation of that theory as it appears in the Ellis-Yeats Quaritch edition of Blake's works. Then, in three chapters, I attempt to review the pattern of Blake's symbolism, with special emphasis upon those symbols Yeats later made his own. In the chapters on Yeats I discuss Yeats's system, having provided the reader with what I hope is an adequate background for the comparison with Blake.

Books on Blake and books on Yeats are numerous, but there is only one book on Blake and Yeats, Margaret Rudd's *Divided Image*, which was published after my own work was well past a first draft. The view of Blake and Yeats which it takes is perhaps not as dissimilar to mine as it may first appear. Miss Rudd deals with Blake and mysticism, and I have tried to steer clear of that term except to call in question its applicability in the comparison between the two poets. Miss Rudd emphasizes spiritual biography. A comparative study emphasizing the poetry is still needed, and this need I have tried to fill.

There are two important shorter studies of Blake and Yeats, Virginia Moore's chapter on Blake's influence in her book on Yeats, *The Unicorn*, and Northrop Frye's essay in the *University of Toronto Quarterly* (October 1947), entitled "Yeats and the Language of Symbolism." Anyone who has read these essays will see that my view of Blake and Yeats more nearly corresponds to Mr. Frye's than to Miss Moore's.

Any student of Blake must be, or should be, influenced by Mr. Frye's *Fearful Symmetry*. Of all the books of its kind on Blake, this study stands out as the best, and I hereby acknowledge my indebtedness to it, not so much in particulars as in the method of looking at Blake which it suggests. Another important book on Blake, David V. Erdman's *Blake: Prophet against Empire*, published in 1954, I was able to see only after my own work was in final form. References to it are limited to one or two explanatory footnotes.

Of the books on Yeats, T. R. Henn's *The Lonely Tower* has influenced me more than my footnotes will show. Mr. Henn makes some interesting suggestions about Blake's influence on

Yeats. Richard Ellmann's recent book, *The Identity of Yeats*, became available to me after my work was in final form. I am pleased to see that we agree that "All Souls' Night" should be defended from Mr. R. P. Blackmur's widely circulated criticism and that the sphere is a much more important image in Yeats's work than has generally been acknowledged. I must, however, disagree with Mr. Ellmann when he argues that Yeats's vortex image is unlike Blake's. My own argument is that the vortex and related images provide a main link between the two poets.

I should like to express my appreciation to those who in one way or another contributed to the completion of this book: Professors E. E. Bostetter (to whom the book is dedicated), Brents Stirling, Malcolm Brown, and Eugene Elliott of the University of Washington; Mr. Bruce R. Park of Cornell University and Mr. James J. Gindin, all of whom read the book in early stages and offered suggestions; Professor Northrop Frye of the University of Toronto, Professor Arthur Mizener of Cornell University, and the members of the Cornell Studies in English committee, who read a late draft and offered suggestions; Mrs. W. B. Yeats, who kindly allowed me to study her husband's manuscripts and library and granted me permission to make quotations both from manuscripts and annotations, including the hitherto unpublished "Michael Robartes Foretells," which appears as Appendix B, and from the published books of W. B. Yeats and *Letters of John Butler Yeats* (1920); Mr. and Mrs. Joseph Hone for various kindnesses while my wife and I were in Dublin, and Mr. Hone for permission to quote from works by him.

Also, I wish to thank the following persons and publishers for granting permission to quote from their books:

Dorothy Wellesley and Oxford University Press for permission to make quotations from *Letters on Poetry from W. B. Yeats to Dorothy Wellesley* (1940).

Oxford University Press and Routledge and Kegan Paul, Ltd., for permission to make quotations from *W. B. Yeats and T. Sturge Moore: Their Correspondence 1901–1937* (1953).

Rupert Hart-Davis, Ltd., and The Macmillan Company of New York for permission to make quotations from *The Letters of W. B. Yeats* (1955).

The Macmillan Company of New York and The Macmillan Company, Ltd., of London for permission to make quotations from the following works of W. B. Yeats (American copyright in parentheses): *The Cutting of an Agate* (1912), *Per Amica Silentia Lunae* (1918), *Four Plays for Dancers* (1921), *Wheels and Butterflies* (1935), *The Ten Principal Upanishads* (1937), *A Vision* (1938), *The Herne's Egg and Other Plays* (1938), *The Collected Poems* (1951), *The Collected Plays* (1952), *The Autobiography* (1953).

T. Werner Laurie, Ltd., for permission to make quotations from the first version of *A Vision* (1925).

Harper and Brothers of New York and London for permission to make quotations from *Language and Myth* by Ernst Cassirer (1946).

Mr. Robert Graves, Faber and Faber, and Farrar, Strauss, and Cudahy for permission to make quotations from *The White Goddess* (copyright 1948 by Robert Graves).

Alfred A. Knopf, Inc., and Allen and Unwin, Ltd., for permission to make quotations from *The Decline of the West* by Oswald Spengler.

The Journal of Aesthetics and Art Criticism for permission to reprint the part of Chapter II which originally was published in somewhat different form in that magazine.

I am grateful to the libraries of the University of Washington, Dublin University, and Cornell University; and to the National Library of Ireland for permission to examine the Yeats collection and to read there.

Finally, I should like to express my deep appreciation to my mother, Mary T. Adams, for criticism and other help; and to my wife, Diana W. Adams, who worked hard and long typing and generally editing the manuscript.

HAZARD ADAMS

Ithaca, New York
June 1955

Contents

BLAKE AND YEATS: THE CONTRARY VISION

May God us keep

From single vision & Newton's sleep!

—WILLIAM BLAKE, to Thomas Butts,
November 22, 1802

If Kant is right the antinomy is in our method of reasoning; but if the Platonists are right may one not think that the antinomy is itself 'constitutive,' and that the consciousness by which we know ourselves and exist is itself irrational?

—W. B. YEATS, to Sturge Moore, June 1928

CHAPTER I

Lineaments and Particulars

For what but eye and ear silence the mind
With the minute particulars of mankind?
—W. B. YEATS [1]*

IN 1917 mysterious "instructors," presumably out of a world very different from our own or—as Blake might have said—very different from what we think our own is like, came to W. B. Yeats with "metaphors for poetry." [2] Yeats himself tells us that during the period of their communication with him the instructors "constantly reproved [him] for vague or confused questions. . . . They shifted ground whenever my interest was at its height, whenever it seemed that the next day must reveal what, as I soon discovered, they were determined to withhold until all was upon paper." [3] Strangely enough, the instructors themselves were frustrated by the slowness of their pupil in the world of time and space, and in their own frustration they doubled his confusion.

A reader of Blake and Yeats is confronted by a world of new dimensions. Having finally entered it, he discovers the great difficulty of returning and writing discursively about it. In a sense he is still in that world, and his efforts to draw his reader to him are frustrated just as the instructors of Yeats were frustrated. Thus,

* Numbered notes appear at the back of the book; they indicate the source of the quotations. Asterisks are used for footnotes.

I begin this book with an apology for what Yeats clearly saw were the present limitations of human understanding. Struggling discursively in time and space, like Blake's Urizen, I know that the symbolic patterns with which I must cope exist in a different kind of time and space—or perhaps ultimately in no time and space at all.

Since this is a study of the symbolical systems of Blake and Yeats, the most important word in this book is "symbol." At the end of Chapter II, when both Blake's aesthetic theory and what Yeats has to say about symbolism and about Blake have been examined, the word will appear in a new light, but it is here that some initial statement about it must be made. It would be easier to explain if, as Susanne K. Langer has pointed out,[4] too many aestheticians had not used the word in too many ways, sometimes defining it, sometimes not. Mrs. Langer, following the lead of the great philosopher of symbolic forms, Ernst Cassirer, does define the word. She writes, "A symbol is any device whereby we are enabled to make an abstraction."[5] Another quotation serves to clarify her words:

A little reflection shows us that, since no experience occurs more than once, so-called "repeated" experiences are really *analogous* occurrences, all fitting a form that was abstracted on the first occasion. *Familiarity* is nothing but the quality of fitting very neatly into the form of a previous experience. I believe our ingrained habit of hypostatizing impressions, of seeing *things* and not sense-data, rests on the fact that we promptly and unconsciously abstract a form from each sensory experience, and use this form to *conceive* the experience as a whole, as a "thing."[6]

Behind these words lies an epistemological problem, and Mrs. Langer's avowed master, Cassirer, explains what epistemology this view of symbolization implies. Cassirer writes:

As compared with other animals man lives not merely in a broader reality; he lives, so to speak, in a new *dimension* of reality. . . . No longer in a merely physical universe, man lives in a symbolic universe. . . . Reason is a very inadequate term with which to comprehend the forms of man's cultural life in all their richness and variety. . . . Hence, instead of defining man as an *animal rationale*, we should define him as an *animal symbolicum*.[7]

A writer on Cassirer, David Bidney, remarks:

For man, all reality is ultimately cultural reality or symbolical reality which the human mind itself has created in the course of historical development, since that is the only kind of reality which it is possible for the human mind to apprehend and evaluate.[8]

Cassirer tried to tell us that it is not possible for us to get behind our symbols to some final reality. Our symbols *are* our reality.

If we return now to Mrs. Langer's short definition, we may well ask just what it is that we are abstracting *from* if we accept Cassirer's assertion that there is no way of knowing what lies beyond our symbols. This is the question Blake asks of all those who use the term "abstraction" and who imply by its use a material reality somewhere out beyond us. We may bypass this question until Chapter II, when Blake tells us what *he* thinks is out there. "Abstraction" in Mrs. Langer's definition is of two kinds. In scientific thought it is generalization which effects further successive generalizations.[9] But in art, says Mrs. Langer, no such intellectual steps are taken. In the evocation of the poetic symbol a whole wealth of analogous experience comes to life in the immediate experience. Blake thought he knew how this happens, and perhaps it is better again to wait until he has had his say, but it must be made clear now that Blake thought that the method of creating the poetic symbol should not be called "abstraction."

Needless to say, I believe that the ideas of Blake and of Yeats about poetic symbolism are very much like those of Cassirer and Langer. Blake would have agreed with Cassirer that the symbolical world is our reality, but his view is importantly different from Cassirer's in two respects. First, Cassirer asserts that the symbolical world is the only reality we can know; Blake asserts that it is the *only reality*. He says that unfortunately, at present, it is a distorted, fallen reality for most of us. Second, while Cassirer posits several symbolic forms by which we intuit the real world —religion, myth, language, science, art—Blake believes there is only one form by which reality can be apprehended. This form is art, which has refined and assimilated to it religion, myth, and language:

A Poet, A Painter, A Musician, An Architect: the Man Or Woman who is not one of these is not a Christian.
  You must leave Fathers & Mothers & Houses & Lands if they stand in the way of Art.
  Prayer is the Study of Art.[10]

The only real symbol is the art symbol, and the artist is a prophet. Science—at least the science Blake knew—is a method which sets up a fictitious world of materiality only because within certain limitations things "work" in such a world.

  Blake substitutes for the conventional materialist processes of identification—measurement of weight, height, etc.—that process of imagination which creates analogy. That analogies can be made, that there are such things as metaphors, suggests that there is some sort of unity in our diverse world; and if our symbolical world is literally the real world, then a metaphor becomes not simply, as we are used to saying, imaginatively true, but literally true—or at least the line between literal and imaginative truth is erased. If a man makes analogies or metaphors, he makes them out of his past experience, and if he sees that one thing now is analogous to something in the past, he has asserted imaginatively that some things are in some way happening more than once, that they return. The more analogies man makes (the more things he finds returning from out of the past), the closer he comes to feeling that things are cyclic, that there is some sort of total configuration in time, which out of time may be a unity. According to Blake, man achieves the greatest imaginative vision when he finally apprehends unity by seeing that all things are analogies of all other things—that the world is a grain of sand, for instance—and by understanding all the steps through which the world must move before man may communally see this vision.

The communal vision is apocalypse, *total resolution* in God, the assertion of reality as a single symbol. When communal vision occurs, time ceases because there is no longer any new analogy to be made with the past. The past has become the present. Blake's poetry was meant to be a complete statement of such a vision from the moment of the bifurcation of thought into the imaginary and the literal to the new achievement of unity yet to occur, the prophecy of which he thought available only in the symbolism of art.

Observed from above, Blake's wheel is similar to Yeats's famous gyre. Conversely, from above, the gyre appears as a wheel shrinking to a point called the vortex, which itself is a central image in both Blake's and Yeats's systems. As more and more analogies are made, as this strange circle shrinks whirling to a point, the world approaches what in Blake's system we may call "apocalypse" and what in Yeats's system we may call that "unity of culture" which he so often associated with his "holy city of Byzantium."

Observed as both wheel and gyre simultaneously, this image illustrates another important Blakean principle, that of the ultimate unity of all divided images. In a circle shrinking as it spins, things opposite on the circumference eventually join one another. Divided images—images of good/evil, body/soul, heaven/hell, etc.—are apparent but unreal. In the circle-gyre, good chases evil and evil chases good until the circle becomes so small that good and evil must embrace and thus assert the unreality of their existence as separate entities. The paradox of the cyclic world is Blake's aphorism, "without contraries is no progression." In this gyring dialectic movement toward apocalypse good *and* evil are cast away as spectral delusions.

Yeats affirmed Blake's principle of the "contraries": "All creation is from conflict, whether, with our own minds or with that of others." [11] Yet from Yeats's point of view there is no progression. Blake believed in progress, not only for any one man but also for Man. But he did not believe that progress would come about through the machinations of "right reason." Instead he thought that it would be achieved as the result of a communal affirmation of faith concurrent with a complete definition of error. In Blake's mythology, as Northrop Frye has pointed out, there are two "narrative structures"—two contraries—at work.[12] The first is the wheel of history. The second is linear progression, guided by poetic prophecy, tenaciously persevering as a link between the fallen and unfallen worlds.

Yeats was fascinated by Blake's wheel image and made it, or something like it, his symbol of symbols. When he had examined Blake's "Mental Traveller," he wrote of its "myth," and he called the myth "the perpetual return of the same thing." [13] Later he spoke of a myth as "one of those statements our nature is compelled to make and employ as truth though there cannot be sufficient evidence." [14] The *order* of Yeats's universe was paradoxically one of eternal conflict. Without conflict, existence as we know it would be impossible.

"When Discord," writes Empedocles, "has fallen into the lowest depths of the vortex"—the extreme bound, not the centre, Burnet points out—"Concord has reached the centre, into it do all things come together so as to be only one, not all at once but gradually from different quarters, and as they come Discord retires to the extreme boundary . . . in proportion as it runs out Concord in a soft immortal boundless stream runs in." And again: "Never will boundless time be emptied of that pair; and they prevail in turn as that circle comes round, and pass away before one another and increase in their appointed turn." It was this Discord or War that Heraclitus called "God of all and Father of all, some it has made gods and some men, some bond and some free," and I recall that Love and War came from the eggs of Leda.[15]

In a sense, then, Blake and Yeats looked at the same world from
different points of view. Yeats focused upon the frustrations of
this world from within this world, and Blake focused upon the
possibilities of this world from a position extremely difficult to
pinpoint anywhere in the delusion we call space. Although
Blake's great influence on Yeats is undeniable, this difference between the two is as important as are the many similarities.

Yet the similarities stand out clearly even for the casual reader
of both poets. Yeats mentions Blake in his letters and prose works
with astonishing frequency. The first appearance of Blake's name
in the *Letters* occurs in a note to Katherine Tynan, written in
1889 during the period when Yeats was at work on the Quaritch
edition of Blake. The last appearance occurs in a letter written to
Ethel Mannin in 1938 not long before Yeats's death on January
28, 1939, and it gives a good indication of the extent to which
Blake's thought held Yeats through the intervening years: *

This idea of death [he comments here on Ethel Mannin's novel,
Darkness My Bride] suggests to me Blake's design (among those he
did for Blair's *Grave* I think) of the soul and body embracing. All
men with subjective natures move towards a possible ecstasy, all
with objective natures towards a possible wisdom.[16]

From Blake's image Yeats moves effortlessly here into the discussion of a central principle in his own system. The casual reader
cannot always make these leaps with him. For Yeats it was second nature; he had worked out over a lifetime the relationship
between Blake's picture of soul and body and his own theory of
subjective and objective man. When he was twenty-eight he had,

---

* Another example is this excerpt from a letter to Olivia Shakespear, written
on March 2, 1929: "Last night I saw in a dream strange ragged excited people
singing in a crowd. The most visible were a man and woman who were I
think dancing. The man was swinging round his head a weight at the end
of a rope or leather thong, and I knew that he did not know whether he would
strike her dead or not, and both had their eyes fixed on each other, and both
sang their love for one another. I suppose it was Blake's old thought 'sexual
love is founded upon spiritual hate'—I will probably find I have written it
in a poem in a few days" (*CL*, 758).

in fact, made a systematic study of all of Blake's works—perhaps the first systematic study ever made. When he was fifty-two, he wrote to Lady Gregory, "I am doing nothing but read Blake for my lecture—working at his philosophy again." [17] In his old age he was again studying Blake carefully.

Yeats's writing abounds with Blakean words—usually those which embody a thought central to Blake's theory of art. A favorite of his was "lineaments" (embodying Blake's principle of outline); it appears over and over again in his prose and even in such poems as "The Gyres" and "The Statues." Another Blakean term which Yeats often invokes as artistic axiom is "minute particular," a central image of Blake's poetic theory. He uses the term in "The Double Vision of Michael Robartes" and follows it with a description of the suspension of time:

> In contemplation had those three so wrought
> Upon a moment, and so stretched it out.[18]

The image comes directly from Blake's prophecies.

But Blake's influence, or at least partial influence, manifests itself within the fabric of Yeats's poetry in more complicated ways, ways so complicated that actual *proof* of influence is impossible. For example, in several poems Yeats uses the word "innocence," immediately recalling Blake's own famous *Songs of Innocence* and his treatment of the imagination of children and fools; but he modifies its Blakean meaning and applies it in new ways to unique circumstances. Two poems in particular demonstrate the Yeatsian use. In "The Second Coming,"

> The ceremony of innocence is drowned,[19]

and in "In Memory of Eva Gore-Booth and Con Markiewicz,"

> The innocent and the beautiful
> Have no enemy but time.[20]

In the first lines Yeats fuses nostalgia for what he conceives to be a more ordered age with his conception of the self-sufficiency of that age. This unity of culture he associates with the imaginative self-sufficiency of the state of innocence, unimperiled by the material world. In the second lines, aristocratic beauty is fused with this concept of innocent self-sufficiency. In his poems Yeats associates the aristocratic ideal with what he calls subjective man. A fool, a beggar, as well as Lady Gregory's son may be an aristocrat. In fact, if the burden of proof of title is upon anyone, it is upon those who are aristocrats in the usual sense of the term. Birth, money, and power (though Yeats by no means denied their significance) are not so important as gesture and state of being.

There is a further qualification: aristocracy is usually observed in Yeats's poems from the outside. What aristocracy is is not so important as what it seems to represent, and from the outside aristocracy appears as a mysterious innocence. As a result, Yeats's images of innocence are his own, not Blake's:

> How but in custom and in ceremony
> Are innocence and beauty born? [21]

Strangely enough, after this metamorphosis of meaning, the idea of aristocratic, solitary innocence (the gesture of the Irish Airman, for example) becomes Blakean in a totally new sense, for it might well be used to describe Blake's heroic figure, Los, as he works in *Jerusalem* to build the great city of art. Los represents, among other things, the prophetic tradition of poetry, the higher innocence of vision isolated from material delusion. In Yeats's poetry aristocracy and innocence are viewed from below or without in awe; in Blake's poetry they are viewed from without and within simultaneously so that their mystery is dissolved. For this reason, the term "mystery" is an evil term in Blake's prophecies; it suggests the enclosure of materialism, the point of view from which Yeats consciously wrote.

There is another means by which Blake influenced Yeats: his paintings and drawings. Just as Blake's image of soul and body embracing lodged in his mind, so did other images.* For example,

---

* The influence of painting upon Yeats is discussed off and on throughout T. R. Henn's provocative study of Yeats, *The Lonely Tower* (London, 1950).

the hands in Blake's pictures of the soul are often together in the position of prayer or perhaps slightly apart in the act of clapping. In his introduction to the Modern Library selection of Blake's poems, Yeats recalls that when in 1787 Blake's brother, Robert, died, Blake "had seen his brother's spirit ascending clapping its hands for joy, and might well sleep content." [22] It is not unlikely that Blake's own paintings and his description of his brother's soul influenced the famous lines from "Sailing to Byzantium":

> An aged man is but a paltry thing,
> A tattered coat upon a stick, unless
> Soul clap its hands and sing, and louder sing
> For every tatter in its mortal dress. [23]

The ambiguity of praying and clapping hands joins two imaginatively related images. The prayer is self-explanatory; the clapping hands suggest a return to childish innocence and spiritual enthusiasm—the new foolhood of the aged.

One suspects that Blake's drawings and, to a considerable extent, his poetry influenced Yeats in another and less concrete way. If one phrase is capable of describing a singular quality of Blake's work, it is the phrase "terrible beauty," used by Yeats to describe the metamorphosis of the Easter rebellion heroes in the poem, "Easter 1916." This "terrible beauty" pervades Blake's poetry —the tortured howlings of Los in the act of creation, the sudden burst of energy that is "The Tyger," the violence of the horse-

---

Mr. Henn has succeeded in showing many instances in which a particular painting has influenced Yeats. Several of these instances involve Blake's work. Mr. Henn's research suggests that much more can be done in this direction. In Appendix II of *The Lonely Tower* Mr. Henn lists certain pictures which probably influenced Yeats, and in Appendix III he lists the contents of Yeats's collection of lantern slides, which includes many Blake illustrations and drawings. It is probably unnecessary to say that Yeats's father was a portrait painter, that his brother is Ireland's leading artist, that Yeats himself studied to be a painter for a time, and that the artistic tradition in the family is carried on now by Yeats's daughter, Anne.

men in that illustration to *Paradise Lost* called "Expulsion from Eden," the fierce form of the crouching Nebuchadnezzar. The same beauty infuses Yeats's later work—the images of Cuchulain, the wisemen in "Lapis Lazuli," Crazy Jane, Old Tom, Ribh.

The fierceness grows in power with Yeats's growth. He assumes the masks of fools, of, as the Irish say, "innocents"; he studies hatred and rage:

> Out of Ireland have we come.
> Great hatred, little room,
> Maimed us at the start.
> I carry from my mother's womb
> A fanatic heart.[24]

In a letter to Ethel Mannin, in 1936, Yeats wrote:

As a young man I used to repeat to myself Blake's lines
>   "And he his seventy disciples sent
>   Against religion and government"
I hate more than you do, for my hatred can have no expression in action. I am a forerunner of that horde that will some day come down the mountains.[25]

The epigrams of his middle period are sometimes remarkably Blakean:

> You say, as I have often given tongue
> In praise of what another's said or sung,
> 'Twere politic to do the like by these;
> But was there ever dog that praised his fleas? [26]

This is very like Blake's blast at his tormentors:

> Hayley, Flaxman & Stothard are also in doubt
> Lest their virtue should be put to the rout.
> One grins, t'other spits & in corners hides,
> And all the Virtuous have shewn their backsides.[27]

Sometimes Yeats's epigrams celebrate nostalgia—the curse of growing old. The poems of his later years gesture more recklessly than those of 1910. One of his later poems is "The Spur":

> You think it horrible that lust and rage
> Should dance attention upon my old age;
> They were not such a plague when I was young;
> What else have I to spur me into song? [28]

Yeats's longer poems exhibit this same ferocity. Examples are "The Second Coming" (to be discussed later) with its "blood-dimmed tide" and "rough beast," and "Nineteen Hundred and Nineteen":

> Now days are dragon-ridden, the nightmare
> Rides upon sleep: a drunken soldiery
> Can leave the mother, murdered at her door,
> To crawl in her own blood, and go scot-free. [29]

Blake's great poem "London" affords us a comparison in attitudes:

> How the Chimney-sweeper's cry
> Every black'ning Church appalls;
> And the hapless Soldier's sigh
> Runs in blood down Palace walls. [30]

The power of rhetoric, the daring of the imagery, and the ferocity of the tone are what often rescue Yeats's poetry from hopeless nostalgia and sentimentality. Both "Nineteen Hundred and Nineteen" and "The Spur" tread close to mawkishness. A severe honesty and a subtle manipulation of point of view maintain their balance.

Blake's influence on Yeats in the matter of ferocity (a vague word in this context) of tone can never be proved; only the complete works of each poet are sufficient evidence to illustrate the point. With a poem such as "Those Images," among the last Yeats wrote, we are on more solid ground. The possible influence of Blake lies in the imagery itself:

> What if I bade you leave
> The cavern of the mind?
> There's better exercise
> In the sunlight and wind.

I never bade you go
To Moscow or to Rome.
Renounce that drudgery,
Call the Muses home.

Seek those images
That constitute the wild,
The lion and the virgin,
The harlot and the child.

Find in middle air
An eagle on the wing,
Recognise the five
That make the Muses sing.[31]

The poem begins with an image which, if more obviously out of Plato's allegory of the cave, is in fact probably closer in spirit to Blake's pictures of the archmaterialist Urizen caught in a material world of his own mental construction and "roofed around" like the angel in Blake's *Marriage of Heaven and Hell.* This angel, who promises to show Blake "his eternal lot," leads him down into a mill and cave:

Down the winding cavern we groped our tedious way, till a void boundless as a nether sky appear'd beneath us, & we held by the roots of trees and hung over this immensity. . . . By degrees we beheld the infinite Abyss, fiery as the smoke of a burning city . . . not many stones' throw from us appear'd and sunk again the scaly fold of a monstrous serpent. . . .

My friend the Angel climb'd up from his station into the mill: I remain'd alone; & then this appearance was no more, but I found myself sitting on a pleasant bank beside a river by moonlight, hearing a harper, who sung to the harp; & his theme was: "The man who never alters his opinion is like standing water, & breeds reptiles of the mind."

But I arose and sought for the mill, & there I found my Angel, who, surprised, asked me how I escaped?

I answer'd: "All that we saw was owing to your metaphysics." [32]

The imagery of the cavern in both Blake and Yeats is obviously meant to symbolize materialist epistemology and the perversion of imagination. Yeats also uses the "mill" image to suggest the workings of the mind, always with derogatory significance:

> Here at life's end
> Neither loose imagination,
> Nor the mill of the mind
> Consuming its rag and bone,
> Can make the truth known.[33]

The childish, loose imagination is not the imagination of old men, nor would it be adequate to the problems of the aged even if it were. Aged innocence and childish innocence only *seem* the same, and then only from the outside. Nor is the reasoning power adequate "at life's end," grinding over and over the same chaff of experience. The answer lies in the elemental images Yeats mentions in the last two stanzas of "Those Images," in a cutting away of the trappings of what Yeats broadly called "politics," in the kind of purgation by fire described in "Byzantium." The images turn out to be those opposites Blake seeks to join in his *Songs of Innocence and Experience* and in *The Marriage of Heaven and Hell:* the lion and virgin described in Blake's "Little Girl Lost" and "Little Girl Found"; the harlot and child of Blake's "London"; the eagle of Blake's proverbs—"When thou seest an Eagle, thou seest a portion of Genius; lift up thy head!" [34] The "five/That make the muses sing" are Blake's "windows of the morning," the senses through which man may escape from the cavern and the mill. These are the basic spare images of a symbolical world, a distillation of the apparent to purity. The drop of dew hanging upon a blade of grass, Yeats's image of reality in a short poem, is Blake's elemental "world in a grain of sand."

The process of growing old brought Yeats closer and closer to the use of the elemental images of Blakean "madness." When he speaks in "The Spirit Medium" of "root, shoot, blossom, or clay," he is dramatizing a return to the earth, not the materialist earth of Urizen but the symbolical earth of Blake's own system (an inaccurate word, for it suggests the mill, but we have no bet-ter). He builds up a doctrine of correspondences, similar to that which he describes in the Quaritch edition of Blake (we shall return to this later), based upon the elemental imagery of air, earth, fire, and water. It is an imagery which, as he says of Blake's, can be read in every area and degree of nature.

Blake, of course, was not alone in influencing Yeats to use elemental images as the basis for a congeries of poetical symbolism. The basic quadruple division of air, earth, fire, and water, how-ever, is closely related by Blake himself to the four central figures, or Zoas, of his own mythology—Los (Urthona), Urizen, Tharmas, and Luvah. These in turn, Yeats was soon to discover, were surely related to certain elements of esoteric thought with which he was acquainted. And all of these quadruple symbolisms for reality (or fallen reality) might well be related to the four talismans of ancient Ireland: the sword, the spear, the stone, the cauldron. Because Blake assimilated what appeared to be a world-wide symbolism and made of it a total poetical system, and be-cause at the same time Blake laid special emphasis upon the "minute particulars" which the four elements seem so well to sym-bolize, it is not difficult to understand why Blake's organization of archetypes appealed so strongly to Yeats. He discovered that wherever he looked Blake's great plan seemed to apply. It en-compassed limited, discursive statement.

We shall later see how important this kind of systematization was to Yeats. For the present the following example of Yeats's thought about the elements will suffice: It is an excerpt from a letter to Olivia Shakespear, July 24, 1934:

Notice this symbolism
    Waters under the earth

The Earth	the bowels etc.	*Instinct*
The Water =	The blood and the sex organ.	*Passion*
The Air =	The lungs, logical thought	*Thought*
The Fire =		*Soul* [35]

It would be impossible to assign one of Blake's Zoas to each of these elements. Nor would it be possible to hold all of Yeats's poetry to this chart of simple equivalence. Although the elements are always present in some symbolical form, in the case of both poets the particular context rules final meaning. With Blake, Luvah (or Orc) is often passion, but he is also often (in one of his roles) fire. In later works Los, too, is often fiery. Urizen represents thought, but his imagery, if it is not that of hard, coarse material, is that of dense clouds; with Yeats, thought is not dense and heavy but light and airy. Some reasons for this difference, which is a difference in point of view, will later emerge.

Like Blake, Yeats developed a theory of history which has as its basic symbolism these elemental images. In each of Blake's historical cycles there is an age of Urizen, an age of Luvah, a generative age of Tharmas, and, transcending these, Los's apocalyptic vision of a timeless reality. In a letter to Mrs. Shakespear, Yeats explains the elemental imagery of his historical theory:

The Earth = Every early nature-dominated civilization
The Water = An armed sexual age, chivalry, Froissart's chronicles
The Air = From the Renaissance to the end of the 19th Century.
The Fire = The purging away of our civilization by our hatred.[36]

In a later letter he quotes his short poem "The Four Ages" in order to show that the symbolism, like Blake's, applies not only to ages of history but also to the life of every man:

> He with body waged a fight;
> Body won and walks upright.
>
> Then he struggled with the Heart;
> Innocence and peace depart.
>
> Then he struggled with the Mind;
> His proud Heart he left behind.
>
> Now his wars with God begin;
> At stroke of midnight God shall win.

They are [he comments] the four ages of individual man, but they are also the four ages of civilization. . . . First age, *earth*, vegetative functions. Second age, *water*, blood, sex. Third age, *air*, breath, intellect. Fourth age, *fire*, soul etc.[37]

It is remarkable how easily the symbolism explained in these letters can be applied to a poem by Blake:

> An old maid early—e'er I knew
> Ought but the love that on me grew;
> And now I'm cover'd o'er & o'er
> And wish that I had been a whore.
>
> O, I cannot, cannot find
> The undaunted courage of a Virgin Mind,
> For Early I in love was crost,
> Before my flower of love was lost.[38]

Here Blake seems to be describing a woman who is looking back from the age of air and intellect (Blake's experience) to the earlier ages of earth and water. The difference from Yeats here is that Blake absolutely rejects the age of intellect as delusory, treating it, for example, in *The Gates of Paradise* as a period of "cloudy doubts & reasoning cares." Yeats, though he mistrusts it, lives in it and follows its ways. Blake is putting words into the mouth of a trapped character.

In startling contrast, Yeats usually treats himself as the trapped character. The point is not that the Yeats described in his poems *wants* to trust the intellect but that, given his situation, he is driven to do so and thus to alienate himself from the condition of fire which he seeks:

> Wine comes in at the mouth
> And love comes in at the eye;
> That's all we shall know for truth
> Before we grow old and die.
> I lift the glass to my mouth,
> I look at you, and I sigh.[39]

A much later poem:

> We are closed in, and the key is turned
> On our uncertainty; somewhere
> A man is killed, or a house burned,
> Yet no clear fact to be discerned.[40]

Many more examples can be found; Yeats's generous use of what seems to be, but really is not, a rhetorical question illustrates the important difference from Blake in point of view.

This difference accounts for the peculiar nostalgia of Yeats's poetry. Blake, viewing the past *sub specie aeternitatis*, is able to treat experience with terrible and prophetic honesty:

> My mother groan'd! My father wept.
> Into the dangerous world I leapt:
> Helpless, naked, piping loud:
> Like a fiend hid in a cloud.
>
> Struggling in my father's hands,
> Striving against my swadling bands,
> Bound and weary I thought best
> To sulk upon my mother's breast.[41]

Time is so much with Yeats that he cannot take exactly the same attitude toward the past. Dramatizing himself, he shows that he thinks Blake's view is right, but he also shows himself still struggling to attain a similar vision. He speaks with a baffled honesty which as his style matures makes a cold yet dramatic statement. In moments when he approaches Blakean prophecy, he manages to free himself from the cave. Sometimes Blake seems to have guided his hand:

> Locke sank into a swoon;
> The Garden died;
> God took the spinning-jenny
> Out of his side.[42]

These lines, as we shall later see, assimilate a whole Blakean system, and they are said with the finality of the prophet. They en-

compass the total vision of history in microcosm. But Yeats adds
another stanza:

> Where got I that truth?
> Out of a medium's mouth,
> Out of nothing it came,
> Out of the forest loam,
> Out of dark night where lay
> The crowns of Nineveh.[43]

The mill of the mind, working in retrospect, causes mystery to
reappear; the certainty of understanding recedes. In a note on
this poem Yeats says that the images came to him "in a sort of
nightmare vision." Blake, it is known, once said that he had had
only one nightmare in all his life, that they seldom came to imaginative men. Here again the difference in point of view is of
primary importance.

More often than not, Blake's direct influence on Yeats cannot
be fully sorted out of the welter of influences which played upon
both. The influence of Plotinus is a case in point. How much
comes to Yeats through Blake and how much comes directly
from the writings of Plotinus (or other Neoplatonists) cannot
be satisfactorily determined. It is just as difficult to determine the
single source for any number of particular images. Yeats's short
poem "His Bargain" gives us an example:

> Who talks of Plato's spindle;
> What set it whirling round?
> Eternity may dwindle,
> Time is unwound.[44]

The winding and unwinding of pernes, spindles, and time in
Yeats's poetry surely has some relation to Blake's image of the
golden thread which, if wound into a ball, will bring us to
Jerusalem. And the ball image has affinities to Yeats's image of
the sphere, made much of in *A Vision*. Yet related images may
also be found in the pre-Socratic poet-philosophers and in
Plotinus.

The well-known "winding path" image from "Byzantium" relates to these, and according to Yeats other images from the poem are Blakean; but when we read Yeats's explanation of the Blakean source, we are back about where we began. In a letter to Mrs. Shakespear he writes:

When I went to London I had just finished a poem in which I appeal to the saints in "the holy fire" to send death on their ecstasy. In London I went to a medium called Cooper and on the way called to my people for their especial wisdom. The medium gave me "a book test"—Third book from R bottom shelf—study—Page 48 or 84. I have only this morning looked it up. The book was the complete Dante designs of Blake. It is not numbered by pages but by plates. Plate 84 is Dante entering the Holy Fire (Purgatorio—Canto 27). Plate 48 is "The serpent attacking Vanni Fucci." When I looked this up in Dante I found that at the serpent's sting Vanni Fucci is burnt to ashes and then recreated from the ashes and that this symbolizes "the temporal Fire." The medium is the most stupid I know and certainly the knowledge was not in my head.[45]

All the resourcefulness of John Livingston Lowes and Harry Price together could not have brought order out of the mystery of such an account.

The important relationship between Blake and Yeats lies not so much in the undeniable and astonishing similarities which the reader of both soon apprehends, but in their modes or forms of experiencing and creating poetic worlds. Blake himself visualized a poetic tradition (in his opinion *the true poetic* and prophetic tradition) beginning in Biblical revelation and even before in Greek myth, moving to Chaucer, Spenser, Milton, Blake himself, and onward to, shall we say, Yeats or those poets who might be expected to renew the arts on Britain's shores. Blake's own theory of art is an attempt to explain the renewal of an archetypal vision in each literary age. As Blake would see it, there is not only a single influence but also a single poetic theme. The influence is that which in romantic terminology is called the "shaping spirit of imagination," the poetic form of experience which opens the window to a timeless and spaceless reality of spirit and is expressed in human terms by a symbolical system or, as Northrop Frye has written, a "set of symbolic conventions." [46] To agree with Blake is to seek the "influences" on Yeats not in Blake alone but in the tradition of which both writers are a part. The question is finally one of their aesthetic principles. It is not at all surprising that, in the Quaritch edition of Blake, Yeats's essay on general principles of poetry applicable to the problem of Blake still stands up as the conveyor of valid insights into Blake's method, while the running commentaries upon specific poems leave much to be desired. Yeats was himself a poet interested in the problems of poetic creation, not a commentator upon poems.

In order to understand what these principles are, it is best to begin with Blake's theory itself and then see it as Yeats saw it when he wrote his essay "The Necessity of Symbolism" for the Quaritch edition. To this we shall proceed, and from this to a brief analysis of Blake's symbolical system.

CHAPTER II

The Blakean Aesthetic

All that we See is Vision, from Generated Organs
gone as soon as come, Permanent in The Imagination,
Consider'd as Nothing by the Natural Man.
—WILLIAM BLAKE [1]

BLAKE'S theory of art is difficult to formulate. He considered
his theory an "image of truth new born," but for most of us it is
only a further complication of the same "endless maze" from
which he would deliver us. Blake tells us that our difficulty in
perceiving truth is simply that we are unable to formulate the
perception of our "maze" in any new way. Our words entangle
us in the same old roots. Our words are no longer our slaves;
they act as tyrants over our abilities to ask new questions and to
overthrow old orientations.

Blake is almost always on the attack, and almost all of his attacks have at their roots an important semantic disagreement
with some intellectual "villain." Peculiarly sensitive to the total
meaning of a word, he believed that the terms chosen by a writer
impose or at least reveal the limitations of that writer's view of
reality. Often it is simply what his terms imply by connotation
that chains a writer to some false epistemology and therefore to
some false theory of art. Among Blake's most cherished villains
are "Bacon, Newton, Locke" and Sir Joshua Reynolds, with "his

Gang of Cunning Hired Knaves." In his annotations to Reynolds' *Discourses*, Blake attacks not only Reynolds' inconsistency but also certain of his basic assumptions. The attack on the latter is the more important of the two, for there Blake is attacking more than Reynolds alone. He is attacking "Bacon, Newton, Locke," symbols for a philosophy. When Blake attacks he always tries to set the culprit right; in his annotations and prose fragments we may find the expression of his own theory of artistic creation.

EPISTEMOLOGY OF VISION

For a man of the late eighteenth and early nineteenth centuries Blake employed a somewhat unusual vocabulary. In revolt against a certain kind of rationalism, he objected to the connotations of words commonly used by the philosophers and poets of his time —"nature," "memory," and "abstraction," for instance. They implied an epistemology with which he could not agree. We must approach Blake's own theory of knowledge knowing that he would not subject himself to the tyranny of what seemed to him a materialistic vocabulary, its conceptual boundaries trapping the thinker in "nets and gins." Blake has been looked upon as an eccentric, as a madman, and—both honorifically and derogatorily—as a mystic; but when the string has been wound into a ball, Blake's thought emerges in a rational system, as much a logical extension of the thought of his time as, for instance, Berkeley's, but an extension contrived to move man out of and beyond the eighteenth-century "endless maze" of "dark disputes and artful teazing." True, Blake's system is based upon intuition or imagination, but it does not therefore dissolve to logical inconsistency.

A major point in Blake's theory of art lies behind a distinction between "allegory" and "vision." Blake does not always use the term "allegory" in the same way, for in one letter he implies a higher and a lower allegory: "Allegory addressed to the Intellectual powers, while it is altogether hidden from the Corporeal

Understanding, is My Definition of the Most Sublime Poetry; it is also somewhat in the same manner defin'd by Plato." [2] But later he makes a less confusing statement: "The Last Judgment [a painting by Blake] is not Fable or Allegory, but Vision. Fable or Allegory are a totally distinct & inferior kind of Poetry." [3] There is a shifting of terms here. "Allegory addressed to the Intellectual powers" becomes "vision." Allegory addressed to, or not hidden from, the "corporeal understanding" corresponds to the "fable or allegory" of the second quotation. If we have unraveled this semantic problem, our understanding of Blake's thought still depends upon the meanings we assign to the terms "intellectual powers" and "corporeal understanding." If we simplify the Blakean language, the following sets of warring contraries appear:

Allegory	Vision
Fable	
Corporeal understanding	Intellect

To the left-hand column we may add, as symbol, the name of Locke, and to the right the name of Berkeley.

Blake makes the name of Locke a symbol for the thinking of a whole age, and then he attacks that thinking. He follows closely Berkeley's *reductio ad absurdum* of the hypothesis of primary and secondary qualities. For Blake the mental image, the form— the very act which creates the image—is the single reality. The world is a world of mental acts: "What is call'd Corporeal, Nobody knows of its Dwelling Place: it is in Fallacy, & its Existence an Imposture. Where is the Existence Out of Mind or Thought? Where is it but in the Mind of a Fool?" [4] The fool is Locke himself, who abstracted the subjective qualities of an experience from the objective, hard material facts. For Blake a visionary truth is the concrete apprehension of an object as it is created in the act of apprehension, not in the impingement of

an outer material object upon a passive subject. We may therefore add the following to our columns of contending words:

Abstraction	Concretion
Passive	Active

Blake objects to the Lockean epistemology in the following comment upon one of Lavater's *Aphorisms:* "Deduct from a rose its
redness, from a lilly its whiteness, from a diamond its hardness,
from a spunge its softness, from an oak its heighth, from a daisy
its lowness, & rectify every thing in Nature as the Philosophers
do, & then we shall return to Chaos. . . ." [5]

Blake summarizes his theory of knowledge in the single statement, "Strictly Speaking All Knowledge is Particular." [6] This
statement follows directly from his attempt to bridge or, better,
disregard the Lockean gap between inanimate object and passive
subject, between nature and mind. It is no surprise to discover
that in the Blakean myth the fall from the visionary state of Eden,
where harmony exists free of nature, is manifested by the creation of Lockean matter. But it is Blake's faith that man's true
state is visionary; that is, his state is potentially above the delusion which is the bifurcated natural world.

It is clear that Blake is not merely quibbling in his criticism
of Wordsworth:

(Wordsworth):   How exquisitely the individual Mind
                   (And the progressive powers perhaps no less
                   Of the whole species) to the external World
                   Is fitted:—& how exquisitely, too,
                   Theme this but little heard of among Men,
                   The external World is fitted to the Mind.

(Blake):   You shall not bring me down to believe such
                   fitting & fitted.[7]

To Blake, Wordsworth's unification of subject and object is tenuous and strained, dependent upon a temporary clutching or an

artificial series of connecting links. The very connotations of "fitting" and "fitted" suggest an outer material reality. Blake, on the other hand, sees reality only in the mental experience, the concrete perceptual act:

(Wordsworth):   Influence of Natural Objects
                  In calling forth and strengthening the Imagina-
                     tion
                  In Boyhood and early Youth.

(Blake):   Natural objects always did & now do weaken,
                     deaden & obliterate Imagination in me.
                  W[ordsworth] must know that what he writes
                     valuable is not to be found in Nature.[8]

Blake abhors the epistemology Wordsworth implies. Again he objects to the material connotation of "nature." From Blake's point of view Wordsworth is unsuccessfully struggling to escape "Bacon, Newton, Locke." He has become the pawn of Blake's mythical goddess Rahab, symbol in the prophetic books of feminine will and of nature separate from and inaccessible to man; he attempts to embrace a Rahab who continually rebukes him but ever beckons. If we follow Blake's argument carefully, we discover that he is quite consistent in saying, with characteristic but meaningful overemphasis,

I see in Wordsw[orth] the natural man rising up ag[ain]st the spiritual man continually, & then he is no poet but a heathen philosopher at Enmity ag[ain]st all true poetry or inspiration.[9]

The vituperative attack upon Sir Joshua Reynolds and the Lockean principles of painting in his *Discourses* is based upon the same general distinction between the natural and the spiritual man. Blake thought, of course, that Reynolds was in far greater error than Wordsworth.

It might be well to borrow here from Northrop Frye, who first quotes Blake's words:

Every eye sees differently. As the Eye, Such the Object.

All of us on earth are united in thought, for it is impossible to think without images of somewhat on earth.

Mr. Frye then comments:

But the reality of the landscape [Blake's "earth," above] even so consists in its relation to the imaginative pattern of the farmer's mind, or of the painter's mind. To get an "inherent" reality in the landscape by isolating the common factors, that is, by eliminating the agricultural qualities from the farmer's perception and the artistic ones from the painter's, is not possible, and would not be worth doing if it were. Add more people, and this least common denominator of perception steadily decreases.[10]

To generalize from a series of these perceptions or to depend upon the memory in order to make these generalizations leads away from the act in which reality momentarily exists: "To Generalize is to be an Idiot. To Particularize is the Alone Distinction of Merit. General Knowledges are those Knowledges that Idiots possess." [11] The argument against Reynolds is rooted in the belief that a generalization is as delusory as the natural world. If one is to employ a generalization, one should assume that it is merely a useful fiction.

One of Blake's most revealing comments is on the following statement by Reynolds:

(Reynolds):   Thus it is from a reiterated experience and a close comparison of the objects in nature, that an artist becomes possessed of the idea of that central form . . . from which every deviation is deformity.

(Blake):   One Central Form composed of all other Forms being Granted, it does not therefore follow that all other Forms are Deformity.
   All Forms are Perfect in the Poet's Mind, but these are not Abstracted nor compounded from Nature, but are from Imagination.[12]

It is quite clear that Blake and Reynolds are talking about two totally distinct "central forms." Reynolds conceives "central form" as a generalization, but a generalization is as meaningless to Blake as the modern American "average voter" or "Mrs. Housewife" should be to us. (As we shall see, Blake calls what we term "generalization" "abstraction.") Blake argues that Reynolds' conception, followed out in art, gives rise to personification and, as in Rubens, to painting in which by allegory and abstraction the "rattle traps of mythology" degrade the imaginative expression.[13] In literature as well as in painting, Reynolds' conception leads to allegory, which is addressed to the "corporeal understanding." But "central form" in Blake has totally different characteristics. It has nothing to do with generalization and abstraction. It is in fact the very opposite. There is a central form available to the visionary imagination, but it is immediately available. All imaginative forms are microcosms of central form. One need not employ the memory in order to build up a set of artificial forms. Blake's central form is the mental or human structure of the world, not the impingement of nature upon a *tabula rasa*.

But how can Blake convince the materialist that all other forms are essentially one with central form, that the microcosm may stand for the macrocosm—in fact *is* the macrocosm? It is here that he affirms the importance of the artist as a religious force in society and especially the importance of the artist's conceptual tool, the poetic symbol. To this affirmation I shall soon return.

Now any discussion which links Blake's idea of the poetic symbol with abstraction seems to me unacceptable in the light of his own vocabulary.* Simply because Blake denies Lockean material nature as the objective reality, we must not assume that his only alternative is to emphasize the abstract rather than the con-

---

* Blake's attack on abstraction may be illustrated by this comment in a letter to Thomas Butts, Sept. 11, 1801: "I labour incessantly & accomplish not one half of what I intend, because my Abstract folly hurries me often away while I am at work, carrying me over Mountains & Valleys, which are not Real, in a Land of Abstraction where Spectres of the Dead wander." (*K*, II, 196.) In mundane language, he is saying that the world of materialism encroaches upon his working time.

crete. In fact to do so is to begin unknowingly in the very pit of Ulro to which Blake consigns Locke and the mythical figure Urizen. It is to do what Blake accuses Reynolds of doing. "Abstraction," to Blake, is a derogatory term; "symbol," though not employed by Blake, may be likened to his word "vision," a highly honorific term.

It is impossible, as Susanne K. Langer has recently pointed out, to use the word "symbol" in any sense acceptable to a majority of writers on the arts. Although Blake does not use the term, nearly all writers on Blake, beginning with Yeats and Ellis, who at least let the reader know what they mean by it, have used it. As we have seen, Mrs. Langer uses "symbol" to mean "any device whereby we are enabled to make an abstraction." Since Mrs. Langer and Blake use the word "abstraction" in crucially different senses, we must seriously qualify such a definition if we are to apply it to Blake's poetry. Mrs. Langer says:

All forms in art, then, are abstracted forms; their content is only a semblance, a pure appearance, whose function is to make them, too, apparent—more freely and wholly apparent than they could be if they were exemplified in a context of real circumstance and anxious interest. It is in this elementary sense that all art is abstract. Its very substance, quality without practical significance, is an abstraction from material existence.[14]

But Blake uses "abstraction" to mean not only the action of Locke in separating the primary from the secondary qualities— the bifurcation of nature—but also "generalization."

Blake would call the building up in poetry of a composite image by selecting the common qualities from a group of objects "abstraction." What we call "generalization" is simply the logical extension of the Lockean way of thinking. Blake would argue that Mrs. Langer allows objects material existence but that material existence is delusion. Thus, what Mrs. Langer calls "material experience" is simply the old "finite organical perception" of the scientist. The infinite perception—the vision of Ezekiel, for example—expressed as symbol is not an abstraction from material existence at all. It never existed materially in the first place. Nor does the vision of a more "realistic" cat or tiger.

Blake never uses the term "abstraction" to mean the act of the artist in transforming experience into expression. In the light of recent epistemology Blake's view may be put this way: The denial of material substance does not necessitate the negation of spatial or temporal vision. Such vision, however, is greatly metamorphosed, becomes something else to us. Our intuitions of the one reality—the world infinite—are, it is true, "symbolic transformations": "It is impossible to think without images of somewhat on earth." [15] We see the infinite all around us symbolized in the forms of space-time. Yet these visions, if read correctly, tell us paradoxically that they are not material forms.

Blake's argument, then, is that the word "abstraction," carrying along past meanings, cannot but imply a material world. Thus the word is a symbol of the basic error in modern thought, the bifurcation of nature. We do not abstract *from* material experience. We intuit *through* visionary forms.

If we follow out Blake's epistemology, the solid, material world falls away, and the terms "abstraction" and "concretion" cease to be useful with their old connotations. The word "concretion" could be admitted into the Blakean world only if it were to lose its hard materiality. It could then be a symbol of immediate perception, the only reality. But there is no possibility of the word's losing its aura, so we are wise to substitute at the beginning a word like "immediate." In the Blakean world there are immediate symbols, produced by the mind, which give reality, and there are abstractions produced by the generalizing memory, which give only a lowest common denominator. As Northrop Frye has aptly put it, "In Blake the criterion or standard of reality is the genius; in Locke it is the mediocrity." [16]

To the abstractions as they appear in art, Blake gives the name "allegory" addressed to the "corporeal understanding." The immediate symbols he dignifies with the word "vision."

THE TRUE VISION AND THE DEBASED VISION

Blake makes no distinction between poet and prophet, poetry and religious prophecy. Both present an intuition of the central form of life. When Isaiah and Ezekiel speak to Blake in *The Marriage of Heaven and Hell*, they simply assume that this correspondence exists:

The Prophets Isaiah and Ezekiel dined with me, and I asked them how they dared so roundly to assert that God spoke to them; and whether they did not think at the time that they would be misunderstood, & so be the cause of imposition.

Isaiah answer'd: "I saw no God, nor heard any, in a finite organical perception; but my senses discover'd the infinite in every thing, and as I was then perswaded, & remain confirm'd, that the voice of honest indignation is the voice of God, I cared not for consequences, but wrote. . . ." Then Ezekiel said: "The philosophy of the east taught the first principles of human perception: some nations held one principle for the origin, and some another: we of Israel taught that the *Poetic Genius* (as you now call it) was the first principle and all the others merely derivative, which was the cause of our despising the Priests & Philosophers of other countries, and prophecying [*sic*] that all Gods would at last be proved to originate in ours & to be the tributaries of the Poetic Genius." [17]

These remarks are packed with significance. First let us explore the implied relationship between poetry and prophecy. The infinite quality of the poetic or prophetic perception is, by its perfect material nothingness, not a process which may be divided up into sections any more than the human body, the *fallen* material manifestation of perception, can be divided into portions capable of separate life.

I have heard many People say, "Give me the Ideas. It is no matter what Words you put them into," & others say, "Give me the Design, it is no matter for the Execution." These People know Enough of Artifice, but Nothing Of Art. Ideas cannot be Given but in their minutely Appropriate Words, nor Can a Design be made without its minutely Appropriate Execution. [18]

The execution of a work of art is not the imposition of an arbitrary form upon the mental experience as it is recollected in tranquillity. It is the immediate apprehension and holding back from time of the central form of that experience.

In Blake's Edenic realm God and man were one. And for him they still are, except that "corporeal" delusion now often prevents us from the realization of that unity. The visionary instinctively knows the fact of unity, and the great works of art are assertions of it. The Poetic Genius may overthrow the bounds of "finite organical perception." The artist in society strives to regain Eden for all men, to leave behind that state of delusion characterized by Lockean nature and spiritual forms fallen into material. Art is thus prophetic in the religious sense. It does not predict, but it does disclose the true central form, the pattern of human life. And it discloses central form, not by viewing the grain of sand and then by means of abstract reason considering its relation to a greater controlling deity, but by visualizing that grain of sand as a symbol of the deity itself, as the central form in microcosm.

In Blake's fallen world of "finite organical perception," instead of the timeless and spaceless unification of the microcosm, which is man or the grain of sand, with the macrocosm, the central form which is God, there is a delusory chain of being in which God, angels, man, animals, and plants are forever separated from one another. To Blake the chain of being is only another aspect of the Lockean dilemma and of the abstract rationalization of the true Christian vision. Without the material delusion which gives more than symbolic reality to matter and time—the chains of Blake's Ulro—the chain of being would cease to exist. Blake writes:

> I give you the end of a golden string,
> Only wind it into a ball,
> It will lead you in at Heaven's gate
> Built in Jerusalem's wall.[19]

So long as the ball exists as a string, it exists as a symbol of linear progression in time and in space. When wound into a sphere it

becomes the traditional symbol of perfection. Unlike Blake's
mythical figure Urizen, who traps himself inside the sphere in
nets and gins, the reader rolling it carefully and finally examining
its perfection sees the chain gone, time ended, and space brought
back to itself, the immediate symbol of heaven remaining. The
reader has slipped out of Plato's cave, the sphere of Urizen, into
vision:

> If the doors of perception were cleansed every thing would ap-
> pear to man as it is, infinite.
> For man has closed himself up, till he sees all things thro' narrow
> chinks of his cavern.[20]

The visionary sees the large in the small because he understands the delusion of taking largeness and smallness literally. The
poetic vision is therefore a vision of apocalypse, *total resolution*,
the return of all things to unity. It begins with a grain of sand
and ends with God, but ideally it begins where it ends and achieves
a single image of reality, shifting by fallen analogy into other
images.

If we are to understand Blake's view of experience, we must
also see that Blake's analogies are not abstractions from a basic
material reality but symbolic assertions of the unity of a reality
into which material is simply never admitted. Blake's world is a
world of hypostasis; Locke's is a world of tenuous correspondences or allegories.

Thus at all times Blake turns to the immediate:

(Swedenborg): The Gentiles, particularly the Africans . . . entertain an Idea of God as of a Man, and say that
no one can have any other Idea of God: When
they hear that many form an Idea of God as existing in the Midst of a Cloud, they ask where
such are. . . .

(Blake): Think of a white cloud as being holy, you cannot
love it; but think of a holy man within the cloud,
love springs up in your thoughts, for to think of
holiness distinct from man is impossible to the

affections. Thought alone can make monsters but the affections cannot.[21]

Blake is trying to show by example that there is a distinct and unbreakable identity between God and man which transcends any barrier raised by nature, that the habit of primitive animation has its own logic. To the human imagination all things grasped and held are microcosms of a single mythic pattern, which Blake finds primarily in the Bible but also in other great bodies of mythology and in the greatest works of art. All things grasped in this manner, as we invest the cloud with human life, are "momentary gods," intimations of reality, personal flashes of intuition which move beyond the illusion of nature into a human, living world; for nature is dead.*

Thus, when Blake says, "A Spirit and a Vision are not, as the modern philosophy supposes, a cloudy vapour," he is not substituting a new cloud of nothingness. He is advancing his theory of imagination to its absolute refinement:

A Spirit and a Vision are not, as the modern philosophy supposes, a cloudy vapour, or a nothing: they are organized and minutely articulated beyond all that the mortal and perishing nature can produce. He who does not imagine in stronger and better lineaments, and in stronger and better light than his perishing and mortal eye can see, does not imagine at all.[22]

The popular philosophy begins with the wrong assumptions. It assumes, but cannot prove, the existence of a material reality out there beyond the mind. It then stretches this assumption illogically and declares that all things which do not seem to have this material reality are by analogy "cloudy vapours." We may take as a peculiarly apt example Hartley's study of the mind and

---

* The term "momentary god" has been suggested to me by Susanne K. Langer's translation of Cassirer's *Language and Myth* (New York, 1946), p. 62, wherein he quotes H. Usener: "According to Usener, the lowest level to which we can trace back the origin of religious concepts is that of 'momentary gods,' as he calls those images which are born from the need or the specific feeling of a critical moment, sprung from the excitation of mythico-religious fantasy."

his attempt to bring the mind and its actions into the "real" material world by explaining them totally in terms of material in extension and movement. He sought to bring thought back into good, solid repute by giving it material reality. But, alas, thought remains nonmaterial, and the thinker remains a dreamer.

Yet, if we have come this far with Blake, we may foresee a difficult problem looming both for the artist and the reader. Will the visionary, having escaped from Plato's cave, be able to communicate a truth so different from the accepted delusion? Will he merely be talking a sign language to the blind? Blake was aware of this problem, for he asks the prophets Isaiah and Ezekiel this very question: "I asked them . . . did [they] not think at the time that they would be misunderstood, & so be the cause of imposition." [23] But Isaiah simply implies that truth cannot compromise with falsehood and maintain its own nature. The Blakean artist must sacrifice himself to Ulro, must howl like Los and stick to his task.

Blake fully understood the risks and proceeded with faith in that thing he called man's "Universal Poetic Genius." Blake believed each man capable of spiritual regeneration through the power of this genius. When he states that "all had originally one language, and one religion," he does not hypothesize the original Indo-European language of the philologists. [24] He means that the vision of all people is of the same pure form. That one pure form is eternally "imagination," pitted against the mundane form called "memory," a product of the delusory finite world of generation and vegetation, which builds up an opaque experience of nature: "There Exist in that Eternal World the Permanent Realities of Every Thing which we see reflected in this Vegetable Glass of Nature." [25]

The mundane world, the world built by nature and memory, is a crazy house of false mirrors, cunningly distorted. If we come into this world a *tabula rasa*, as Blake thought both Locke and Reynolds believed, then it is the memory alone upon which we

depend. Our experiences are multiple, diverse; we are hurled out
alone into a world where separate entities jostle about without
single purpose and form. Blake could not accept this view. Against
Reynolds he defends innate ideas: "Reynolds Thinks that Man
Learns all that he knows. I say on the Contrary that Man Brings
All that he has or can have Into the World with him. Man is Born
Like a Garden ready Planted & Sown. This World is too poor to
produce one Seed." [26] There is a human form of experience and
ideation which is common to us all and in which we are conceived.
It is not learned; it is part and parcel of our very existence. We
have spiritual form, symbolized in space and time but unrestricted
by them. Blake's form denies the careening, soundless, scentless
world of matter.

But even the productions of the Poetic Genius have been debased. Greek myth as we know it, once pure vision, is an example:

Reality was Forgot, & the Vanities of Time & Space only Remember'd & call'd Reality. Such is the Mighty difference between Alle-
goric Fable & Spiritual Mystery. Let it here be Noted that the Greek
Fables originated in Spiritual Mystery & Real Vision, which are lost
& clouded in Fable & Allegory, while the Hebrew Bible & the Greek
Gospel are Genuine, Preserv'd by the Saviour's Mercy. The Nature
of my Work is Visionary or Imaginative; it is an Endeavour to
Restore what the Ancients call'd the Golden Age.[27]

The Blakean "golden age" is no more a past period than it is a
future period. It is simply the timeless reality. To Blake, then,
apocalypse is the ultimate communal assertion of spiritual reality,
of central form.

Debased vision usually manifests itself in moral allegorization,
or allegorical interpretation, the turning of mythic vision into
moral law. Interpreters of the Bible have lost the true Biblical
significance, though "by the Saviour's mercy" the truth remains
for the intellectually active reader. How the deathlike process of
abstraction occurred is visualized by Blake in *The Marriage of
Heaven and Hell:*

The ancient Poets animated all sensible objects with Gods or Geniuses, calling them by the names and adorning them with the properties of woods, rivers, mountains, lakes, cities, nations, and whatever their enlarged & numerous senses could percieve [*sic*].

And particularly they studied the genius of each city & country, placing it under its mental deity;

Till a system was formed, which some took advantage of, & enslav'd the vulgar by attempting to realize or abstract the mental deities from their objects: thus began Priesthood;

Choosing forms of worship from poetic tales.

And at length they pronounc'd that the Gods had order'd such things.

Thus men forgot that All deities reside in the human breast.[28]

It is now a short step to the "Proverbs of Hell": *The apple tree never asks the beech how he shall grow; nor the lion, the horse, how he shall take his prey.*[29] Everything should act according to its own form.

Yet here Blake must face up to the "contrary" nature of the fallen world. If every eye sees according to its own form, can there be any communally acceptable standard of truth, can there be any true central form? Blake answers "Yes," but he denies that the truth must be an artificial abstraction of the common qualities perceived by every eye. The first step toward the communal apprehension of true central form is for each individual to comprehend the delusory nature of matter, its projection, and all the tricks of the fallen world. The second step is to visualize the world, relieved of these encumbrances, as a timeless reality in which entities are no longer separated, because material and temporal configurations have disappeared, the world has moved toward unity: the great is the small, the old the young, microcosm is macrocosm. Central form is accessible through the cleansed or uncorrupted eye.

To the materialist, Blake's vision is merely symbolical (in the materialist's sense of the word), an assertion of possibility which might be achieved through the supernatural intervention of great controlling deity, but to Blake that which is symbolical is a door opening upon the real world. In fact, that real world is evoked only by poetic symbols, which may escape the chains of time and space. The poetic symbol is an image of unity shining through to the fallen world and apprehensible as such by all souls if only read correctly.

We should not dignify with the word "symbol" the abstraction Blake calls "allegory." Such an "allegory" is totally inconsistent with Blake's epistemology. It tends to break into pieces the human life pattern, which to the intellectual powers remains unified and complete. It presents an arbitrary system of analogies. Any value can be assigned to the term "x."

The Last Judgment is not Fable or Allegory, but Vision. Fable or Allegory are a totally distinct & inferior kind of Poetry. Vision or Imagination is a Representation of what Eternally Exists, Really & Unchangeably. Fable or Allegory is Form'd by the daughters of Memory. Imagination is surrounded by the daughters of Inspiration, who in the aggregate are call'd Jerusalem. Fable is allegory, but what Critics call The Fable, is Vision itself. The Hebrew Bible & the Gospel of Jesus are not Allegory, but Eternal Vision or Imagination of All that Exists. Note here that Fable or Allegory is seldom without some Vision. Pilgrim's Progress is full of it, the Greek Poets the same; but Allegory & Vision ought to be known as Two Distinct Things, & so call'd for the Sake of Eternal Life.[30]

Blake argues that there may be *some* vision in allegory and that there is a partial truth in Greek myth as we know it today. He argues that each human being must strive against corporeality. Each human being is a microcosm of the great dialectic: "Without contraries is no progression." The dialectical battle resounds through Blake's poetry, "The Mental Traveller," "My Spectre Round Me . . . ," the great prophecies. It is the battle of devils and angels in *The Marriage of Heaven and Hell;* it is the battle of Urizen and Orc; it is the problem which Los must solve.

In the bulk of Blake's writing there are at least three places where he implies that a battle has occurred within an artist and has led to a peculiar contradiction within his work. One of these artists is Reynolds, who is upbraided, not without a diabolic humor, for inconsistencies:

The Contradictions in Reynolds's Discourses are Strong Presumptions that they are the Work of Several Hands, But this is no Proof that Reynolds did not Write them. The Man, Either Painter or Philosopher, who Learns or Acquires all he knows from Others, Must be full of Contradictions.[31]

Another, as a previous quotation has shown, is Wordsworth: "I do not know who wrote these Prefaces: they are very mischievous & direct contrary to W[ordsworth]'s own practice." [32] The third is Milton: "The reason Milton wrote in fetters when he wrote of Angels and God, and at liberty when of Devils & Hell, is because he was a true Poet and of the Devil's party without knowing it." [33]

Blake implies that the god of abstraction, symbolized in the Blakean myth as Urizen, the giver of law, restrains the true Poetic Genius. When Urizen is at work, the poet is forcibly separated from the prophet. Both art and religion suffer. Vision perishes. Those who write in a violently Urizenic age sometimes come very near the completely mundane view of life. It does not take a great deal of imagination to decide what Blake must have thought of Pope's work; he mentions it once. We know very well his view of Rubens'. Blake applies to Rubens' paintings the very criticism which he levels at Greek mythology; for when the mythical figures of a now abstract mythology become accoutrements of painting, the result can only be a subjugation of vision to allegory, and probably bad allegory. Blake's antagonism toward Rubens is immense. His attack is characteristically excessive in vehemence; but his objection, with violence discounted, is significant:

Rubens's Luxembourg Gallery is Confessed on all hands to be the work of a Blockhead: it bears this Evidence in its face. How can its Execution be any other than the Work of a Blockhead? Bloated Gods, Mercury, Juno, Venus, & the rattle traps of Mythology & the

lumber of an awkward French Palace are thrown together around
Clumsy & Ricketty Princes & Princesses higgledy piggledy.[34]

Others, who have the prophetic temperament, unconsciously
revolt and join the "Devil's party," since in a Urizenic age the
devils are the upholders of "vision." In *The Marriage of Heaven
and Hell,* Blake speaks of an angel who has been defending the
materialist view of life and whom Blake has finally converted:
"This Angel, who is now become a Devil, is my particular friend;
we often read the Bible together in its infernal or diabolical
sense, which the world shall have if they behave well." [35]

Although Blake thinks of a poet as a visionary, he sees him also
as a human being in whom the contraries battle. Blake himself
was subject to vacillation between the visionary and the mundane,
the traditional Western duality.

I am under the direction of Messengers from Heaven, Daily &
Nightly; but the nature of such things is not, as some suppose, without trouble or care. Temptations are on the right hand & left; behind, the sea of time & space roars & follows swiftly; he who keeps
not right onward is lost.[36]

As a visionary the poet must evade time and space and see into
the Edenic realm of harmony.

Blake not only condemns (1) the gradual allegorization of
Greek myth into abstraction and (2) the tendency to interpret
"vision" allegorically; he also makes clear the depths to which a
debased vision may fall: "Allegories are things that Relate to
Moral Virtues. Moral Virtues do not Exist; they are Allegories
& dissimulations." [37] According to the Blakean premise, the fundamental visionary form of a poem is violated by an allegory which
proposes an artificial morality. Blakean "perfect unity" breaks
down. The writer's imagination—Blake's Los in his mythology
—is locked in battle with his tendency toward the assumption of
an abstract morality—Blake's "spectre." These two, hero and
spectre, work at cross-purposes; the poet finds himself caught between revelation rationalized and a new imaginative reason re-

vealed. If he is pulled toward the former, as Blake admits that
he sometimes was, he becomes lost in a "Land of Abstraction"
where all form is dead form, where, in the words of Messrs. Sloss
and Wallis, "the 'spectre of the dead' is apparently the abstract
idea for which the artist cannot, save by inspiration, find the living form. . . ." [38] This is the maze from which the Ancient Bard
in *Songs of Innocence* seeks to lead men:

> Youth of delight, come hither,
> And see the opening morn,
> Image of truth new born.
> Doubt is fled, & clouds of reason,
> Dark disputes & artful teazing.
> Folly is an endless maze,
> Tangled roots perplex her ways.
> How many have fallen there!
> They stumble all night over bones of the dead,
> And feel they know not what but care,
> And wish to lead others, when they should be led. [39]

Folly here is female, for she is really the goddess of nature, Rahab.
More men are chained by the spectre than are not; the tangled
roots of nature take a sorry toll:

> Each Man is in his Spectre's power
> Untill the arrival of that hour,
> When his Humanity awake
> And cast his own Spectre into the Lake. [40]

In Blake's fallen world all things are bifurcated, all images
divided. The spectre of Blake's evil is good; the spectre of his
good is evil. In Blake's real world—for the materialist the unreal
symbolic world—the abstract ideas of good and evil disappear
even as all spectres disappear. All things are one. The genius,
free of his spectre—or better, unified with it so that it ceases to
exist as entity—recognizes this situation: "He who can be bound
down is No Genius. Genius cannot be Bound." [41] The forms of
memory, of time, of space are the chains of the spectral life, of
nature, of reason triumphant over faith:

The Negation is the Spectre, the Reasoning Power in Man:
This is a false Body, an Incrustation over my Immortal
Spirit, a Selfhood which must be put off & annihilated alway.
To cleanse the Face of my Spirit by Self-examination,
To bathe in the Waters of Life, to wash off the Not Human,
I come in Self-annihilation & the grandeur of Inspiration,
To cast off Rational Demonstration by Faith in the Saviour.[42]

These are the words of Blake's symbolical Milton in the
prophecy named for that great poet. In another place, where
Blake is not speaking of the symbolical Milton, but presumably
of the Milton who walked our fallen material earth, he attacks
Dryden's "improving" of Milton as the chaining of human imagination by the mundane and opaque: "Now let Dryden's Fall &
Milton's Paradise be read, & I will assert that every Body of Understanding must cry out Shame on such Niggling & Poco-Pen
as Dryden has degraded Milton with." [43] We may then imagine
Dryden as Milton's symbolical spectre. For Blake to use him thus
—he uses "Bacon, Newton, Locke" in a similar way—would
not be surprising.

For another poet, Spenser, the perfect symbolical spectre could
be a spitting, hermaphroditic, double-mouthed creature much
like his own blatant beast. One mouth would serve to represent
a composite image of Spenser's allegorical interpreters, who dis-
mantled the *Faerie Queene* as if it were a great machine, interpreted the pieces independently with strict rationality, and then
frustrated themselves over and over by their inability to put the
pieces back into a rational whole. They overlooked the organic
unity of a work of art; they violated the Blakean premises. The
second mouth would represent Spenser's personal difficulty in
dealing with an ecclesiastical moral doctrine where rational con-
sistency—itself based originally on faith and imagination—was
sacrificed for political expediency. Thus a compromising mundane, abstract, opaque morality was forcibly grafted on a Los-
like imagination. Yeats was aware of this tendency toward the

rationalized imagination in Spenser when he dubbed him "the first salaried moralist among poets" and found himself bored by Spenser's allegory.[44]

The important principles of Blake's thought are these: He finds reality in the immediate mental experience, not in the passive joining of an inanimate object to a chained subject. "Where man is not, nature is barren." The "corporeal" world is delusion caused by the passive reception of an inanimate, nonexistent nature by a race of the spectral dead. "Active Evil is better than Passive Good." All abstraction from sense data is unreal and must be considered as such. "Bacon's philosophy has ruin'd England." God and man are identical in the sense that macrocosm and microcosm are identical. "All deities reside in the human breast." The symbolical world is the real world. "One thought fills immensity."

In great art the vision of apocalypse, total resolution, is available. The Bible, preserved by "the Saviour's mercy," is the greatest receptacle of the Poetic Genius, but it has been subjected to perverse, corporeal interpretation. Greek myth, on the other hand, became distorted as it was handed down through centuries; but originally it was evolved from pure vision.

Blake based his hope for the communication of his vision on the truth of his theory of the Poetic Genius. He based this theory upon a carefully thought-out epistemology. He saw in mythology an archetypal religious vision created again and again in traditional poetic symbols forming a single pattern of human experience, the one thought which "fills immensity." This to Blake was the true central form. Blake's poetry combined with his painting was an attempt to bring alive that archetypal vision, free of debasement by false interpretation and allegorical presentation, for the edification of a debased world: "The Religions of all Nations are derived from each Nation's different reception of the Poetic Genius, which is every where call'd the Spirit of Prophecy." [45]

Although Blake's theory of the Poetic Genius is a logical extension of his theory of knowledge, it appears that it was either evolved simultaneously with or, at least, substantiated inductively by a rather extensive study of comparative mythology. Blake had read the great mythologies and the awkward and inaccurate works of contemporary mythologists. He discovered in all myths statements of central form.

Blake was one of the first modern artists not only to articulate fully man's loss of spiritual community but also to seek an answer both in the communal myths of the past and the personal poetic symbols of the present. He sought to recreate for men out of a *personal* vision a communal vision both new and old. His faith in art led him to a form of reality which denied the final truth of nature and of abstraction from it. It led him to express that form as a pattern of symbolism distilled from the debased visions of past mythologies, cleansed and unified in his own imagination. Blake would have argued that, if both he and Yeats were successful in this effort at expression, their work would be similar, not only in visionary form but also in minute particulars.

YEATS'S BLAKE

If one wishes to amass evidence of Blake's direct influence upon Yeats, the primary external exhibit is the three-volume Quaritch edition of Blake's works, published in 1893. A collaboration between Yeats and Edwin J. Ellis, the edition contains Blake's works, commentaries upon the poems, a life of Blake, and essays on Blake's system.*

The Quaritch edition was an ambitious undertaking, the first

* Edwin John Ellis (1848–1918), a poet and painter, was a friend of Yeats's father, the author of two volumes of poetry and a verse drama. He edited Blake's works in a two-volume edition of his own in 1906, and he published a book on Blake, *The Real Blake*, in 1907. The collaboration with Ellis was not Yeats's first venture into Blake. Yeats tells us that his father had introduced him to Blake when he was fifteen or sixteen years old.

attempt by anyone to interpret Blake's system in detail. In their Preface Ellis and Yeats make clear, somewhat pompously at the expense of Swinburne, who had written on Blake, that this was a pioneering effort:

Two principal causes have hitherto kept the critics,—among whom must be included Mr. Swinburne himself, though he reigns as the one-eyed man of the proverb among the blind,—from attaining a knowledge of what Blake meant.

The first is the solidity of the myth, and its wonderful coherence. The second is the variety of terms in which the sections of it are named. . . .

Mr. Swinburne, Mr. Gilchrist, and the brothers, Dante and William Rossetti, deserve well of literature for having brought Blake into the light of day and made his name known throughout the length and breadth of England. But though whatever is accessible to us now was accessible to them when they wrote, including the then un-published "Vala" [Blake's first name for *The Four Zoas*], not one chapter, not one clear paragraph about the myth of Four Zoas, is to be found in all that they have published.[46]

Ellis and Yeats were the first to publish *The Four Zoas*, the manu-script of which they discovered in the possession of the Linnell family; and they held that it was the focal document in any in-terpretation of Blake's symbolism. Unfortunately for the text of the poem, they took the liberty of improving upon some of the original lines:

Blake had not, though he says in the first lines that he had done so, marshalled the long-resounding, long-heroic verse, in order of in-tellectual battle. He had, however, left many passages of perfect sound and emphasis. The restoration of the halting or stumbling lines to a condition in which they could equal the musical quality and cadence of their neighbours was an exceedingly irksome task, but not, in most cases, particularly difficult.[47]

It was perhaps poetic justice that some years later Ezra Pound altered without Yeats's permission some of Yeats's poems for *Poetry* magazine. Yeats was at least alive and able to defend himself at the time. After Yeats's attack on Blake's text the following attack on Swinburne and others seems harmless indeed:

Everyone who has looked at Blake has been struck with possible origins for this, that, and the other story, name, symbol, or poem. Some have gone so far as to maintain that Blake was a mere foolish patchwork of spoiled morsels, gathered with an ignorant hand from the treasure houses of all the great to whom he had access. Such is the burden of the only really clever article about him ever contributed to a magazine . . . but the writer's ability was wasted in an attempt to overthrow Blake, just as that of Mr. Swinburne, Mr. Gilchrist, and Mr. Rossetti has been wasted in the attempt to raise him up, and for the same reason in every case. The critics had not read their author.[48]

But the words did not seem harmless to Swinburne, and thirteen years later when his own work was reissued he leveled this broadside in typical alliterative fashion:

Some Hibernian commentator on Blake, if I rightly remember a fact so insignificant, has somewhere said something to some such effect that I, when writing about some fitfully audacious and fancifully delirious deliverance of the poet he claimed as a countryman, and trying to read into it some coherent and imaginative significance, was innocent of any knowledge of Blake's meaning. It is possible, if the spiritual fact of his Hibernian heredity has been or can be established, that I was: for the excellent reason that being a Celt, he now and then too probably had none worth the labour of deciphering—or at least worth the serious attention of any student belonging to a race in which reason and imagination are the possibly preferable substitutes for fever and fancy.[49]

Ellis actually wrote the lines disparaging Swinburne's interpretation, but the counterattack was directed against Yeats, who had gone to some trouble to try to prove that Blake was descended from Irish ancestors. The theory was built on the shakiest of evidence. In an annotation to his own volume of the Quaritch edition Yeats later wrote, "My authority for Blake's Irish extraction was Dr. Carter Blake who claims to be descended from a branch of the family that settled at Malaga and entered the wine trade there." [50] Yet Yeats had received a letter from the daughter of Carter Blake stating, "I am afraid I can give you little help as to the tradition you mention in your book." She added, "Two brothers of John O'Neill [supposed by Yeats to be Blake's grand-father, who took his wife's name] suffered the extreme penalty of the law in Dublin Castle for political offenses; their heads adorning the gate." [51] No proof to substantiate Yeats's claim has yet turned up, and Swinburne's explanation for Blake's Irish madness remains only wit.

In spite of textual inaccuracies and such wild assumptions, the Ellis-Yeats interpretation is often brilliant and provocative, an adequate reflection of both the limitations and powers of the authors. Writing to Joseph Hone on July 17, 1938, Geoffrey Keynes, whose own edition of Blake is the most trustworthy yet published, commented, "This is a very fine book, but it was a work of enthusiasm rather than of accurate scholarship and the text suffered accordingly." [52] In his Blake bibliography Mr. Keynes had already made a most gentlemanly evaluation of the work:

The chief value of these volumes lies in the interpretation of the symbolism, the paraphrased commentaries and the lithographic re-productions which they contain. The memoir introduces a new theory of Blake's ancestry, according to which he is supposed to be of Irish origin. The value of the printed text is reduced by the large number of inaccuracies which occur in them; some of these are intentional alterations. [53]

On May 3, 1900, Yeats wrote in his personal copy of the Blake volumes a short note on their composition and his own criticism of their content:

The writing of this book is mainly Ellis's. The thinking is as much mine as his. The biography is by him. He wrote and trebled in size a biography of mine. The greater part of the "symbolic system" is my writing; the rest of the book was written by Ellis working over short accounts of the books by me, except in the case of the "literary period" the account of the minor poems, and the account of Blake's art theories which are all his own except in so far as we discussed everything together.

WBY—May 3, 1900

P.S.—The Book is full of misprints. There is a good deal here and there in the biography, etc., with which I am not in agreement. I think that some of my own constructive symbolism is put with too much confidence. It is mainly right but parts should be used rather as an interpretitive [sic] hypothesis than as a certainty. The circulation of the Zoas, which seems to me unlike anything in traditional symbolism, is the chief cause of uncertainty, but most that I have written on the subject is at least part of Blake's plan. There is also uncertainty about the personages who are mentioned by him too seldom to make one know them perfectly; I here and there elaborate.[54]

If they lacked scholarly tact, Yeats and Ellis possessed some qualifications for their study—considerable interest in certain mystical philosophers known to Blake (Boehme and Swedenborg) and much occult lore (the Cabala and eastern myths). Yeats had acquired some learning from occultists, including Mme. H. P. Blavatsky, who was a veritable storehouse of mythology; but it was a random, unsystematized learning. In an annotation to his own copy of the Quaritch edition, opposite a comparison between Blake's symbolism and a Hindu myth, he wrote, "Authority H. P. B. a doubtful authority—I would never quote her now." [55] Yeats's qualification was thus ultimately his weakness. Northrop Frye has written in an important essay on Yeats that Yeats and Ellis "approached Blake . . . from the wrong side of Blavatsky: that is, they had already acquired a smattering of occultism, and they expected to find in Blake an occult system or secret doctrine instead of a poetic language." [56]

Nevertheless, the Ellis-Yeats interpretation—especially if we remember the state of Blake studies in 1893—is much better than has generally been allowed. It is all too true that the editors run afoul of the word "mysticism" in their commentary, but later commentators have done worse by Blake in this matter. The truth is that when Yeats speaks of mysticism and the mystical vision of experience, he is in spite of his terminology speaking of the language of poetic symbolism, what Northrop Frye calls a set of "symbolic conventions." In the Quaritch edition Yeats discusses the problem:

Whoever has understood the correspondence asserted by Blake between (say) sight, hearing, taste and smell, and certain mental qualities, feels at once that much in his own intellect is plainer to him, and when Shakespeare compares the mind of the mad Lear to the "vexed sea," we are told at once something more laden with meaning than many pages of psychology. A "correspondence," for the very reason that it is implicit rather than explicit, says far more than a syllogism or a scientific observation. The chief difference between the metaphors of poetry and the symbols of mysticism is that the latter are woven together into a complete system. The "vexed sea" would not be merely a detached comparison, but, with the fish it contains, would be related to the land and air, the winds and shadowing clouds, and all in their totality compared to the mind in its totality.[57]

Yeats's distinction between "the metaphors of poetry" and "the symbols of mysticism" simply does not survive scrutiny, for some metaphors can become a part of a pattern of symbolism within a work of literature and yet remain metaphors of poetry. To call any poet who develops a pattern of symbolism in his work a mystic is to purge the term of any useful meaning. Yeats's treatment of the term "mysticism" is itself vague and misleading. By his use of the term he seems to imply that mysticism follows from putting into practice a certain kind of theory of knowledge. Yet when we analyze his conception of this theory we find that it is simply that same denial of naïve materialism made by Blake and already described in this chapter. This denial is so generally made in one form or another by poets and philosophers that to classify it as mysticism is simply to render the word useless. And yet Yeats could say with some accuracy in a letter to John O'Leary, "I have been busy with Blake. You complain about the mysticism [Yeats's esoteric studies]. It has enabled me to make out Blake's prophetic books at any rate." [58] His esoteric study did teach him much about myth and symbol.

If we read Yeats's essay "The Necessity of Symbolism" in Volume I of the Quaritch edition and substitute "poet" for "mystic," we shall not be fully satisfied, but we shall discover that Yeats apprehends the central form of Blake's vision and tells us a great deal about the language of poetic symbolism in general. We shall discover also, in spite of Yeats's description of Blake's symbolism as mystical and occult, that Yeats's argument itself shows Blake's work to be essentially poetic rather than esoteric.

The editors were the first to deal intelligently with Blake's use of the term "nature," a key word in understanding the whole system. Their Preface clears up a semantic problem:

Nature, he tells (or rather he reminds) us, is merely a name for one form of mental existence. Art is another and a higher form. But that art may rise to its true place, it must be set free from memory that binds it to Nature.

Nature,—or creation,—is a result of the shrinkage of consciousness,—originally clairvoyant [here we have the first intimation of Yeats's interest in the occult],—under the rule of the five senses, and of argument and law. Such consciousness is the result of the divided portions of Universal Mind obtaining perception of one another.[59]

Here the editors introduce us to Blake's symbolism of self-enclosure—the globe, the "womb of nature." They write that Blake saw nature itself as a symbol: "Art and poetry, by constantly using symbolism, continually remind us that nature itself is a symbol. To remember this, is to be redeemed from nature's death and destruction." [60] Over and over again throughout "The Symbolic System" Yeats defines "nature" as a nonmaterial symbol. He writes that Blake saw the natural body as a symbol, also. When Blake speaks of "man," he means, according to Yeats, "the highest ideal, 'the human form divine,' as he calls it, and not the extrinsic body." [61] Man's own bodily life is itself symbolical: "The growing genius of the child forms about it by affinity a complex series of thoughts, and these in their turn have much to do in moulding unconsciously the no less complex symbol, or series of symbols, known as the physical body." [62]

In the Preface the editors write: "Imagination may be described as that which is sent bringing spirit to nature, entering into nature, and seemingly losing its spirit, that nature being revealed as symbol may lose the power to delude." [63] Here the editors suggest perhaps too strongly the spiritual existence of nature as a positive force rather than as a negative creation in the mind of divided man, but the important point of nature's delusory power is emphatically made throughout the volumes.

No less important to the interpretation is a description of the nature of the "symbol," for "nature" itself is really a vast symbolism, a "mirror" of infinity refracted into particular images. [64] The essay "The Necessity of Symbolism," which precedes a discussion of specific Blakean symbols, lays the foundation for intelligent study:

To hear a man talking, or to watch his gestures, is to study symbolism, and when we restate our impressions in what are thought to be straightforward and scientific sentences, we are in reality giving a more limited, and therefore more graspable, symbolic statement of this impalpable reality. Mysticism, poetry and all creative arts, for the very reason that they explain but seldom, are more profound than the explanatory sciences. Sometimes the mystical student, bewildered by the different systems, forgets for a moment that the history of moods is the history of the universe, and asks where is the final statement—the complete doctrine. The universe is itself that doctrine and statement. [65]

We create the real, mental world—a central form of experience which is the only unity, a macrocosm of symbols in itself. A description of the single unit which is simultaneously both doctrine and statement, world and expression of the world in language, is achieved on the analogy of organism:

It is the charm of mythic narrative that it cannot tell one thing without telling a hundred others. The symbols are an endlessly inter-marrying family. They give life to what, stated in general terms, appears only a cold truism, by hinting how the apparent simplicity of the statement is due to an artificial isolation of a fragment, which, in its natural place, is connected with all the infinity of truths by living fibres.[66]

Faced with the necessity of isolating fragments in order to explain Blake to a Urizenic audience, Yeats seeks to do as little violence as possible to the structure of the great myth. He recognizes that a major problem in understanding Blake's symbolism is presented by the paradoxical nature of his cosmos, where things expand inward and contract outward. When he first attempts to deal with Blake's denial of materialist space, he fails to overcome the paradox: "The mood of the seer, no longer bound in by the particular experiences of his body, spreads out and enters into the particular experiences of an ever-widening circle of other lives and beings." [67] But in Blake the expansion described above does not enlarge the circle. Instead it turns the circle inside out, or better still it corrects the inside-outness of the circle which came about in the fall. To correct the circle's inside-outness is to free the mind from any boundaries whatever instead of simply enlarging the area within the boundaries. In another place Yeats comes closer to Blake's view: "The perception of the senses apart from symbol, limits us down to the narrow circle of personal experience." [68] Later, in Volume I, when he examines Blake's symbol "the centre," which he calls a paradox, he writes:

The apparent contradiction disappears when looked at in the light of Blake's religious belief in the essential brotherliness of Imagination, and the essential egotism and isolation of Reason. The one being Christ, the other Satan. . . . Each is endowed with a centre and a circumference. The centre of brotherhood, or its essence, is its quality of expansiveness. But this is an inner expansiveness. Each man opens his own mind inwards into the field of Vision and there, in this infinite realm, meets his brother-man.[69]

In the conception of enclosure and in the hope of escape into the realm of a universal mind, Yeats's interpretation of Blake approaches Yeats's own later interpretation of life. On page 305 of Volume I there appears a chart called "Chart of the Descending and Ascending Reason," which pictures the travel of Blake's Urizen through his world, through the seven days of his creation to the zenith of his power and then suddenly "falling down a terrible space" back to the nadir. This spiraling circle is Yeats's first gyre, drawn long before the supernatural events leading to his writing of *A Vision*. The path of Urizen is the path of Yeats's falcon in "The Second Coming," the path of all history in the charts and graphs of *A Vision:*

Then "Adam begins again in endless circle," and the first Church comes once more in some new form. This is purely Blakean. With the finality of the sectary and reformer Swedenborg believed that his new revelation was to last for ever and not to be merely a new turn of the old wheel. Blake's mind was infinitely more subtle. . . . Blake dared to see that the serpent must always keep its tail in its mouth, and creed follow creed, no matter how bitter be our longing for finality. Into this ever-revolving circle Christ only can descend and draw man upward out of nature.[70]

Upwardness and inwardness in Blake are identical, and Christ is the symbol of imagination. Again Blake's imagery suggests the later Yeats, though there is no conventional Christ for Yeats— only the wheel and Urizen seeking release.

The concept of inward expansion suggests the disappearance of common spatial concepts, and Yeats tells us that the whole idea of symbolism tends to violate our concepts of extension. Everything is really happening at once. A symbolical statement is not fully linear:

It must always be remembered that when Blake speaks of any of these personages [the characters of his prophetic books] he does not mean merely this or that particular attribute, but all the attributes in various degrees according to the point of view from which we choose to take the story. A perfect mystical [can we not read "poetical" here?] symbol or fable can be read in any region of nature and thought—mineral, meteoric, religious, philosophical—it is all one. Things we have to give in *succession* in our explanatory prose are set forth *simultaneously* in Blake's verse. From this arises the greater part of the obscurity of the symbolic books. The surface is perpetually, as it were, giving way before one, and revealing another surface below it, and that again dissolves when we try to study it.[71]

Yeats's later essays on Blake in *Ideas of Good and Evil* continue to deal with the problem of understanding symbolism and its defiance of material forms. Yeats writes that Blake spoke in a strange way "because he spoke of things for whose speaking he could find no models in the world about him." [72] Our vocabulary too easily implies a materialistic view, and Blake's work becomes the receptacle of mystery, just as Urizen comes to treat religion as mystery. To have become the darling of a cult would have irritated Blake. He would even have objected to the use of the word, "invisible," in the following words of Yeats: "A symbol is indeed the only possible expression of some invisible essence, a transparent lamp about a spiritual flame; while allegory is one of many possible representations of an embodied thing." [73] To Blake the symbol is always immediately visible, and the symbol is the essence. It is allegory that makes things "invisible," by raising a wall of words between object and subject. The relation of symbol to mind is immediate for Blake; symbols *are* mind. It is ironic that Yeats, Blake's first real interpreter, should shroud the Blakean truth of this relationship in mystery:

It is happily no part of my purpose to expound in detail the relations he believed to exist between symbol and mind, for in doing so I should come upon not a few doctrines which, though they have not been difficult to many simple persons, ascetics wrapped in skins, women who had cast away all common knowledge, peasants dreaming by their sheepfolds upon the hills, are full of obscurity to the man of modern culture.[74]

For Yeats, Blake was the first prophet of the religion of art "of which no man dreamed in the world about him," [75] but Yeats himself was a "man of modern culture," by no means able to escape the circle of reason, especially after reason had achieved such astonishing scientific success. Despite his sensitive study and understanding of Blake, Yeats came from Blake's system with hope instead of full assent. The vein of skepticism in Yeats made him seek for some demonstrable proof of the relation of symbol to mind and mind to mind. For Yeats, Blake was a man fighting against great odds, "a symbolist who had to invent his symbols." [76] Yeats wanted to follow in Blake's tradition and to discover a mythology of transcendent significance: "The systems of philosophy and the dogmas of religion are to the mystic of the Blakean school merely symbolic expressions of racial moods or emotions—the essences of truth—seeking to express themselves in terms of racial memory and experience." [77] But Yeats wanted proof that there was such a thing as a racial memory and a Universal Poetic Genius. While he was studying Blake he was also studying magic, where symbolism was tested empirically. In the Blake volumes Ellis writes:

While this work is going through the press some curious experiments have been commenced with persons who, on receiving a symbol, have the power of seeing and conversing with visionary forms raised by that symbol. Some of these seers have beheld personages that are recognizably identical with those of Blake's myth, though differing a little, as Blake himself said visions differ with the eye of the visionary. Orc, for instance, was viewed by one seer as black, instead of glowing, and by another as a wolf in armour.[78]

Yeats was hoping to find proof in magical experimentation that, as Arthur Symons later wrote, symbolism is the "establishing of the links which hold the world together." [79]

Strangely enough, magical and symbolical experimentation is foreign to Blake's whole concept of truth. To him it would have been Baconian experimentation, Lockean materialism, Newtonian sleep. On the other hand, Blake's work is a striking example of symbolist method, and Yeats wrote to John O'Leary in July 1892, "If I had not made magic my constant study I could not have written a single word of my Blake book." [80] If Blake was not a magician, magicians were symbolists.

With the false Yeatsian picture of Blake as mystic and magician dismissed, Blake the symbolist remains. In spite of Yeats's intelligent discussion of the principles of Blake's symbolism and of certain Blakean symbols themselves, the running accounts of the prophetic books, written by Ellis from notes by both editors, are inaccurate because they are based upon an inadequate, specialized learning and a superficial study of the particulars of the prophecies. To what extent Yeats was responsible for the deficiencies of this section it is difficult to say. It appears likely, however, that in writing up the accounts Ellis may have tended to limit Blake's symbolism to that which Blake himself defined as hated allegory. Because these accounts are not trustworthy, the next three chapters of this book (approaching Blake, it is hoped, from the right side of Mme. Blavatsky) present a brief analysis of the symbolic pattern of the prophecies. Chapters VI through IX consider Yeats's own symbolism and its important similarities to Blake's.

CHAPTER III

"A Complete Corpus
of Poetic Reference"

If it were not for the Poetic or Prophetic character
the Philosophic & Experimental would soon be at the
ratio of all things, & stand still, unable to do other than
repeat the same dull round over again.

—WILLIAM BLAKE [1]

IN HIS remarkable book *The White Goddess*, Robert Graves
writes that William Blake was the only poet known to him who
ever tried to institute "Bardism" in England. By "Bardism" Graves
probably means allegiance to a great, controlling mythology in
which the history and total value of every word used are known
to the poet and to his colleagues. Graves believes that such an
allegiance inevitably brings the poet to one universal system of
archetypes—"a single poetic theme." Graves claims for Blake
that "he intended his Prophetic Books as a complete corpus of
poetic reference, but for want of intelligent colleagues was
obliged to become a whole Bardic college in himself, without
even an initiate to carry on the tradition after his death." [2]

Certainly, Blake sought to create a "complete corpus of poetic
reference." He sought to do it by correcting two past errors simul-

taneously. First, he would reinterpret the greatest source of prophecy, the Bible. Second, he would present anew—purified by a personal vision—the truths of the old mythologies. In "A Descriptive Catalogue" he writes:

The antiquities of every Nation under Heaven, is no less sacred than that of the Jews. They are the same thing, as Jacob Bryant and all antiquaries have proved. How other antiquities came to be neglected and disbelieved [or distorted, he might have added], while those of the Jews are collected and arranged, is an enquiry worthy both of the Antiquarian and the Divine.[3]

One of the antiquities is, of course, the great saga of Arthur. In the catalogue for his ill-fated exhibition of 1809, Blake explains the symbolism of one of his paintings called "The Ancient Britons," and he asserts, "The British Antiquities are now in the Artist's hands; all his visionary contemplations, relating to his own country and its ancient glory, when it was, as it again shall be, the source of learning and inspiration." [4] He means that he now understands the true symbolical meaning of the ancient British legends, which when read correctly celebrate a time before time, before the fall, when England was eternity, not simply a false, delusory, clouded island, the home of many oppressions:

> But most thro' midnight streets I hear
> How the youthful Harlot's curse
> Blasts the new born Infant's tear,
> And blights with plagues the Marriage hearse.[5]

The Britons of the Golden Age were, according to Blake, wise "naked men"—naked in order to symbolize the divestation of false materiality—but they were overwhelmed in the fall from eternity (or Eden, as Blake calls it). The symbol of that lost golden England is Arthur, and in the day of apocalypse Arthur will return. Blake discovers that, "Arthur was a name for the constellation Arcturus, or Boötes, the keeper of the North Pole." [6] This suggests that the Arthur of the legends we now know is greatly changed, that originally he was some figure óf cosmic proportions and great spiritual significance, topping the world, so to speak. It would appear that the Arthur of legend is a mortal symbol for a greater figure.

According to Blake's description of "The Ancient Britons," after the fall only three men escaped into space-time as we now know it. These were three archetypal creatures which Blake would have us believe are every man—the "Beautiful," the "Strong," and the "Ugly":

The Strong Man represents the human sublime. The Beautiful Man represents the human pathetic, which was in the wars of Eden [the fall] divided into male and female. The Ugly Man represents the human reason. They were originally one man, who was fourfold. He was self-divided, and his real humanity slain on the stems of generation, and the form of the fourth was like the Son of God. How he became divided is a subject of great sublimity and pathos. The artist has written it under inspiration, and will, if God please, publish it; it is voluminous, and contains the ancient history of Britain, and the world of Satan and of Adam.[7]

The fourth creature symbolizes the fallen unity, God. Blake calls him Albion because England is the microcosm of all things, because Albion is the true Arthur, the dead hero who must be revived: "The giant Albion, was Patriarch of the Atlantic; he is the Atlas of the Greeks, one of those the Greeks called Titans. The stories of Arthur are the acts of Albion, applied to a Prince of the fifth century, who conquered Europe, and held the Empire of the world in the dark age, which the Romans never again recovered."[8] Blake's prophecies apply the events in contemporary Europe to the acts of Albion. Blake has reinterpreted the myth in what he calls its "poetical vigour."

In Blake's terms all of British history presents to the active reader the same meaning which is preserved "by the Saviour's mercy" in the Bible, especially in the Old Testament myths of genesis. In Blake's description of his painting "The Last Judg-

ment" we are told that "an Aged patriarch is awakened by his
aged wife—He is Albion, our Ancestor, patriarch of the Atlantic
Continent, whose History Preceded that of the Hebrews & in
whose Sleep, or Chaos, Creation began." [9] The old, distorted
legends and the usually misinterpreted Bible are really a unity
creating a single cosmogonic myth which tells the whole story
of creation, fall, history, apocalypse from a specific point of
view or focus. That focus suggests paradoxically that the whole
story is a delusion, that to see a series of acts in a false time, spread
through a false extension, is to see reality clothed (as the naked
Ancient Britons were not) in error. In truth, reality is a timeless, spaceless symbol—a single symbol. To prove this point Blake
shows us that there are two ways to look at our world.

SPACE, TIME, AND SYMBOL

The first way is to look at history, the charting of time past,
as a single linear movement stretching from some moment of
creation endlessly into infinity. Another way is to see time moving cyclically, things repeating themselves, progress qualified
by return. Each of these, as Blake sees it, is a half-truth. The first
vision allows no end for our delusions, no boundaries for our
actions, no consummation for our hopes. The second is perhaps
nearer the truth, but stated as above it is subject to most of the
same objections. But if we look for a moment at the cycle as the
legendary symbolic serpent, which bites its own tail and seeks to
consume itself, we see that in this symbol there is finally a moment
of no return, of action ceased, where the serpent must stop or
supernaturally consume itself and thus disappear. Here a certain kind of progress impresses itself upon the cycle. To the
visionary, then, the circle is not totally hopeless—it is really a
spiral going somewhere—but to the corporeal eye, the circle
forms a limit to time even more severe than the thought of progression *ad infinitum*. The visionary arrives at the same conclu-

sions about time if (as I have suggested in Chapter I) he can see all things as analogies of all other things. The view of things as cyclical in time is thus a view lacking its logical completion in unity.

As for looking at space, the problem is perhaps slightly more complicated. Without material substance space becomes the inward expansion of the mind, a Blakean paradox. In the Blakean cosmos objects expand inward to vision, contract outward to materiality. In *Jerusalem*, Blake's prophet-hero Los speaks to the sleeping Albion:

> We live as One Man; for contracting our infinite senses
> We behold multitude, or expanding, we behold as one. . . .[10]

This is the double vision which Blake dramatizes in all of his poetry. We can see the world one way as a unity and another way as a multiplicity. One of these views is truth, the other delusion. Yet knowing which is which, I might still assert that I see on a beach millions of grains of sand, each a minute particular, each unique—where is the unity? Blake replies that each grain of sand, if looked at as a symbol of reality, divested of material substance, weight, mass, extension, ceases to have the same kind of uniqueness it has in a material world. It is an idea, and as an idea it can stand for things in the way a metaphor stands for things, and if the world is a symbolical world the metaphor is literally true. The grain of sand is the microcosm, the world itself the macrocosm:

> To see a World in a Grain of Sand
> And a Heaven in a Wild Flower,
> Hold Infinity in the palm of your hand
> And Eternity in an hour.[11]

To live in a world of symbols is to live in a world where the multiplicity of minute particulars is not the multiplicity of material objects, jostling about in space.

The problem of space, time, and symbol is thus central to an understanding of Blake. In the Blakean cosmos objects expand, contract, become opaque or transparent. And yet they do these things symbolically, depending on the way they are looked at: A grain of sand may be the world, or it may be something most irritating to the corporeal eye. Blake's system depends on a denial of our conventional views of space and time and a belief that we can know the macrocosmic pattern and can see it repeated symbolico-literally in the microcosm.

The view of space-time expressed above quite naturally leads to certain controlling metaphors, which themselves beget new metaphors. For instance, the cyclic idea of time most certainly suggests a wheel or some other circular object. Space suggests some kind of physical object. Combining space and time we get a globe. And since our globe symbolizes not only the creation of error but also the vehicle of eventual apocalypse, perhaps it is an egg waiting to be hatched, acting both as a prison and incubator of new life. In space human beings are obviously bodies; and since all human beings are in reality one being, the fallen humanity can easily be thought of as a primordial giant, hints of whom appear in the Bible. He is also the Adam Kadmon of the Cabala, and Ymir of the Edda. In Blake he is Albion, the universal man. The symbol proliferates and he becomes, as we have seen, patriarch of the Atlantic. Legend has it that the Atlantic ocean at one time rolled over a golden continent called Atlantis. This is, of course, the flood of Biblical myth too, symbolizing the fall of all things into opacity, down into materiality. But note also that water is a traditional symbol of rebirth, purification. So the great flood which wiped out the eternal golden age is also the vehicle of a cleansing ritual by means of which apocalypse may reappear. Here again the mundane symbol of water, like the symbol of the globe, holds within it ambiguous but not incompatible meanings.

There are other ambiguities which in the fallen world appear to be incompatible, but they are merely broken images of a basic unity. Old Chinese symbolical thought saw reality as a circle, the *ovum mundi*, the great monad, which is divided by two arcs with opposite centers. These two halves, perpetually whirling after one another, were the material or feminine principle *yin* and the spiritual or masculine principle *yang*. They are Blake's "contraries" without which "is no progression." We can arrive at a similar conclusion about the contraries by recognizing that if we symbolize time as a wheel, the fallen world, like the astrologist's circle, sets up opposites staring across at each other, following each other in a mad, pointless chase as the wheel spins. As long as the contraries maintain the chase and as long—to change the metaphor—as the serpent who forms the wheel consumes himself, the contraries do create progression toward some finality, where the opposites are married, all things joined.

As Blake's mythology develops, he is able to see a good many of the faults of the fallen world in the form of these contraries. Good and evil have been so distorted as no longer to have useful designatory power as symbols, yet their clash—or pseudoclash —keeps the circle moving. Another opposition symbolized by the Chinese circle is that of male and female, which suggests man striving for completion of self. The feminine creature comes to symbolize not only the error of materiality (for material creates separation) but also a perverted chastity. In his poems Blake attacks false moral codes:

> And Priests in black gowns were walking their rounds,
> And binding with briars my joys & desires.[12]

Blake's archetypal female figure is the great frustrator who has enclosed man in his "corporeal" senses. Sometimes she is called "Nature," at other times "Mystery," for mystery is a "corporeal" idea; there is no mystery to vision. In the description of "The Last Judgment," Blake writes:

Beneath these is the Seat of the Harlot, nam'd Mystery in the Revelations. She is siezed [*sic*] by Two Beings each with three heads;

they Represent Vegetative Existence; as it is written in Revelations, they strip her naked & burn her with fire; it represents the Eternal Consummation of Vegetable Life & Death with its Lusts. . . . Those who are blessed with Imaginative Vision see This Eternal Female & tremble at what others fear not, while they despise & laugh at what others fear.[13]

This harlot, whom Blake usually calls "Rahab, the Whore of Babylon," serves to represent material substance and thus what Blake castigates as "reason."

The belief in material substance has led to the following errors:

1. That Man has two real existing principles: Viz: a Body & a Soul.
2. That Energy, call'd Evil, is alone from the Body; & that Reason, call'd Good, is alone from the Soul.[14]

We have come full circle here (the symbol is apt), for we now know how Lockean epistemological error is intertwined with errors of morality, errors of false contrariety. "The Last Judgment [will be] when all those are Cast away who trouble Religion with Questions concerning Good & Evil or Eating of the Tree of those Knowledges or Reasonings which hinder the Vision of God, turning all into a Consuming Fire." [15]

Throughout his work, then, Blake is always battling the same monster, a Spenserian Blatant Beast which turns up in all phases of human activity—representing the powers of generalization, materialism, literalness—to destroy all vision. This monster has attempted to frustrate all art, to distort the magical power of the great archetypal symbols, by creating a false distinction between *symbolical* and *real*.

Where did such error begin? Far back in time, though in recent centuries there has been a shift in the nature of the error. In *The Seventeenth Century Background*, Professor Basil Willey has taken as an example of the changing conception of one of our most powerful poetic symbols the views of the nature of the moon from the Scholastic period to the period of the New Philosophy. According to the medieval world view the moon was perfect, spherical, a heavenly body—heaven meaning not simply a body out in space but a body of supernatural quality. After Galileo the moon became a natural object of a quite different kind, as imperfect as our own euphemistically designated "globe." Professor Willey writes:

[Lunar mountains] would be abhorrent to the Peripatetic as derogations from the moon's "perfection," which implied her perfect sphericity (the "sphere" being the most "perfect" of solids). Galileo makes it his affair to deny that incorruptibility, inalterability and sphericity are necessary attributes of "perfection." It is more "noble" for the earth, for example, to be as it is than to be like a lump of crystal; . . . we should note this as a good early example of the veneration for "things-as-they-are" rather than "things-as-they-can-be-conceived." [16]

It is not difficult to determine with whom Blake would tend to side in this argument. For Blake, nothing exists unless it is conceived. But Blake can agree only partially with the Scholastic view, for the Scholastic view, if nearer to a philosophy of mental things, nevertheless misconstrues the nature of mental existence by ascribing to it materiality distinct from spirituality. Nevertheless, in the Scholastic view the moon maintained at least vestiges of its symbolical reality. Today as a symbol for poetry the moon must be abstracted from material reality. In poetry the moon symbol thus becomes merely a stylization; the poet is easily caricatured as a spinner of false dreams or an ornamentor of a basically drab material world. The duty of the poet is naïvely thought to be imitation, not creation. But Blake dissents: " 'What,' it will be Question'd, 'When the Sun rises, do you not see a round disk of fire somewhat like a Guinea?' O no, no, I see an Innumberable company of the Heavenly host crying, 'Holy, Holy, Holy is the Lord God Almighty.' " [17]

A last judgment, when the false material view of things is finally abolished, will be, in Blake's words, "an overwhelming of Bad Art and Science," for bad art and science are the logical results of the materialist view whereby reality is misplaced.

Although Blake is battling a single monster, he is at the same time forcing it to work for him. Paradoxically, apocalypse, says Blake, will appear only when the form of degradation is complete and perceptible to all. No one can fully understand error until he has seen it symbolized in its clear and proper outlines. Furthermore, error as it operates in the fallen world can do nothing but consume itself just as the serpent consumes itself. Eventually error's bid for power is its own downfall. As long as it remains clouded and unformed, it is pernicious, but in this state it cannot fully assert itself. When it achieves completed form, the corporeal eye can understand it for what it is. If, says Blake, the multiplicity of errors is ever seen communally as a unity, then apocalypse will have been effected, the trumpet blown.

This paradoxical theory leads to Blake's theory of art as prophecy, which demands the "vision of these eternal principles or characters of human life" created with "minute discrimination" with special emphasis upon outline: "Without Minute Neatness of Execution The Sublime cannot Exist! Grandeur of Ideas is founded on Precision of Ideas." [18]

The most important thing about Blake's vision, however, is that it presents what is basically a single image or central form of experience into which can be drawn all minute particulars, where what have always been looked upon as contraries are unclothed and shown to be "equally true." The globe which narrows and narrows and becomes more and more confining makes existence within intolerable. The shell cracks, the inhabitant leaps into the real world. The circle, sphere, egg—anything which becomes part of cyclic movement consuming itself—is an image in microcosm of central form. This form can be viewed as unity, as a timeless ideal. Microcosms of it are what Blake calls "the bright sculptures of Los's halls," creations of the artistic imagination (re-creations of a collective unconscious, perhaps), re-creations

of the Poetic Genius. Any symbolic representation of these timeless ideals in time is what Blake calls prophecy: "Prophets, in the
modern sense of the word, have never existed. Jonah was no
prophet in the modern sense, for his prophecy of Nineveh
failed." [19] A modern poet can speak well for Blake on this point
—Hart Crane in his essay on modern poetry: "Poetic prophecy
in the case of the seer has nothing to do with factual prediction
or with futurity. It is a peculiar type of perception, capable
of apprehending some absolute and timeless concept of the imagination with astounding clarity and conviction." [20] Blake would
have objected only to the word "peculiar." To him this kind of
perception was the real common denominator of human existence.

A poem, then, or a painting was to Blake, as it is to C. Day
Lewis, "a total image," [21] microcosm of another image, the world.
This image cannot be "expressed in general propositions." As
Northrop Frye has written of Blake, "The units of poetry are
images rather than ideas, and a poem's total meaning is therefore
a total image, a single visualizable picture." [22]

GLOBE AND CAVERN

The total image Blake worked toward in his great prophecies
was the image of reality. As long as it was not a total image it
would be a series of images in multiplicity and thus merely an
unsatisfactory patchwork of past errors. All of Blake's works are
attempts to achieve total image or, as he called it, "vision." His
self-imposed task was to outline all existence from creation to
apocalypse in this single visualization.

One of Blake's greatest total images is the *Book of Urizen*,
his first attempt to deal with creation and fall. In *Urizen* we see
the Blakean imagery in its most stunning power—a vast, primeval
world of giants, globes, trembling noises, and depths. The sounds
crash in great shapes and ages. The vastness of this world is

symbolized not only visually but also audibly, for in *Urizen* the sound is successfully a part of the symbol:

> what Demon
> Hath form'd this abominable void,
> This soul-shudd'ring vacuum? . . .
>
>   .   .   .   .   .
>
> . . . & the rolling of wheels,
> As of swelling seas, sound in his clouds,
> In his hills of stor'd snows, in his mountains
> Of hail & ice; voices of terror
> Are heard, like thunders of autumn
> When the cloud blazes over the harvest.[23]

All the powers of language are brought to bear here, the alliteration enforcing the fury, the visual image enforced by the movement from vowel to vowel wrenched in controlled dissonance:

> cloud blazes over the harvest

In the previous long quotation Blake plays upon similar sounds to achieve the effect of violent convulsion and swooping fall through a vast spacelessness:

> Soul shudd'ring vacuum

The words have a palpable texture; the lines charge swiftly, race, revolve, slow with the images:

> Times on times he divided & measur'd
> Space by space in his ninefold darkness,
> Unseen, unknown; changes appear'd
> Like desolate mountains, rifted furious
> By the black winds of perturbation.[24]

Urizen, the busy architect—"The Ancient of Days" as Blake titles a painting of him—moves mysteriously, methodically; the whipping wind symbolizes in speed the horrifying results of his labor. Blake's universe is a falling universe, and the wind—palpable, powerful—is also a state of mind, black and cold like Lockean material. The mountains are extensions of the mind; visual images become symbols in a world where rightly there is nothing else but a symbol, where time is not our time and space not our space.

The *Book of Urizen* begins in eternity. Here the imagination reigns supreme without the intervention of the fallen forms of space and time between the perceiver and the perceived. Blake's problem in writing *Urizen* was to communicate a vision of eternity while denying at the same time what we have come to think of as its conventional existence. The problem had worried men before Blake—Boehme, for example:

It is only our feeble mind which is compelled to place one thing after another, because, otherwise, we could not comprehend it. But the real state of the case is different. In eternity there is no temporal succession, but everything is in "circular" movement; nothing is first, nothing last in point of time; but everything is simultaneous.[25]

According to Boehme, then, the question of what is going to happen, like the question of whether God knows what is going to happen, is a fallen question, woefully distorted. God is the greatest of prophets, but a prophet does not predict; he simply sees reality as a single unit; he thinks in a form which symbolizes time as circular, but he sees the circle from without or above. He is not trapped within it. In *Urizen* what we see is the gradual erection of a prison, for Urizen eventually finds himself trapped within the circle of time. The eternity in which Urizen acts at the beginning is a realm of the imagination, where reality is unity, where everything is an extension of the mind, a symbol of thought. If man creates out of that extension a system of abstract ideas, or if he begins to think of the extension as material, he begins to trap himself. He must look at the world as if it were symbolical, not as if it were a soulless chaos of particles. And the pre-fall world must also be seen as a receptacle for the symbols of imagination created by a communal man. All ideals exist there. Blake says:

Many suppose that before the Creation [Blake thinks of the Creation and the Fall as synonymous] All was Solitude & Chaos. This is the most pernicious Idea that can enter the Mind, as it takes away all sublimity from the Bible & Limits All Existence to Creation & to Chaos, To the Time and Space fixed by the Corporeal Vegetative Eye, & leaves the Man who entertains such an Idea the habitation of Unbelieving demons. Eternity Exists, and All things in Eternity, Independent of Creation. . . .[26]

In *Urizen,* where the fall emerges from eternity, there are four basic clusters of imagery, all of which contribute to a total image. They are images of (1) circularity, (2) division, (3) enclosure, and (4) material, such as rock, mountain, water, chain, and body. So coherent is this body of imagery that the existence of all the clusters can almost be imaginatively deduced from the knowledge of the existence of any one of them. Each cluster is a microcosm of the whole.

The first intimation of circularity occurs at the very beginning of the poem. The Eternals describe Urizen as "self-clos'd, all-repelling," "dark revolving" in self-contemplation. These, as Boehme says, are images of the perfect "circularity" of eternity, where time is not linear, space nonexistent, reality mental. But Urizen's contemplation is totally egocentric; he inhabits his own forests apart from the total unity. He broods, he rationalizes, he divides all things. Soon he begins to attribute some new kind of existence to his ideas; they take the form of mountains whipped by black winds. He begins to think of these extensions of his imagination as existing in some way beyond himself. Apart from him they become strange and dangerous, and he battles them as if they are his enemies: "beast, bird, fish, serpent and element." He prepares to assert himself now, not only against these creatures but against the Eternals themselves. He imagines seas, clouds, snows, mountains, and ice. The rolling of wheels sounds through his new cosmos—images of war, division, new circularity, the going-nowhereness of his action.

In this period of time or circular not-time Urizen has unhappily succeeded in thinking out the first steps toward the fall. Material earth has not yet formed. Urizen battles ideas still:

> Earth was not: nor globes of attraction;
> The will of the Immortal expanded
> Or contracted his all flexible senses;
> Death was not, but eternal life sprung.[27]

No images of enclosure, no separated globes or circles, no material entities yet exist; but Urizen in his dark contemplation has begun to suspect that there are separate material entities. Some of these beliefs, metamorphosed into suspicions, he calls "evil." Somewhere in the dark past, he tells us, he has already fought with evil, which he symbolizes as fire, an image of good transvaluated. Having emerged victorious, he claims that he has plumbed the depths of existence—the communal mind of man and thus his own mind, though unrecognizable to him. He claims to have found there an enclosure, the womb of nature, a world of water and solids:

> First I fought with fire, consum'd
> Inwards into a deep world within:
> A void immense, wild, dark & deep,
> Where nothing was: Nature's wide womb;
> And self-balanc'd, stretch'd o'er the void,
> I alone, even I! the winds merciless
> Bound; but condensing in torrents
> They fall & fall; strong I repell'd
> The vast waves, & arose on the waters
> A wide world of solid obstruction.[28]

Having created his globe and having fallen within its hollow spaces so that he is enclosed as in a womb, he is ensphered in what seems to his distorted perception a void. Out of the liquid of nature's womb he manages to create, like the Elohim, a more

solid material which he symbolizes as books "form'd of metal."
They hold the "secrets of wisdom" created and hidden in smoke
and cloud by his own contemplation. From these books of
sounding brass he deduces abstract moral commandments which
he means to enforce within his closed world. Urizen symbolizes
the enormity of his error in a speech to the world in which he
asserts that he has battled against terrible monsters, the seven
deadly sins. These monsters are, of course, bred from his own
wilderness, brought into existence by the powers of his own perverse imagination. When he fights them he is fighting his own
divided self, turning in wheels. He himself is the dragon, the
fierce attacker. His circular, deterministic thought recalls the
cavern and mill of Blake's *Marriage of Heaven and Hell* and
predicts the unprolific "mill of the mind" of Yeats's poetry, consuming over and over again the same intellectual rubbish. Just
as according to old physical theory matter can be neither created
nor destroyed, the powers of reason in both Blake and Yeats
work with a given amount of material and are thus held down
to making the same dull round over and over again with no
escape.

Attributing independent material existence to all of his own
symbolism, Urizen is mentally sick. He attempts to bring all
separate entities back together artificially under a single law by
the power of abstract reasoning. The fall is imminent:

> Sund'ring, dark'ning, thund'ring,
> Rent away with a terrible crash,
> Eternity roll'd wide apart,
> Wide asunder rolling.[29]

Through this breach Urizen falls into a void between "frowning
cliffs," and again we see him, this time past all possible immediate
redemption:

> And a roof vast, petrific around
> On all sides he fram'd, like a womb.[30]

From his point of view he is enclosed, roofed over in a world of mountains and rivers essentially "petrific." To the Eternals viewing their fallen brother, his world is divided from them, a "globe," a "human heart":

> . . . & like a black globe,
> View'd by sons of Eternity standing
> On the shore of the infinite ocean,
> Like a human heart, struggling & beating,
> The vast world of Urizen appear'd.[31]

The "Eternal Prophet," Los, has been assigned the difficult task of controlling this potentially dangerous world, and he watches over the globe, seeking to keep it separate from eternity so that it cannot wreak further havoc. Suddenly Blake shifts the image of the fall, and we see the still-amorphous mass of Urizen rent (like Adam's rib) from the side of Los, symbol of eternal vision. The cosmic genesis myth of globe and flood gives way to the genesis myth of mortal creation. But both myths are really the same, and Blake puts them side by side so that we may understand their identity. In the fall the body of Urizen becomes, instead of an extension of imagination, a symbol of enclosure associated with caverns and chains. This amorphous, indefinite creature falls into "stony sleep" through the great geologic ages of the earth's formation. Then Los, the blacksmith, attempts to give Urizen's formlessness some distinct outline. Molding material, he seeks to create an image which will allow man to visualize the usurping powers of matter and reason in their true form. Los seeks, as Blake seeks in his own art, "precision, outline, distinctness of form."

By attempting to "build" with amorphous, vile matter, Los symbolizes the central paradox of fall and redemption. Not until degradation is complete can the error which is creation be seen for what it really is and be dispelled. In helping to create the world's body as we know it, Los is thus hastening complete fall and at the same time preparing for the communal apocalyptic vision, which strangely enough is every bit as much a clear view of error as it is a clear view of eternity. "Without contraries is no progression." Los is the symbol of progress in time. As the builder, Los is also the artist, and his actions throughout the prophetic books symbolize Blake's own theory of art opposed to the Urizenic theory of Reynolds: "Broken Colours & Broken Lines & Broken Masses are Equally Subversive of the Sublime." [32]

The blacksmith must wrestle with hard images—chains, tongs, iron—

> The Eternal Prophet heav'd the dark bellows,
> And turn'd restless the tongs, and the hammer
> Incessant beat, forging chains new & new,
> Numb'ring with links hours, days & years. [33]

These material images symbolize in turn the creation of time; for time, like material, forms a limit beyond which the fall may not proceed. It is through God's mercy, says Blake, that the creation as we know it exists, for otherwise man would fall eternally through a void. Therefore Los builds the body of Urizen in order to give it clear form, in order to bring order out of non-entity, even if at first that order must be a fallen order.

The images describing Urizen's body are again those of circle and enclosure, material and division. The body begins to take form within an orb, where Urizen's thoughts are enclosed. Suddenly springing from his mind, a writhing spine appears, and ribs shoot out, circularly enclosing an interior space, a cavern for bodily organs. Then in the cavern a globe pulsates and metamorphoses into veins and arteries surrounding the ribs. Fast on this a third development occurs:

> His nervous brain shot branches
> Round the branches of his heart;
> On high, into two little orbs,
> And fixed in two little caves,
> Hiding carefully from the wind,
> His Eyes beheld the deep. [34]

Urizen is a mass of microcosmic globes and caverns, a tenuous unity. From any point of vantage in his own fallen world he appears as a congeries of elements; from eternity he is simply encompassed, a void in a globe, his own perceptions limited to the boundaries of his body.

In the violence of his own work, Los, who really sacrifices himself to the fallen world and laborious creation in time, falls down into a material world, which is split between him and Urizen. In pity for Urizen, Los creates from his own imagination a globe of blood from which springs a female form, his other self divided from him. The Cabala and much esoteric thought tells us that man in eternity is androgynous, that man in the world is split into sexes—"hermaphroditic" (Blake's term), because the old unity is now represented by two sexes. Blake takes up the symbolism of this idea and develops it. "Time is a Man, Space is a Woman," he says.[35] The female "emanation" of Los is Enitharmon, space. She is the first of the great female figures of the Blakean myth. In her creative state she contributes to the creation of art and gives birth to heroes. In her unprolific state she repels the prophet, helps enforce Urizen's laws, changes her name and becomes a harlot.

With the building of Urizen's body, the introduction of Los into the fallen world, and his division into male and female, the first stages of creation are completed. The Eternals, Blake's chorus, enclose this new multiplication of divisions in a new shell:

> "Spread a Tent with strong curtains around them.
> Let cords & stakes bind in the Void,
> That Eternals may no more behold them."

> They began to weave curtains of darkness,
> They erected large pillars round the Void,
> With golden hooks fasten'd in the pillars;
> With infinite labour the Eternals
> A woof wove, and called it Science.[36]

Before proceeding further, it is best to stop here to re-examine the nature of the symbolism. The four major images are inter-related. The total image to which they contribute may be formulated from the point of view of the visionary. It is a circular image imprisoning material which Los attempts to beat into forms with distinct outlines, but these forms are really half-forms and thus in a sense dead because divided. This total image is the world itself, rolling through a void which Blake later calls "Ulro." It is a great egg-sphere filled with vegetal life, globes of blood, waiting perhaps to be hatched into the golden age. Urizen himself is a microcosm of this egg, a great rough creature pictured in the illustrations sometimes as a skeleton, sometimes as a stocky human form with a gross body. His images are the globe or the cave depending upon the point from which the images are seen. As a globe Urizen is still revolving in perfect circular thought, but he has interpreted that thought corporeally. As a cave Urizen is the chained human being of Plato's allegory symbolizing the problem of knowledge, the answer to which Blake thought he knew, having escaped from the cave into the labyrinth of his own spirit.

BEAM AND SERPENT

When time begins, man, divided into man and woman, begets more men and women. Los and Enitharmon, symbols of this division, give birth to something which symbolizes, as they themselves do, a life-force of some kind, a state of existence. This force is called Orc, and his symbol is a serpent. Meanwhile Urizen and presumably Ahania, his female counterpart or emanation, beget Fuzon; and his symbol is the Old Testament pillar of fire. By this time we have advanced into the realm of human history as it is revealed to us by the Bible. The births of Orc and Fuzon create in both cases a tension between parent and son. Orc is a Prometheus, or rather Prometheus is the Orc figure distorted in Greek mythology. His parents chain him to a rock "beneath Urizen's dreadful shadow." Fuzon, however, very nearly gets the better of his father.

At this time Urizen's law has conquered the earth's people. Men's senses have "contracted"; the giants hinted at in the old myths are no more; the human form is low and reptilian. The people live in a parched land called Egypt, surrounded by salt floods. As the *Book of Urizen* ends, Fuzon, finding life in this land intolerable, leads a group of followers out of it, asserting his own individuality and his independence from his father and the fatherly law. In the *Book of Ahania* the results of this action are explored, and they are grim results indeed. Fuzon calls to his people:

> "Shall we worship this Demon of smoke,"
> Said Fuzon, "this abstract non-entity,
> This cloudy God seated on waters,
> Now seen, now obscur'd, King of sorrow?" [37]

As he speaks he molds his wrath into a globe of fire and hurls it with great speed through the void: "Burning it flew, length'ning into a hungry beam." It succeeds in rending Urizen's "disk," redividing the father, piercing the globe. Urizen's symbol, the solar disk here, suggests that this episode, read historically, presents Urizen as the Egyptian sun-god-pharaoh, the oppressor. No one knows how many slaves perished in order that his great temples and tombs might be built.

Here the two primal figures of the fallen world lock in battle: globe and beam, circle and spear, father and son, old and new. Fuzon appears as a hero; his actions are those of energy. Yet as hero he is perhaps hopelessly englobed like his father by the fallen world. As a beam or pillar of fire Fuzon seems to represent the straight line of progress, but the straight line he represents is a beam imbedded in a globe. In order to close in battle with his father and to wound him, Fuzon is forced to attach himself to his father. So Urizen's globe and Fuzon's beam are two parts of a single picture. The defect of both is evident. The globe in the fallen world cannot really go anywhere, for it returns ever to itself in one vast, spinning circle. The beam, on the other hand, moves forward endlessly from an infinite past into an infinite future, but it reaches no conclusion. Only together do these two images come under some kind of control, and that control is a tension of opposites. The double symbol can perhaps best be explained in the terms of the traditional maypole dance described by E. K. Goldsmith in *Life Symbols:* "In this symbolism of pole and circle, the dominant, forceful upright was looked upon as Creator, and the circle was the 'regulator or bridle of time and motion.' " [38]

It may well be remembered now that Urizen, even before the fall, claimed to have battled with fire:

> First I fought with fire, consum'd
> Inwards into a deep world within. [39]

His present battle with Fuzon hints unmistakably at some vast cyclic return in which both he and fire are trapped. There are other hints too. Urizen finally succeeds in conquering Fuzon by force, but only after Fuzon, having led the people from Egypt, proclaims his own divinity—becomes Urizen, so to speak. Urizen then succeeds in crucifying him, but Fuzon, nailed to the tree, though suffering terribly does not seem to die; while Urizen, if not nailed to the tree, is at least tortuously hemmed in by trees:

> Amaz'd started Urizen when
> He beheld himself compassed round
> And high roofed over with trees. [40]

As the *Book of Ahania* ends, things remain in a state of unrelieved tension. Fuzon, in the act of dividing the loins of Urizen with his beam, has succeeded in separating Ahania from him. She has become the moon to Urizen's earth:

She fell down a faint shadow wand'ring
In chaos and circling dark Urizen,
As the moon anguish'd circles the earth,
Hopeless! Abhorr'd! a death-shadow,
Unseen, unbodied, unknown,
The mother of Pestilence.[41]

The division is merely a further step in complete degradation, complete fall. Ahania, as symbol of that female will who becomes a central character of the later prophecies, contributes to the enclosure of Urizen by encircling him. She becomes an image of nature separate from man, with whom man seeks communion without success. She is the great frustrator, the distorter of imagination, the enchantress.

In the other minor prophetic books Fuzon plays no part. It is probable that Blake, recognizing that he had created not really a hero but simply a young energetic Urizen liable to the same delusions, decided to develop his other symbol of youth, Orc, about whom he had written in *America* (1793), a year before *Urizen*, and in *Europe* (1794). The minor prophecies other than *Urizen* picture an Orc inevitably associated with political reform and revolution. His gradual disappearance from Blake's later writings, along with the gradual metamorphosis of his significance, symbolizes Blake's shifting attitude toward the apocalyptic potentiality of political reform. At the same time Blake was developing a cyclic view of history consistent with his circular view of reality, and in history Orc was becoming something Blake did not want his hero to become.

In *Urizen* and *Ahania* there are definite suggestions of a cyclic view of history; both of these books seem to deal with history up to the coming of Christ, but in the light of *Europe* and *America* it becomes increasingly evident that *Urizen* and *Ahania* together symbolize the central form or "outward circumference" of history seen as a unit. History, being circular, comes back to itself. Modern history as it is described in *Europe* and *America* is simply the microcosm of this central form. Its minute particulars may differ from those of the Old Testament, but in outline there is no difference.

Europe is Blake's first attempt to describe the minute particulars of that cycle of history in which he himself lived, the cycle beginning with Christ. As the prophecy begins, a "secret child" representing Christ and microcosmic images of him "descend[s] thro' the orient gates of the eternal day." He is the culmination in fire of the Jewish inspiration, once killed already by the appearance of cold moral law on Sinai. Christ is the new bearer of fire, and he, like Fuzon, is sacrificed to law. This new death of energy is symbolized by the sleep of Enitharmon, the emanation and inspiration of Los. Her sleep echoes the nightmarish sleep and enclosure of Urizen in primordial times:

> Enitharmon slept
> Eighteen hundred years. Man was a Dream! [42]

Blake is saying that Urizen again controls the mundane world. But during this period all is not quiet. There are violent wars, microcosmic battles between Urizens and Orcs:

> Shadows of men in fleeting bands upon the winds
> Divide the heavens of Europe.[43]

Our history books tell of the building and decline of great empires, the wars for land. All of these movements are really microcosmic symbolizations of the one great form of division, the fall from eternity. Blake calls the first great fall the "wars of Eden."

One microcosm of central historical form is the "glorious revolution" in England, where the Orcian flame spirit momentarily bursts forth (the "Angels of Albion," below, are England's leaders):

> . . . Albion's Angel, smitten with his own plagues, fled with
> his bands.
>
>   .   .   .   .   .

In council gather the smitten Angels of Albion;
The cloud bears hard upon the council house, down rushing
On the heads of Albion's Angels.

One hour they lay buried beneath the ruins of that hall;
But as the stars rise from the salt lake, they arise in pain,
In troubled mists, o'erclouded by the terrors of struglin [*sic*]
   times.

In thoughts perturb'd they rose from the bright ruins, silent
   following
The fiery King. . . .[44]

The political history of England from the ruin of the monarchy
up through the Restoration is itself a rolling tension of opposites
in microcosm. The King's followers are "Angels," and angels in
Blake's cosmos are agents of the god of this world, Urizen. (See
The Marriage of Heaven and Hell for the best example of this
typical Blakean inversion.) Yet in the passage cited above,
strangely enough, Blake associates his Urizenic angels with the
Orc-Fuzon image of flame. The return of monarchy is evidently
a reassertion of energy, but it brings back only another Urizen.
Blake's symbol of energy seems, in this world at least, wed to
stultification. The suspicion is confirmed almost immediately.
With Urizen again in control,

Then was the serpent temple form'd, image of infinite,
Shut up in finite revolutions, and man became an Angel,
Heaven a mighty circle turning. . . .[45]

If the fire image of the beam is suspect, so is the serpent image
of Orc. It hardly ever travels in a straight line. It is more likely
to consume itself in circles—the symbols of Urizen himself.
Though the serpent is associated with procreation, it is also associated with poison and death, "the worm of corruption." Despite
its ability to give life, it manages only to recreate itself, sloughing
its dead skin, burning itself from Urizen back to Orc. It is not
only the worm in the womb, it is also the "great snake father"
of the material world. It is the creature who must be overcome

by the forces of some constant light, by Ra in Egypt, by Apollo in Greece. The great trouble is that Ra and Apollo are distorted, allegorized figures. Who is left to bring order but a pure mythological hero created by Blake himself—Los, whose own name is an anagram of the sun's name, and in fact the sun's name reversed?

The Ancient Guardian or Angel of England is thus either Orc or Urizen, depending upon whether he represents the forces of revolt or reaction. In the late eighteenth century he is Urizen. Orc is imminent, however, for the prospect of revolt flares through France and America. In Blake's *Europe*, Orc is still sometimes associated with apocalypse:

> But terrible Orc, when he beheld the morning in the east,
> Shot from the heights of Enitharmon,
> And in the vineyards of red France appear'd the light of his
>   fury.
>
> The sun glow'd fiery red!
> The furious terrors flew around
> On golden chariots raging with red wheels dropping with blood!
> The Lions lash their wrathful tails!
> The Tigers couch upon the prey & suck the ruddy tide,
> And Enitharmon groans & cries in anguish and dismay.
>
> Then Los arose: his head he rear'd in snaky thunders clad;
> And with a cry that shook all nature to the utmost pole,
> Call'd all his sons to the strife of blood.[46]

But strangely enough it is not Orc who sets this world-shaking revolution—perhaps the last—in motion. It is another figure:

> A mighty Spirit leap'd from the land of Albion,
> Nam'd Newton: he siez'd [*sic*] the trump & blow'd the
>   enormous blast! [47]

Newton blows the trumpet of apocalypse because he symbolizes the completed form of error, set down in its necessary clear outline. "Surely," as Yeats wrote in "The Second Coming," "some revelation is at hand!"

But nothing comes. Orc is only Urizen. The French Revolution is a failure, and Blake has already stopped work on the epic which was to have been a visionary description of that glorious event. He had etched *America* in 1793, before *Europe*, but now even that Orc-flourish had much the same character. In fact, the imagery of *America* is identical to that of *Europe*. In both prophecies the "Guardian Prince of Albion" is "smitten with his own plagues." Yet no final trumpet sounds.

Certainly the poem by Yeats which one thinks of in relation to Blake's early prophecies is "The Second Coming." It presents us with a dismal picture of history very much like that which Blake (although he did not mean to make it appear dismal) actually presents. The world is cyclical, no savior is imminent, the revelation is a revelation not of the spirit but of the body. Enitharmon's sleep in *Europe* is echoed by the "twenty centuries of stony sleep" in Yeats's poem. The great and bloody battle which ends Blake's *Europe* is rather like what we might expect from Yeats's "rough beast." And yet the attitudes of the two poems are totally different, for Yeats's poem is pessimistic with a bitter gaiety, while Blake's is a prediction of apocalypse, which, in retrospect, has gone wrong.

On May 24, 1804, several years after he had composed these early prophecies, Blake sent to William Hayley a letter of thanks for some books:

Dear Sir,

I thank you heartily for your kind offer of reading, &c. I have read the book thro' attentively and was much entertain'd and instructed, but have not yet come to the *Life of Washington*. I suppose an American would tell me that Washington did all that was done before he was born, as the French now adore Buonaparte and the English our poor George; so the Americans will consider Washington as their god. This is only Grecian, or rather Trojan, worship, and perhaps will be revised [?] in an age or two. In the meantime I have the happiness of seeing the Divine countenance in such men as Cowper and Milton more distinctly than in any prince or hero.[48]

If Blake's interest in politics as the vehicle of apocalypse had dimmed, his interest in history certainly had not. Indications are that he now sought a hero in another area of human endeavor, art. No wonder then that Newton did not really bring about the complete formulation of error! No wonder that Blake did not stop writing when he had completed the minor prophecies! The real hero must be an artist—Los, or perhaps Blake himself.

Blake's effort to write the great English myth, which would tell the complete story of Albion the Ancient Man, not only outlining the central form but also holding allegorically all of the microcosmic actions of that Man within its form, was now under way. The poetry, as it tried to encompass more and more, became more and more complex. In later poems Blake was working from the circumference of his vision toward the center; that is, he would begin with his great archetypal form and demonstrate how this form could be acted out by historical personages. And since each man is a microcosm of Albion, Blake's own life would be the most minute of particular representations of that central form.

The microcosmic particulars of Blake's prophecies are usually veiled by names created from Blake's imagination. In general the particular actions, the historical and autobiographical substrata, are subordinated to the archetypal structure, as if Blake wished to emphasize the larger form or macrocosm.* Instead of taking the acts of Albion and applying them to those of a particular character, Blake took the acts of a particular character and showed how they were in microcosm the acts of Albion.

The poem by Yeats which this method most nearly suggests is an early long work, "The Wanderings of Oisin," in which Yeats allegorized both the events of his own life and the English oppression of Ireland. But the resemblance to Blake stops short

---

* *Jerusalem*, in which Blake appears in the first person, is an exception. Here he seems to be moving toward the microcosm. In *Milton*, also, there is naked personal statement.

here. Yeats's aim seems to be a kind of secrecy rather than an attempt to emphasize any particular aspect of the symbolism. In all other respects—tone, style, etc.—"Oisin" is much further from Blake than almost any of Yeats's later poetry. Poems such as "No Second Troy" and "Easter 1916" wear no mask of personae or artifice. The speaker is Yeats, perhaps a contrived Yeats such as we find in *A Vision*, but nevertheless someone we cannot mistake for a hypothetical character consciously imagined by the author. The central figure of "Easter 1916" from the first line ("I have met them at close of day") is Yeats himself; the initial world of the poem is a world which, if personal, is the world even an archmaterialist might be expected to call real.

In some of his later poems Yeats created personae—Ribh, Crazy Jane, Old Tom—but even here these characters have a closeness to conventional conceptions of reality that Blake's Los and Urizen and lesser characters never have. The distinction is again a distinction of point of view. Yeats characterized himself as a common man, caught like Urizen in what Blake called the fallen world—the world known to other fallen creatures. In "Easter 1916" he shows us that world from within and then that world metamorphosed into the ideal. Utter denial of both the actuality and the reality of the fallen world led Blake in another direction.

Yet when Blake and Yeats are working from different points of view, their work is more nearly alike than when their methods are superficially similar.

CHAPTER IV

The Growing Image

Also out of the midst thereof came the likeness of
four living creatures. And this was their appearance;
they had the likeness of a man.   —Ezekiel 1:5

BLAKE'S long unfinished prophetic book, *The Four Zoas*, is
a world in itself, a world of chaos, half-built and confused, a
mine of images and passages for the later poems, *Milton* and
Jerusalem. Although it is often incoherent, *The Four Zoas* is
sometimes more complete in its communicated statement than
Blake's later elaborations, in which his symbolism grows more
personal and obscure. In *The Four Zoas*, Blake again attempts
to express macrocosmic central form, to unravel the paradoxes
and contrarieties of fallen life, to differentiate between the delusions and visions of human perception. The total structure of
the work grew naturally out of the story of creation and fall in
Urizen, of history in *Ahania*, and of apocalypse in the other
minor prophecies. The major change of attitude is expressed by
the new role of Orc and the gradual development of Los as the
central figure and hero of the whole mythology. A major development is the appearance of new figures and controlling symbols.

THE CIRCLE OF DESTINY

The macrocosmic image of *The Four Zoas* is a giant body or communal man, much like Adam Kadmon of the Cabala. He is Albion, the world, the single human imagination. The fall is represented by his falling asleep; his female portion, named "Jerusalem," is separated from him, and his body is enclosed in a great globe called the "Mundane Shell" or "Mundane Egg." He is also divided into four creatures called the "Zoas":

> Four Mighty Ones are in every Man; a Perfect Unity
> Cannot Exist but from the Universal Brotherhood of Eden,
> The Universal Man, To Whom be Glory Evermore.[1]

In the Edenic unity of Albion these creatures are both communal and individual. After the fall their unity becomes a multiplicity like the body of Osiris, and they become spectres of themselves. Their names are Los (Urthona, when he lived in Eden), Tharmas, Luvah (called "Orc" in history), and Urizen. In fallen spectral form, Los symbolizes the artist, Tharmas the generative powers, Luvah the spirit of revolt, and Urizen rationalism and law.

In Eden the Zoas begin to war upon one another, and all fall. Then each·Zoa in turn tries to take over the world and bring some sort of order out of its chaos, but each fails and suffers separation from his female portion or emanation. Gradually, however, after the extreme limit of the fall has been set by God and reached, things begin to move slowly back toward perfection, where the circle is again consumed. The appearance of Jesus on earth symbolizes in history the major shift in balance from fall toward such a vision, complete only when error has achieved a form by which it can be understood. Then Albion rends the Mundane Shell and leaps back into eternity:

> But the bright Sun was not as yet; he, filling all the expanse,
> Slept as a bird in the blue shell that soon shall burst away.[2]

Each night is an image of our fallen world, each sunrise an image of the new birth through an opaque, blue, star-flecked shell.

The Four Zoas tells the story of a world where all images are turned upside down, all eternal ideas transvaluated. The world-circle of destiny is a world of paradoxes where generation is strangely enough decay, where life is death. *The Four Zoas* is the story of Albion, of

> His fall into Division & his Resurrection to Unity:
> His fall into the Generation of decay & death, & his
> Regeneration by the Resurrection from the dead.[3]

The major "contrary" of *The Four Zoas* is the antagonism between Urizen and Orc. The major crisis of the poem is their meeting in Night VII, for here they are, like Yeats's Demon and Beast, finally revealed as two aspects of a single principle, the two halves of which are too often mistakenly thought of as unrelated to each other: law and revolt, withdrawal and return.

By the time that Urizen and Orc meet each other, much has already happened in the fallen world. Urizen, the architect, has already declared that he is the only God. In the "wars of Eden" he has already quarreled with Luvah, and the first violent separation of the Zoas has occurred:

> But perverse roll'd the wheels of Urizen & Luvah, back revers'd
> Downwards & outwards, consuming in the wars of Eternal
> Death.[4]

Later we see him building the enclosure for Albion, which he calls the "Mundane Shell around the rock of Albion." As the "vehicular form" of rationalism and materialism, he creates solid matter and catches life within innumerable gins, traps, and nets —the subtle net of his own logic:

> Then rose the Builders. First the Architect divine his plan
> Unfolds. The wondrous scaffold rear'd all round the infinite,
> Quadrangular the building rose, the heavens squared by a line,
> Trigons & cubes divide the elements in finite bonds.

Multitudes without number work incessant: the hewn stone
Is plac'd in beds of mortar mingled with the ashes of Vala.
Severe the labour; female slaves the mortar trod oppressed.[5]

The great architectural plan, from the beginning a vehicle of
oppression, is not limited to earth. The whole starry system of
the heavens is the shell of the great egg: "Thus were the stars
of heaven created like a golden chain." All things, like the stars
themselves, are caught in a series of seasonal cycles:

> In sevens & tens & fifties, hundreds, thousands, number'd all
> According to their various powers, subordinate to Urizen
> And to his sons in their degrees & to his beauteous daughters,
> Travelling in silent majesty along their order'd ways
> In right lined paths outmeasur'd by proportions of number, weight,
> And measure, mathematic motion wondrous along the deep,
> In fiery pyramid, or Cube, or unornamented pillar square
> Of fire, far shining, travelling along even to its destin'd end;
> Then falling down a terrible space, recovering in winter dire
> Its wasted strength, it back returns upon a nether course,
> Till fir'd with ardour fresh recruited in its humble season,
> It rises up on high all summer, till its wearied course
> Turns into autumn. Such the periods of many worlds.[6]

But even in his stronghold Urizen is uneasy. He has fallen;
he has lost strength; he has been given a body, but that body
has been enclosed within his own edifice. It is, in effect, the
Mundane Shell—a mass of globes and caverns described in *The
Four Zoas* almost verbatim from the *Book of Urizen*. He is
haunted by a vision of his adversary, Orc. Furthermore, he is
divided and alone, having cast out Ahania. In this uneasy state
he decides to explore the world he has built. Early in his travels
he comes upon three women, the triad which Blake elsewhere
calls the "Goddesses of Destiny." Instead of receiving some
revelation from them he simply discovers that they are extensions of himself—his own daughters, "rocky forms." His whole
journey is a series of similar frustrations: he is set upon by

"hideous monsters," thwarted by deep chasms, horrified by visions of tortures. Gradually and pathetically he begins to understand the woeful extent of his self-imprisonment, now out of his control. He hides in caves safe from those who curse him:

> Here he had time enough to repent of his rashly threaten'd curse.
> He saw them curs'd beyond his Curse: his soul melted with fear.
> He could not take their fetters off, for they grew from the soul,
> Nor could he quench the fires, for they flam'd out from the heart,
> Nor could he calm the Elements, because himself was subject. . . .[7]

He begins to realize his fate, but he is not yet sure where to lay the blame. He is locked in the cycle of generation and decay, space and time. His world is a world of wheels going nowhere:

> "Can I not leave this world of Cumbrous wheels,
> Circle o'er Circle, nor on high attain a void
> Where self sustaining I may view all things beneath my feet?
> Or sinking thro' these Elemental wonders, swift to fall,
> I thought perhaps to find an End, a world beneath of voidness
> Whence I might travel round the outside of this dark confusion.
>   When I bend downward, bending my head downward into the deep,
> 'Tis upward all which way soever I my course begin;
> But when A Vortex, form'd on high by labour & sorrow & care
> And weariness, begins on all my limbs, then sleep revives
> My wearied spirits; waking then 'tis downward all which way
> Soever I my spirits turn, no end I find of all.
> O what a world is here, unlike those climes of bliss
> Where my sons gather'd round my knees! . . .
>
>   . . . . .
>
> And if, Eternal falling, I repose on the dark bosom
> Of winds & waters, or thence fall into a Void where air
> Is not, down falling thro' immensity ever & ever,
> I lose my powers, weaken'd every revolution, till a death
> Shuts up my powers; then a seed in the vast womb of darkness

I dwell in dim oblivion; brooding over me, the Enormous worlds
Reorganize me, shooting forth in bones & flesh & blood,
I am regenerated, to fall or rise at will, or to remain
A labourer of ages, a dire discontent, a living woe
Wandering in vain." [8]

Trapped within the shell like a fly caught in a vase, Urizen
stumbles on through a world both infinite and bounded. He
never comes to any final precipice; but he never goes anywhere
either. One of Blake's epigrams—this one strangely bitter—is
relevant to his plight:

To God

If you have form'd a Circle to go into,
Go into it yourself & see how you would do. [9]

Urizen, as the "Ancient of Days" and "Old Nobadaddy" of another poem is Jehovah, the deity of natural religion, the creator
of manacles, time cycles, bounded space. In the circle Urizen,
himself, cannot do very well.

Toward the end of Night VI, Urizen begins to hear Orc,
chained by Los to a rock, howling somewhere in the distance,
and he goes to seek him out as a scapegoat for his difficulties.
The meeting takes place in Night VII (a), the second of two
versions of this chapter. In some ways it is a meeting similar to
that between Blake and the angel in *The Marriage of Heaven
and Hell*.* The angel is a kind of Urizenic figure who attempts
to show Blake a vision of eternal damnation; Blake subjects him
to fuddling indignities and proves him to be a son of Urizen:

So I remain'd with him, sitting in the twisted root of an oak; he was
suspended in a fungus, which hung with head downward into the
deep. [10]

As Urizen faces Orc, he discovers himself "compassed round/
And high roofed over with trees." † Somewhat startled and con-

* Part of this episode is quoted in Chapter I, page 13.
† A line repeated from *Ahania*, by Blake.

fused, he arranges his books of brass around him and addresses Orc, invoking his laws; but Orc does not fear him, calls him a hypocrite, holds him responsible for his imprisonment. As Orc speaks, Urizen recognizes that the creature before him is really a fallen spectre of Luvah, with whom he has battled in eternity. Orc-Luvah's symbols are serpent, flame, blood, bull, pulse, and violence. Urizen's are circle, book, rock, metal, and snow. In Night VII, Blake shows that in a topsy-turvy cyclical world the opposites are fragments of a broken unity. The serpent with tail in mouth is a circle. Blake often refers to nature as a vast serpent form, and in Night III, Albion says to Luvah:

> I will turn the volutions of your Ears outward, & bend your
>   Nostrils
> Downward, & your fluxile Eyes englob'd roll round in fear;
> Your with'ring Lips & Tongue shrink up into a narrow circle
> Till into narrow forms you creep.[11]

Luvah's new body, as we shall later see more clearly, is imagistically related to Urizen's. Here it is clear that Blake relates the serpent form to the circle, a symbol of Urizenic enclosure. The serpent image traditionally associates contrary powers. It has always been ambivalent. Its sloughing of skin suggests rebirth, but not formal change; its crawl in the dust suggests materialism. "In allegory one meets as constantly with the Evil as with the Good Serpent." [12] Blake's denial of the reality of abstract ideas such as good and evil suggests that these two serpents are really one.

Orc and Urizen illustrate the cycles of time and space. In time they represent a mundane deterministic history—the Circle of Destiny. A young and fiery Orc becomes a gray and impotent Urizen. In space they represent a materialistic world of chains and frustration—globe and cavern.

The opposite figures of Blake's poem represent a traditional duality (but in Blake's work divided and subdivided to infinity), and we find similar dramatic confrontations in all of literature. There are numerous examples of such moments in Yeats. In one of these, "The Man and the Echo," the man, still trapped in life with only the vaguest notion of what comes after death, confronts his own spectre, a "Rocky Voice" whose only advice is that he should die. The scene is Blake's fallen world:

> In a cleft that's christened Alt
> Under broken stone I halt
> At the bottom of a pit
> That broad noon has never lit,
> And shout a secret to the stone.
> All that I have said and done,
> Now that I am old and ill,
> Turns into a question till
> I lie awake night after night
> And never get the answers right.[13]

This is the mill of the mind, the Urizenic traveler observed from the point of view of Urizen himself.

Orc and Urizen are opposites within a larger unity which is more completely demonstrated in Nights VIII and IX, and we shall return to this demonstration after an examination of the other Zoas, Los and Tharmas.

THE MUNDANE EGG

The figures of Los and Tharmas are not so clearly related to one another as are the figures of Urizen and Orc. Tharmas seems to have played a greater part in early versions of *The Four Zoas*, and Los becomes more and more independent of all the Zoas as the myth progresses. The generative powers of Tharmas do not seem to be confined, like Orc's powers of revolt, to the time cycle. The artist Los may employ them in his regenerative labors. In fact, Tharmas seems to have been Los's father, the symbol of procreation. He is a sea god, associated with sea monsters, and he rises from the great archetypal floods of history as the first element of new life. But the world of Tharmas is a limited

world of no real value except in so far as Los, the great spiritual-
izer, is capable of formalizing it. It is the world which Yeats rejects in "Sailing to Byzantium":

> That is no country for old men. The young
> In one another's arms, birds in the trees
> —Those dying generations—at their song,
> The salmon-falls, the mackerel-crowded seas,
> Fish, flesh, and fowl. . . .[14]

It is the world across which Plotinus must swim:

> Behold that bold Plotinus swim,
> Buffeted by such seas.[15]

Though as a monster Tharmas is certainly ambivalent, he has
to do with complex evolutionary generation, and Los is its formalizer. On the other hand, Orc is the great destroyer and Urizen
the great stultifier. We may associate the deterministic Circle of
Destiny with Orc and Urizen. The apocalyptic egg belongs to
Los and Tharmas.

Beyond Urizen's world, and surrounding it, lies the chaos of
life, unorganized and rent from eternity:

> For many a window ornamented with sweet ornaments
> Look'd out into the World of Tharmas, where in ceaseless tor-
> rents
> His billows roll, where monsters wander in the foamy paths.[16]

When Urizen has overstepped his powers, the Western Land
(Atlantis, the golden country) is drowned by floods. Tharmas,
riding on the storms, howls and curses, maintains some vague control over life, seeks to bring life out of chaos. He calls to Los, the
great formalizer:

> But thou, My Son, Glorious in brightness, comforter of Thar-
> mas,
> Go forth, Rebuild this Universe beneath my indignant power,
> A Universe of Death & Decay.[17]

Of course, Los cannot accept the rule of Tharmas any more than he can accept the rule of Urizen. He rebels, chastises Tharmas for his distorted vision, tries to show him his place in the total scheme of life. Tharmas only half understands; he has been separated from his emanation; and though his instincts are correct, he threatens Los with his great, unorganized natural powers at the same time as he asks him to create order:

> Take thou the hammer of Urthona: rebuild these furnaces.
> Dost thou refuse? Mind I the sparks that issue from thy hair?
> I will compell thee to rebuild by these my furious waves.
> Death choose or life; thou strugglest in my waters; now choose life,
> And all the Elements shall serve thee to their soothing flutes:
> Their sweet inspiriting lyres thy labours shall administer,
> And they to thee; only remit not, faint not thou, my son.
> Now thou dost know what 'tis to strive against the God of waters.[18]

Los accepts this challenge, perhaps half out of fear, half out of duty. He also is divided and fallen. He builds the body of Urizen, creates from it a sharply delineated form of globes and caves which become the Mundane Shell in proper outline.

Urizen's body is, however, only one image of the Mundane Shell. The total macrocosm is a congeries of ideas: The shell is time, space, man, protoplasm, and the extension of God's imaginative powers. The congeries is Albion. The Four Zoas each represent symbolically the parts of Albion's body (Luvah, the loins; Urizen, the head; Tharmas, the heart; Los, the legs). Sometimes Albion is the world; simultaneously he is what lies trapped in the world, just as man is trapped in his body. The Circle of Destiny, which appears early in *The Four Zoas*, is probably the time-form of the Mundane Shell. The human body is a part of the space-form; and Blake's image of the vast Polypus of life and death also suggests the space concept. Related images are Urizenic rock, the tent, the Covering Cherub. All are the albumen of the great egg.

These images are put to various uses in *The Four Zoas*. They are all images of delusion, but they are also images of creation:

> Then Eno, a daughter of Beulah, took a Moment of Time
> And drew it out to seven thousand years with much care
>   & affliction
> And many tears, & in every year made windows into Eden.
> She also took an atom of Space & opened its centre
> Into infinitude & ornamented it with wondrous art.[19]

The image is purposely ambiguous. It illustrates the stretching out of the circle of time, like a rubber band, into a progression of years—a linear delusion sustained by misreadings of the Bible. The space of the great Circle of Destiny expands inward instead of outward, budding inversely back into the mind. Infinity and eternity are apprehensible not by looking to the opaque shell we call the sky. We discover infinity by diving into the bud of imagination, by forcing the bud to proliferate.

Another time image is what Blake, and the Cabala before him, call the "Eye of God": creative movement as an extension of God's own imagination, refracted by the fall into images of Albion's nightmares. As Los says when he predicts the appearance of Christ:

> Tho' in the Brain of Man we live & in his circling Nerves,
> Tho' this bright world of our joy is in the Human Brain.[20]

In the time-world the Eyes of God are the seven major historical cycles, stages in redemption assigned by the Divine Family:

> The Family Divine drew up the Universal tent
> Above High Snowdon. . . .
> . . . Then they Elected Seven, Called The Seven
> Eyes of God & the Seven Lamps of the Almighty.
> The Seven are one within the other; the Seventh is named
>   Jesus.[21]

Later in *The Four Zoas,* Los gives each eye its name:

> . . . And those in Eden sent Lucifer for their Guard.
> Lucifer refus'd to die for Satan & in pride he forsook his charge.
> Then they sent Molech. Molech was impatient. They sent
> Molech impatient. They sent Elohim, who created Adam
> To die for Satan. Adam refus'd but was compell'd to die
> By Satan's arts. Then the Eternals sent Shaddai.
> Shaddai was angry. Pachad descended. Pachad was terrified.
> Then they sent Jehovah, who leprous stretch'd his hand to Eter-
> nity.
> Then Jesus came & Died willing. . . .[22]

Albion is thus chained round by time and space in its ever-shifting metaphorical form. He is caught in the products of looms, encased in a cavelike human body, surrounded by chains of stars, incubated preborn in a great egg. He struggles in vile albumen, seeks to gain wings, dreams nightmarish images created by God. The parts of his body are in disequilibrium, warring against one another. He is really dead, rent from eternity:

> The Corse of Albion lay on the Rock; the sea of Time & Space
> Beat round the Rock in mighty waves, & as a Polypus
> That vegetates beneath the Sea, the limbs of Man vegetated.
> In monstrous forms of Death, A Human polypus of Death.[23]

The fallen human form is ambivalently dead and vegetal. It holds to the possibility of life in the state which may be called "Tharmas." Surely the human mind lies in the state called "Urizen."

The strangeness of this great Polypus is its delusory physical existence in a nonphysical universe. But given the mournful fact of war in heaven the creation is an "act of mercy," and Blake, following Boehme, repeatedly refers to it as such. The limitations of the fall are really states of mind. Blake calls them "Satan" and "Adam." Satan represents the "limit of opacity"; Adam represents the "limit of contraction." Presumably, had these limits not been created, man would have been rent in pieces like Osiris and flung in eternal fall through a chaos of not-space. Or, if

things had become more and more and more opaque, finally all
mental movement would have ceased, like cooling lava, and all
existence would have been stultified.

Inside the Mundane Shell, where opacity and contraction are
limited, the seeds of life, the Polypus, and the primordial ocean
are really parts of a monstrous formlessness, an ugly embryo,
hardly the hope of the world. If Tharmas provides the seed and
Orc and Urizen the fearful symmetry of history, someone else
must create out of this protoplasm the real bird of apocalypse.
That creator is, of course, Los; but even the Los of *The Four
Zoas* is not always what he should be. The concept of Los as
the agent of divine providence was only in the process of development when Blake began to write *The Four Zoas*. In *Jerusalem*,
Los is clearly the great artist, the "Labourer of Ages." His job
is twofold—to create out of the matter at hand a form for all
states of mind so that they may be immediately understood and
to create a city of imagination as a stronghold against the assaults
of error. It is Los, therefore, who must drive the tiger from the
forests.

THE CRACKING SHELL

Having rolled through six cycles called the "Eyes of God,"
the great egg approaches new birth. In Night VIII of *The Four
Zoas*, the savior Jesus sets in motion the final cycle. In the robes
of Luvah—revolt—he enters a world stultified by Urizen's law;
but there is something unique about him:

> When Urizen saw the Lamb of God clothed in Luvah's robes,
> Perplex'd & terrifi'd he stood, tho' well he knew that Orc
> Was Luvah. But he now beheld a new Luvah, Or Orc
> Who assum'd Luvah's form & stood before him opposite.[24]

The world now accelerates toward new form. Even Urizen
begins to see his opponents in a new way. Ready for battle, he
discovers that Orc is no longer his antagonist but his ally, that

Jesus is something greater than any previous Orc-Urizen convolution. In a rage he turns his wrath against Los and communes with Orc:

> Communing with the Serpent of Orc in dark dissimulation,
> And with the Synagogue of Satan in dark Sanhedrim,
> To undermine the World of Los & tear bright Enitharmon
> To the four winds, hopeless of future.[25]

Until Jesus appears, Urizen has successfully confused and conquered simply because—cloudy, dark, and caverned—he has never been forced to show himself completely. But now unnerved, he tries to do battle in the open.

> And Urizen gave life & sense by his immortal power
> To all his Engines of deceit: that linked chains might run
> Thro' ranks of war spontaneous: & that hooks & boring screws
> Might act according to their forms by innate cruelty.
> He form'd also harsh instruments of sound
> To grate the soul into destruction, or to inflame with fury
> The spirits of life, to pervert all faculties of sense
> Into their own destruction, if perhaps he might avert
> His own despair even at the cost of every thing that breathes.[26]

Nature itself begins to animate, builds for itself a single form and thus becomes Rahab, representative of Urizen's mysteries unclothed. Her appearance suggests completion of error. She sits among the judges at the trial of Jesus:

> A False Feminine Counterpart, of Lovely Delusive Beauty
> Dividing & Uniting at will in the Cruelties of Holiness,
> Vala, drawn down into a Vegetated body, now triumphant.
> The Synagogue of Satan Clothed her with Scarlet robes & Gems,
> And on her forehead was her name written in blood, "Mystery."
>
> . . . . .
>
> The Synagogue Created her from Fruit of Urizen's tree
> By devilish arts, abominable, unlawful, unutterable,
> Perpetually vegetating in detestable births
> Of female forms, beautiful thro' poisons hidden in secret

Which gave a tincture to false beauty; then was hidden within
The bosom of Satan The false Female, as in an ark & veil
Which Christ must rend & her reveal. Her daughters are call'd
Tirzah; She is named Rahab. . . .[27]

Only to Los she is no mystery. He has spent six thousand years
since his fall trying to give form to this world and to her:

Los sat upon his anvil stock; they sat beside the forge.
Los wip'd the sweat from his red brow & thus began
To the delusive female forms shining among his furnaces:
"I am that shadowy Prophet who six thousand years ago
Fell from my station in the Eternal bosom. I divided
To multitude, & my multitudes are children of Care & Labour.
O Rahab, I behold thee. . . ."[28]

Rahab's appearance in unclothed form clarifies the Orc-Urizen
relationship, for it now becomes clear, as Blake says, that "her
cup of fornication" is the "food of Orc & Satan." She also "com-
mun[es] with Orc in secret." [29] Then, after Los confronts her,
she "communes" with Urizen:

Rahab, burning with pride & revenge, departed from Los.
Los drop'd a tear at her departure, but he wip'd it away in hope.
She went to Urizen in Pride. . . .[30]

In the degradation of the final cycle of history Urizen himself assumes the body of a dragon, an Orcian reptilian form:

Urizen sitting in his web of deceitful religion
Felt the female death, a dull & numming stupor, such as ne'er
Before assaulted the bright human form; he felt his pores
Drink in the deadly dull delusion; horrors of Eternal Death
Shot thro' him. Urizen sat stonied upon his rock.
Forgetful of his own Laws, pitying he began to embrace
The shadowy Female; since life cannot be quenched, Life ex-
    uded;
His eyes shot outwards, then his breathing nostrils drawn forth,
Scales cover'd over a cold forehead & a neck outstretch'd
Into the deep to sieze [*sic*] the shadow; scales his neck & bosom
Cover'd & scales his hands & feet; upon his belly falling

Outstretch'd thro' the immense, his mouth wide opening,
 tongueless,
His teeth a triple row, he strove to seize the shadows in vain,
And his immense tail lashed the Abyss; his human form a Stone.[31]

When the last judgment finally arrives, the circle is consumed
to a center. Orc and Urizen are one. Urizen allows Orc to escape
from time and retain his youth. Urizen himself becomes young
Orc:

"Rage Orc! Rage Tharmas! Urizen no longer curbs your rage."

So Urizen spoke; he shook his snows from off his shoulders &
 arose
As on a Pyramid of mist, his white robes scattering
The fleecy white: renew'd he shook his aged mantles off
Into the fires. Then, glorious bright, Exulting in his joy,
He sounding rose into the heavens in naked majesty,
In radiant Youth.[32]

The cycle named Jesus contains within it the microcosmic
cycles of Paul, Constantine, Charlemagne, Luther, and Milton.
In each period the Phoenix Orc rises from the ashes of Urizen
only to age into images of Babylon and Rahab. Rahab is the
goddess of the present cycle. She is also the real deity of the
medieval cult of female worship, the mystery which was burned
in the Reformation and arose like a Phoenix as again

The Ashes of Mystery began to animate; they call'd it Deism
And Natural Religion; as of old, so now anew began
Babylon again in Infamy call'd Natural Religion.[33]

The final consummation of error is expressed in images of a
debased sexuality. The sexual communion of Orc-Urizen with
Rahab, the nature goddess, brings about the joining of all mundane things in a single apprehensible configuration, the mighty
hermaphroditic form which when fallen signifies the Satanic
state—joined in unprolific prostitution:

. . . When the Male & Female
Appropriate Individuality they become an Eternal Death.
Hermaphroditic worshippers of a God of cruelty & law. . . .[34]

In the dream of Albion all aspects of the great hermaphroditic form of error—Rahab, Vala, Babylon, Orc-Urizen, the fallen Zoas separated from their emanations—are combined by the symphonic movement of images. What we have seen is the evolution of this symbol out of the chaos of the "wars of Eden." *The Four Zoas* ends with the remarkable and beautiful Night IX describing the last judgment, where the consequences of the apprehension of a sharply delineated central form are explored. Blake's symbols converge upon this point so that the "loud trumpet thundering along from heaven to heaven" may collapse all entities into the equilibrium of material nothingness where "sweet Science reigns." [35]

CHAPTER V

The Circle Consumed

> But mark,
> I will compell thee to assist me in my terrible labours: To beat
> These hypocritic Selfhoods on the Anvils of bitter Death.
> I am inspired . . . —WILLIAM BLAKE [1]

ALTHOUGH Blake's final long poem, *Jerusalem*, grew out of his vision of *The Four Zoas*, appropriating whole passages from it, there are important new developments. First, Blake no longer strongly emphasizes the fourfold nature of man. Of the Zoas, only Los is really an important character in *Jerusalem*. Second, Los the artist is sharply delineated as hero at all times. Only through him is any progress achieved or anything ever built. Third, Blake drastically shifts the focus of his myth. He becomes a figure in his own story; everything the reader sees is communicated through the personal pronoun "I." When Blake is not acting in the poem he clearly identifies himself with Los. Fourth, Blake develops a peculiar topographical symbolism employing British place names. The whole poem, though often hopelessly obscured by this new system of symbolic reference, is more direct in its expression of Blake's apocalyptic idealism and his identification of poetic with prophetic inspiration.

In three respects *Jerusalem* and, to a lesser degree, *Milton* present us with interesting similarities to important aspects of Yeats's poems. The first is Blake's treatment of time and the symbolism which expresses it. The second is Blake's creation of a mythical city of art and imagination, which may be compared to Yeats's similar creation in the Byzantium poems and in *A Vision*. And the third is the development of the highly personal symbolism in which Blake himself appears as a figure, either disguised or not. This we may compare to Yeats's treatment of himself in his later poems.

INTO TIMELESSNESS

Jerusalem may be taken as an explanation of the true nature of visionary experience. In one respect its creation is the culmination of Blake's attempt to rid his communication of temporal and spatial chains by creating a single image. The result is a certain disregard for strict narrative sequence. Blake sought to project the myth not as a story but as an expanding and contracting unity of images. His attempt to destroy narrative is consistent with his metaphysical view of time. He breaks down his narrative into a cyclic pattern so that any one cycle can stand for any other, and then he strongly implies that each cycle (or *the* single cycle) is itself a point rather than a wheel, a single archetype— the timeless and spaceless reality.

Yeats's treatment of time is very similar to Blake's, and both are probably influenced by Plotinus, who saw the soul as an eternal entity generate a time in which what the soul conceives has its symbolical before and after. Yeats, who read the great historical theorists, also read "profound McTaggart," who denied the reality of time and space in a long and complicated argument which in spirit arises from a view of things very similar to Blake's.

Yeats views time (or its illusion) as he views everything else —from within the globe. His intuitions of the timeless reality are momentary, fleeting intuitions. Like Blake's, his major symbol of not-time is the vortex in its many disguises—the point of a gyre, the drop of dew, and the whirling dancer. Blake's presentation of the vortex image and its related images (all minute particulars are vortexes) is most complete in *Jerusalem*, where his strange treatment of time creates a new obscurity and a new coherence.

Certainly every imaginative advance is both a clarification and a complication, depending upon the point of view from which the reader begins to examine. Blake states his own views on the obscurity of his work in a letter of August 23, 1799:

You say that I want somebody to Elucidate my Ideas. But you ought to know that What is Grand is necessarily obscure to Weak men. That which can be made Explicit to the Idiot is not worth my care. The wisest of the Ancients consider'd what is not too Explicit as the fittest for Instruction, because it rouzes the faculties to act. I name Moses, Solomon, Esop, Homer, Plato. . . . But I am happy to find a Great Majority of Fellow Mortals who can Elucidate My Visions, & Particularly they have been Elucidated by Children, who have taken a greater delight in contemplating my Pictures than I even hoped.[2]

Blake rightly demands an active participation by the reader. His use of the word "explicit" should not lead one to assume that he artificially hid his ideas behind a simple allegory. He believed that truth does not come easily to the "corporeal understanding." In the diary of Crabb Robinson, dated July 24, 1811, a case of "corporeal" rather than imaginative reading is well illustrated. Robinson writes, "He [Blake] showed S[outhey] a perfectly mad poem called *Jerusalem*. Oxford Street is in Jerusalem."[3] Evidently neither Southey nor Robinson was prepared to imagine anything more than a completely mundane structure. Both of them demanded of Jerusalem a standard floor plan, and Blake was not willing to give them one. Southey and Robinson, like poor Urizen caught in his dens, simply could not impose one symbol upon another. It follows that they never attained even to the simpler meanings in the poem.

One aim of *Jerusalem* itself is to do for the reader what Urizen himself is unable to accomplish in *The Four Zoas*. The difference between Urizen and those in Blake's time who thought *Jerusalem* "mad" is simply that Urizen recognizes his difficulties while they did not: "Can I not leave this world of Cumbrous wheels?" In *Jerusalem* we are to stand at what Blake calls a "vortex" so that we may see things all at once, from within and without, so to speak. Each Orc strives for this vortex; but, unable to hold to it once he arrives, he gyres back into Urizenic old age. Blake mentions the vortex image in *Milton:*

> The nature of infinity is this: That every thing has its
> Own Vortex, and when once a traveller thro' Eternity
> Has pass'd that Vortex, he perceives it roll backward behind
> His path, into a globe itself infolding like a sun,
> Or like a moon, or like a universe of starry majesty,
> While he keeps onwards in his wondrous journey on the earth,
> Or like a human form, a friend with whom he liv'd benevolent.[4]

Although, as Blake illustrates it, the vortex is a difficult image, it is instructive as a guide to the focus in *Jerusalem*. Blake says above that every object which we imagine with our perceptive faculties (our eyes are of course simply mundane symbols for types of imaginative powers) creates for us a vortex. For example, if we look at a pencil point our two eyes form beams creating a point upon which we look, and these points, or vortexes, are symbols of a unified perception. They expand inward as the two beams projected back from the pencil point into the mind finally encompass an infinite area, form a single imaginative plane. That infinite area is the mind itself, and it is also the only reality of the image seen. Thus a center expands inward to infinity, and all images are really infinite perceptions, unified extensions of mind. The pencil point is interpreted by the corporeal understanding as existing materially. It is really an image of infinity. (See drawing.)

Unfortunately most people have the corporeal or materialistic view of perceptual existence and think of the vortex as something beyond the mind. For them each vortex is not infinitely encompassing. It remains only a point in space. Blake says that every traveler who passes his vortex sees it roll behind him like a globe; and, passing a number of vortexes, he creates like Urizen a multiplicity of globes in a vast heaven. Now the body is a symbol for man's imaginative form, and we remember that Urizen's

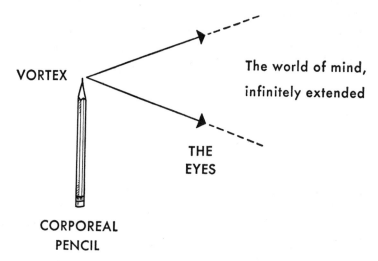

VORTEX

The world of mind,
infinitely extended

THE
EYES

CORPOREAL
PENCIL

body itself is a mass of globes. The Urizenic traveler miscalculates. He sees an extension of his own concepts rolling behind him as globes which are really broken sections of the image which should really be his own body. In the poem *Milton*, Blake writes that the world of imagination should be symbolized as a flat world, that is, the visionary sees all things as symbols created out of an infinite and unbounded mind, a single unified plane flowing endlessly behind the eyes.* The Urizenic traveler creates

---

* J. Bronowski (*William Blake: A Man without a Mask*, republished by Pelican, 1954) sees Blake's cosmos as an answer to Newton's abstract universe. See pp. 145–148.

units instead of unity. He is really breaking his own body symbols into pieces just as Osiris was broken into pieces. One area
of Blakean symbolism is the mass of bodily images. The world
itself is a sleeping giant; time is the beat of blood through his
veins, space the globules of his blood:

> Every Time less than a pulsation of the artery
> Is equal in its period & value to Six Thousand Years,
> For in this Period the Poet's Work is Done, and all the Great
> Events of Time start forth & are conciev'd [*sic*] in such a Period,
> Within a Moment, a Pulsation of the Artery.
> The Sky is an immortal Tent built by the Sons of Los:
> And every Space that a Man views around his dwelling-place
> Standing on his own roof or in his garden on a mount
> Of twenty-five cubits in height, such space is his Universe:
> And on its verge the Sun rises & sets, the Clouds bow
> To meet the flat Earth & the Sea in such an order'd Space:
> The Starry heavens reach no further, but here bend and set
> On all sides, & the two Poles turn on their valves of gold;
> And if he move his dwelling-place, his heavens also move
> Where'er he goes, & all his neighbourhood bewail his loss.
> Such are the Spaces called Earth & such its dimension.
> As to that false appearance which appears to the reasoner
> As of a Globe rolling thro' Voidness, it is a delusion of Ulro.[5]

Our two eyes do not act together upon an outer object (from
two points in space); instead, we are really the object itself, expanding like a spiral into the mind, and then whirling out to a
vortex. There the idea is refracted into a minutely particular
symbol for mental activity.

The great trouble with Urizen, Southey, and Robinson was
that they could never hold to this vortex. Climbing toward it,
gyring nearer, they would suddenly shoot through and out into
the other trap of the hourglass. Robinson in his diary was frustrated in this way: "He [Blake] declared his opinion that the
earth is flat, not round, and just as I had objected the circumnavi-
gation, dinner was announced." [6] Thus is reality sacrificed to the
corporeal.

The reader no doubt is reminded of Yeats's symbol of the interlocking cones. In his *Autobiography*, Yeats recalls that a follower of Mme. H. P. Blavatsky once said to him:

H. P. B. has just told me that there is another globe stuck onto this at the northpole, so that the earth has really a shape something like a dumbbell.[7]

The north pole in Mme. Blavatsky's myth is Blake's vortex, Yeats's "centre" in "The Second Coming." From such a position the visionary may stop time (see history as unity), stop space (see in all directions at once). In *The Four Zoas* the Daughters of Beulah, Blake's prophetic chorus, stand at a vortex when they see the Saviour. The time of the Saviour's appearance on earth was itself a vortex created by the "Eye of God":

For whether they look'd upward they saw the Divine Vision,
Or whether they looked downward still they saw the Divine
    Vision
Surrounding them on all sides beyond sin & death & hell.[8]

They stand at Mme. Blavatsky's symbolical north pole; their imagination ceases to be three dimensional, "single vision and Newton's sleep." Instead it is infinite and fourfold, encompassing all four cardinal points of the universal mind.

In *Jerusalem*, Blake begins a communication of his vision in the first person, invoking the aid of divine spirit:

Of the Sleep of Ulro! and of the passage through
Eternal Death! and of the awakening to Eternal Life.
This theme calls me in sleep night after night, & ev'ry morn
Awakes me at sun-rise; then I see the Saviour over me
Spreading his beams of love & dictating the words of this mild
    song.[9]

He describes himself at his task:

Trembling I sit day and night, my friends are astonish'd at me,
Yet they forgive my wanderings. I rest not from my great task!
To open the Eternal Worlds, to open the immortal Eyes

Of Man inwards into the Worlds of Thought, into Eternity
Ever expanding in the Bosom of God, the Human Imagination.[10]

The image is again that of the vortex expanding inward to the
infinite world of imagination, broadening back into mind behind
the symbols of perception (eyes, ears, tongue, hand). Elsewhere
in *Jerusalem*, Blake says that his vision enables him to "see the
Past, Present & Future existing all at once/Before me." [11] The
communication of such a vision is extremely difficult, refracted
as it is into broken images for divided people and into simultaneous projections of temporal and eternal worlds. The communication is, in fact, so difficult that Yeats's whole canon of
poetry, written from another point of view, dramatizes as its
main theme the difficulty even of achieving such a vision, let
alone passing the particulars of it along to others.

THE CITIES OF IMAGINATION

In *Jerusalem*, in addition to the English topographical references, there are three cities representing mental states: Babylon,
Golgonooza, and Jerusalem itself. In the preface to Chapter III
of *Jerusalem*, Blake writes:

He never can be a Friend to the Human Race who is the Preacher
of Natural Morality or Natural Religion; he is a flatterer who means
to betray, to perpetuate Tyrant Pride & the Laws of that Babylon
which he foresees shall shortly be destroyed, with the Spiritual and
not the Natural Sword. He is in the State named Rahab, which State
must be put off before he can be the Friend of Man.[12]

The natural religionist confuses Babylon with Jerusalem,
seeks Babylon as if it were Jerusalem. His temptress is Rahab.
The artist's vision is ultimately of Jerusalem, but he gets to
Jerusalem from Golgonooza. The natural religionist is a subject
dealing with an object which has never been a part of him. The
artist is a Los creature who, though separated from his emanation, Enitharmon, knows that this separation is simply a delusion

of a fallen world in which he is compelled to work. In Golgonooza, the city of art, Los and his emanation are really one.

The third city is Jerusalem, but Jerusalem is also a woman.
She transcends the concept of the emanations of all the Zoas.
She is the vision of apocalypse, holy marriage with man, *total
resolution*. In the ninety-ninth plate of *Jerusalem* she and Albion
are locked in embrace. Unhappily, in the fallen world she becomes a spectre of herself and is represented by the great earth
mother Vala, who acts as her evil demon. Vala is a creation out
of Rahab:

> Man is adjoin'd to Man by his Emanative portion
> Who is Jerusalem in every individual Man, and her
> Shadow is Vala, builded by the Reasoning power in Man.[13]

Generally speaking, Jerusalem is a symbol for eternity, Vala a
symbol for nature, and Rahab a symbol for the reasoning power
in man which creates nature. Rahab's communing with Urizen
is therefore "natural." Both Rahab and Urizen represent the unprolific quality of opaque matter. Urizen forsakes his proper
emanation for the harlot. When Blake says, early in Chapter I,
that "Jerusalem is scatter'd abroad like a cloud of smoke thro'
non-entity," he is describing the envelopment of eternal vision
in a cloudy amorphous world of multiplicity.[14] The reason has
made a mystery of the clear and sharply outlined. Albion cannot find Jerusalem by counting the stars; he must discover her
in himself. The world and the great chain of stars is a vast serpent
form, the pet and steed of the Whore of Babylon, who is Rahab
herself. It is a seven-headed monster, each head an Orc and a
time cycle. Babylon is the city of nature, Jerusalem is the city of
eternity, and Golgonooza is the city of art, where our experience
is freed of Rahab and expressed symbolically.

In *The Four Zoas*, Golgonooza represents the more rudimentary concept of creative work. It is associated with art, but not so
specifically with art as it is in *Jerusalem*:

. . . Los perform'd
Wonders of labour—
They Builded Golgonooza, Los labouring builded pillars high
And Domes terrific in the nether heavens, for beneath
Was open'd new heavens & a new Earth beneath & within.[15]

Los continues to build Golgonooza all through *Jerusalem*. It is
an eternal task, but Blake with his prophetic power over time can
raise his hand and let us see the great city in its completed form.

The cosmology of Golgonooza cannot be understood fully
without an understanding of its builder, and the Los of *Jerusalem*
is significantly different from the Los of *The Four Zoas*. In
Jerusalem, Blake recapitulates Los's separation from the total
Zoa, Urthona, and describes his continuous attempt to hold the
prophetic vision unprofaned against the attacks of human delusion. In *Jerusalem*, Los is consistently the true spirit of prophecy,
for he is gifted with an understanding of the world he has helped
to create. He can say:

I know that Albion hath divided me, and that thou, O my
    Spectre,
Hast just cause to be irritated; but look stedfastly upon me;
Comfort thyself in my strength; the time will arrive
When all Albion's injuries shall cease, and when we shall
Embrace him, tenfold bright, rising from his tomb in immor-
    tality.[16]

If Los is the Eternal Prophet, it should be he who builds Albion's
body. Orc-Urizen builds within the fallen world by destroying.
Los destroys the fallen world by building it. Each truly creative
act within the sleep of Albion must be forged in some manner
that expresses its freedom from the Orc-Urizen cycle. Los must
hammer the solidification of falsehood. That is why in *Jerusalem*
it is Los, not Urizen, who builds the Mundane Shell. That is
why it is Los who takes "his globe of fire to search out the dark
interiors of Albion's bosom." Both of these actions are great

imaginative ventures; they transcend in time the unprolific build-
ings and searchings of Urizen.

Golgonooza stands at the center of the Mundane Shell. Los is
the builder of both the shell and the city, which are the twofold
possibilities of man. Spatially the shell encompasses all:

> Around Golgonooza lies the land of death eternal, a Land
> Of pain and misery and despair and ever brooding melancholy
> In all the Twenty-seven Heavens, number'd from Adam to
> Luther,
> From the blue Mundane Shell, reaching to the Vegetative
> Earth.[17]

But it does not really encompass its own core:

> The Vegetative Universe opens like a flower from the Earth's
> center
> In which is Eternity. It expands in Stars to the Mundane Shell
> And there it meets Eternity again, both within and without.[18]

Man may choose one of two courses. He may attempt to break
past the stars and through the shell alone; although until apocalypse it is inevitable that he will be unsuccessful. Like the fly in
the glass vase, he will merely battle materiality, and he will fall
into the Orc-Urizen cycle by exploring the shell's complete con-
cavity. On the other hand, he may choose to look for the minute
particular at the heart of the shell, the very essence of Golgonooza itself, budding flowerlike back into the infinitude of the
mind's eye—the vortex again. Apocalyptic thought is paradoxical. The individual breaks the egg not by beating "upon the wall/
Till Truth obey[s] his call," [19] as Yeats once erroneously but
revealingly described Blake's action, but by creating vortexes
which expand into the infinite mental world. See the grain of
sand as an imaginative vortex, a metaphor for thought, and then
the grain discloses its secrets:

> Mock on, Mock on Voltaire, Rousseau:
> Mock on, Mock on: 'tis all in vain!

> You throw the sand against the wind,
> And the wind blows it back again.
>
> And every sand becomes a Gem
> Reflected in the beams divine;
> Blown back they blind the mocking Eye,
> But still in Israel's paths they shine.
>
> The Atoms of Democritus
> And Newton's Particles of light
> Are sands upon the Red sea shore,
> Where Israel's tents do shine so bright.[20]

The gemlike vortex expands in divine beams into eternal life. Of course, to be accurate we should say that the eternal expresses itself symbolically in our experience as vortex images or microcosms of a central unity; but to the "mocking eye" the sands are simply irritating. To the visionary eye they are what they are made to be. Every microcosm is a vortex, and every vortex is an image of eternity; every microcosm is the macrocosm. The sands blown by the wind are those same sands which formed delusory pillars and befuddled the Egyptians, but as gems of fire they led the Israelites into the promised land.

In *Jerusalem*, Blake, suggesting that he is the eternal prophet Los and that Golgonooza lies in Lambeth, writes:

> There is a Grain of Sand in Lambeth that Satan cannot find,
> Nor can his Watch Fiends find it; 'tis translucent & has many
>   Angles,
> But he who finds it will find Oothoon's palace; for within
> Opening into Beulah, every angle is a lovely heaven.[21]

The world, as the "corporeal understanding" sees it, is really inside out. Running to its delusory shell, Urizen spins in a circle. In order to get out of the circle Urizen must turn himself outside in; he never succeeds and instead merely irritates his eyes with globes of sand and remains spiritually blind.

Since the real world is nonmaterial, the city of art does not hold within itself material creations. Instead it treasures the communal memory of mankind in images representing acts, not corporeal things:

> . . . all that has existed in the space of six thousand years,
> Permanent & not lost, not lost nor vanish'd, & every little act,
> Word, work & wish that has existed, all remaining still.[22]

Everything is an act; nothing is passive or inanimate except the Lockean delusion called Ulro. All acts are symbolic. They have a reality when separated from the fallen encumbrances of time and space. The "corporeal understanding" cannot fully grasp the real significance of an act because it is confused in a welter of impressions caused by cyclic flux. To the imaginative vision an act exists in its archetypal reality free of fallen perceptual forms. It transcends the cyclic flux. The acts of imaginative vision are the archetypal symbols of art, images in the mind of God:

> All things acted on Earth are seen in the bright Sculptures of
> Los's Halls, & every Age renews its power from these Works
> With every pathetic story possible to happen from Hate or
> Wayward Love; & every sorrow & distress is carved here,
> Every Affinity of Parents, Marriages & Friendships are here
> In all their various combinations wrought with wondrous Art,
> All that can happen to Man in his pilgrimage of seventy years.
> Such is the Divine Written Law of Horeb & Sinai,
> And such the Holy Gospel of Mount Olivet & Calvary.[23]

Blake projects through Los and his work symbols of all things creative. Los not only defines the possibility of individual apocalyptic vision but also builds and formalizes the rudimentary structure of error. He acts the artist hero in the face of turmoil, life and death, withdrawal and return.

In the poem *Milton*, Blake suggests that the symbol of Los himself is one of the great "sculptures" or archetypal forms. These forms perpetuate themselves in changing minute particulars throughout the seven historical cycles. Each contributor to the great tradition of poetic prophecy is a minute particular of the great archetypal artist hero. Springing from the foot of Milton, Blake himself perpetuates the Los symbol in society. As Los reborn, he sees "the Past, Present & Future existing all at once/Before me." [24] His is "the Voice of the Bard!/Who Present, Past, & Future, Sees." [25] Blake is convinced that, since all men are one man, his vision should be available to all men: "An Universal Poetic Genius exists." In *Jerusalem* he pleads the possibility of its immediate communal manifestation. Until this occurs he will "keep the divine vision in time of trouble."

The idea of the great city of art and the epiphanic nature of art is not unique with Blake, so we cannot assume that Blake alone influenced Yeats's conception of Byzantium. But certain similarities are worth careful consideration. Blake sees the true reality as the "bright sculptures of Los's halls." There is really no difference between the image of these sculptures and the idea of apocalypse. Apocalypse is merely a vision of these sculptures from somewhere in time. The nearest Yeats comes to an outright assertion of apocalytic vision occurs in the Byzantium poems and in the comments upon Byzantium in *A Vision*. The poems will be discussed later; here is the major part of the comment in *A Vision*:

I think that if I could be given a month of Antiquity and leave to spend it where I chose, I would spend it in Byzantium a little before Justinian opened St. Sophia and closed the Academy of Plato. I think I could find in some little wine-shop some philosophical worker in mosaic who could answer all my questions, the supernatural descending nearer to him than to Plotinus even, for the pride of his delicate skill would make what was an instrument of power to princes and clerics, a murderous madness in the mob, show as a lovely flexible presence like that of a perfect human body.

I think that in early Byzantium, maybe never before or since in recorded history, religious, aesthetic and practical life were one, that architect and artificers—though not, it may be, poets, for language had been the instrument of controversy and must have grown abstract—spoke to the multitude and the few alike. The painter, the mosaic worker, the worker in gold and silver, the illuminator of sacred books, were almost impersonal, almost perhaps without consciousness of individual design, absorbed in their subject-matter and that the vision of a whole people.[26]

The last few lines above are especially important because they posit a kind of unity which we find described in the conclusion of Blake's *Four Zoas* and *Jerusalem*, but there is an important difference. Byzantium exists *in* time, and the drama of the Byzantium poems is Yeats's effort to remove Byzantium from time. Knowing that time gyres away the momentary Byzantine unity of culture, Yeats dramatizes himself in poem after poem as unsure of the timelessness of his imaginative visions, which themselves seem transitory. Blake's vision of unity, represented by images of artist, smith, and city, seems in his earlier prophecies to be a vision of the future; but in *Jerusalem* the vision is timeless—an apocalypse in time or even at the end of time is really a contradiction in terms.

In the troubled ages during which Los keeps the vision, all things seem turned upside down. Jerusalem is cursed by the people; Rahab is deified as Vala,

> . . . by Sacrifice of the Lamb
> And of his children before sinful Jerusalem, To build
> Babylon the City of Vala, the Goddess Virgin-Mother.
> She is our mother! Nature! [27]

Even the Zoas cannot distinguish between the contrary cities: "Whether this is Jerusalem or Babylon we know not./ All is confusion. All is tumult." [28] The great whore Rahab is herself an archetype—the white goddess; but she is also a chameleon creature—a Circe as well as a hag:

> Imputing Sin & Righteousness to Individuals, Rahab
> Sat, deep within him [Albion] hid, his Feminine Power unreveal'd,
> Brooding Abstract Philosophy to destroy Imagination, the Divine—

Humanity: A Three-fold Wonder, feminine, most beautiful,
    Three-fold
Each within other. On her white marble & even Neck, her Heart,
Inorb'd and bonified, with locks of shadowing modesty, shining
Over her beautiful Female features soft flourishing in beauty,
Beams mild, all love and all perfection, that when the lips
Recieve [*sic*] a kiss from Gods or Men, a threefold kiss returns
From the press'd loveliness; so her whole immortal form three-
    fold,
Three-fold embrace returns, consuming lives of Gods & Men,
In fires of beauty melting them as gold & silver in the furnace.
Her Brain enlabyrinths the whole heaven of her bosom & loins
To put in act what her Heart wills. O who can withstand her
    power!
Her name is Vala in Eternity: in Time her name is Rahab.[29]

Rahab in her threefold character is best described by Blake in
"The Mental Traveller," where she is lover, mother, and killer.
Blake discovers her in *Macbeth* as a triad: "I instance Shakspeare's
Witches in Macbeth. Those who dress them for the stage, consider them as wretched old women, and not as Shakspeare intended, the Goddesses of Destiny." [30] Blake suggests that Jerusalem separated from Albion is Rahab. Crowned ruler of earth
"round Golgonooza" by the sons of Albion during the Jesus
cycle, she represents the separated female will of which each
emanation is a minute particular: "The Emanations of the griev-
ously afflicted Friends of Albion/Concenter in one Female
form." [31] For example, it was she as "an aged pensive female"
who created time and space. Before Los finally rends the veil of
her falsehood, she,

. . . like a dismal and indefinite hovering Cloud,
Refus'd to take a definite form; she hover'd over all the Earth
Calling the definite, sin, defacing every definite form
Invisible or Visible, stretch'd out in length or spread in breadth
Over the Temples, drinking groans of victims, weeping in pity
And joying in the pity, howling over Jerusalem's walls.[32]

In her supreme moment she makes even Enitharmon part of her, but Los is the great artist capable of defining her; and when he succeeds, error must disintegrate and fulfill the paradox of its self-clarification. Los speaks:

> . . . We Shall not die! we shall be united in Jesus.
> Will you suffer this Satan, this Body of Doubt that Seems but
>   Is Not,
> To occupy the very threshold of Eternal life? If Bacon, Newton,
>   Locke
> Deny a Conscience in Man & the Communion of Saints & Angels,
> Contemning the Divine Vision & Fruition, Worshipping the
>   Deus
> Of the Heathen, the God of This World, & the Goddess Nature,
> Mystery, Babylon the Great, the Druid Dragon & hidden Harlot,
> Is it not that Signal of the Morning which was told us in the
>   Beginning? [33]

Thus the Circle of Destiny and its triple goddess are simultaneously consumed in the fire of Los's smithy. Los's symbols are the anvil and the forge. Instead of fighting fire as Urizen did, he makes fire work for him. He is the true archetype of the Greek god Hephaestos. He falls to Lemnos, overcomes his lameness and the derisive abuses of other gods, and escapes the wheel. He carves the mental sculptures called the Seven Eyes of God and makes "living form eternal existence." The sculptures of great art stand boldly in the face of time, sharply delineated, unclouded by material "vapours."

The Poetic Genius is eternal in the time world. It appeared in Chaucer:

> The characters of Chaucer's Pilgrims are the characters which compose all ages and nations: as one age falls, another rises, different to mortal sight, but to immortals only the same; for we see the same characters repeated again and again, in animals, vegetables, minerals, and in men; nothing new occurs in identical existence; Accident ever varies, Substance can never suffer change nor decay.
>
> Of Chaucer's characters, as described in his Canterbury Tales,

some of the names or titles are altered by time, but the characters themselves forever remain unaltered, and consequently they are the physiognomies or lineaments of universal human life, beyond which Nature never steps. Names alter, things never alter. I have known multitudes of those who would have been monks in the age of monkery, who in this deistical age are deists.[34]

From Chaucer through others to Milton and Blake the Poetic Genius perpetuates itself as the great worker, the prophetic blacksmith. Even today the artist seeks out the Los in his soul. James Joyce, for example, concludes *A Portrait of the Artist as a Young Man* as follows:

I go to encounter for the millionth time the reality of experience and to forge in the smithy of my soul the uncreated conscience of my race.
Old father, old artificer, stand me now and ever in good stead.

As the serpent circle consumes itself, the ages of history convene in Los's Halls. In *The Four Zoas* there were seven eyes of history appointed. In *Jerusalem* an eighth is named. The divine vision is capable of naming the moment of its startling appearance:

> . . . I behold him,
> But you cannot behold him till he be reveal'd in his System.
> Albion's Reactor must have a Place prepar'd. Albion must Sleep
> The Sleep of Death till the Man of Sin & Repentance be re-
> veal'd.
> Hidden in Albion's Forests he lurks . . .[35]

According to Blake, when the Eternals met to elect the Eight Eyes of God, "They nam'd the Eighth: he came not, he hid in Albion's Forests." [36] The Eighth Eye of God is the single vast illumination, a "momentary god," fallen man in the forests of Albion, the tiger "in the forests of the night." It is the sudden brightening of a shadow in the jungle of the speeding, expanding, and contracting flux of space-time. When caught and held it appears as the spring of the beast—the self, separated off from the soul by the "vegetable glass of nature"—crashing through in violence to *total resolution*. The emergence of man's tiger-demon from the forests is among other things the shattering emergence of history into eternity where the seven eyes become the Eighth Eye, where all are one.

THE PERSONAL SYMBOL

Even the reader with considerable poetic sensibility and wide understanding of mythological themes is brought up short by the intrusions of some of the personal symbols in Blake's poems. When Blake identified himself with Los, he made symbolic use of everything that happened in his own life. His trouble with a soldier named Schofield, which forced him to defend himself in court against a trumped-up charge of treason, becomes a micro-cosmic image of the war between reason and inspiration in *Milton*. In developing this personal symbolism, Blake seems to have turned dangerously in the direction of the very errors for which he chastised others in his comments on allegory. Ill-defined names clutter *Milton* and *Jerusalem*. The whole of the mundane universe eventually collapses into what seems a catalogue of English cities and counties inhabited by obscure people known to Blake but forgotten by history. Even when the reader recognizes a name, the association made by Blake is so personal that the reader's recollection of the name may lead him further astray than simple ignorance.

Blake's error was his attempt to make the foundations of his plan carry more and more weight without strengthening the buttresses of communication. The very nature of his marvelous imagination must have been responsible in part for the defects of his communication. His was the flash of insight, the enlargement of the minute to the status of totality. Each new perception demanded its elaboration as part of the whole—as the whole. Thus what Blake saw was the whole, and what he saw was England. The Englishman, especially "English Blake," who had never traveled, had to create all things out of his own perception. Never having been to the Holy Land, Blake brought the Holy Land to him. On one level, then, such English symbols as Mt. Snowdon and the counties of Ireland are part of a system of correspondences between British history or legend and Biblical legend. The interminable catalogues of the Old Testament are repeated in the prophetic books with new names. In addition, certain English names are related to the cardinal points of the compass and therefore to the Four Zoas themselves. The following correspondences appear:

North	Urthona (Los)	Edinburgh
South	Urizen	Verulam
East	Luvah	London
West	Tharmas	York

Then we find London further subdivided with undeveloped correspondences to the Jerusalem of Biblical times. Although Blake bent over backward to escape creating a map plan, these references are limited, by the chains of a rationalistic order. Beyond certain directional significances Los and Edinburgh have little in common. York, it is true, can be related to Tharmas and the West through the idea of the newly generated New York, but the original city has little to do with the West, except by opposition signifying delusion. The symbolic relationships fail to proliferate and remain allegorical. And what of this catalogue?

> Kox has Oxford, Warwick, Wilts; his Emanation is Estrild;
> Join'd with Cordella she shines southward over the Atlantic.

> Kotope had Hereford, Stafford, Worcester, & his Emanation
> Is Sabrina; join'd with Mehetabel she shines west over America.

> Bowen had all Scotland, the Isles, Northumberland & Cumberland;
> His Emanation is Conwenna; she shines a triple form
> Over the north with pearly beams gorgeous & terrible.
> Jerusalem & Vala rejoice in Bowen & Conwenna.

But the Four Sons of Jerusalem that never were Generated
Are Rintrah and Palambron and Theotormon and Bromion.
  They
Dwell over the Four Provinces of Ireland in heavenly light,
The Four Universities of Scotland, & in Oxford & Cambridge
  & Winchester.[37]

The complexity of Blake's English symbolism is not always a
fruitful complexity and is almost never immediately fruitful
even to the erudite reader. It is ironic that this is so, for the English names incorporated into Albion's sleep are the logical culmination of the Blakean vision. He wished to create an English
mythology, not only because England was the environment for
his imagination, but also because he thought that England needed
a mythology, "a corpus of poetic reference" which would correspond in power to other racial expressions of the Poetic Genius.
Professor Denis Saurat's view, that Blake was indulging in some
"strange mystic imperialism," is a distorting half-truth.[38] Blake
certainly did not literally believe, as Professor Saurat seems to
assert, that "primitive humanity was formed in England, and in
England humanity will reach its supreme goal." [39] Instead, he
was forming a mythology by means of which, according to
Yeats, he "meant to assert the sacredness of England, as a part
of the whole," as a microcosm of the whole, to be exact.[40] Yeats's
annotation to Professor Saurat's chapter "Celts and Druids" in
Blake and Modern Thought sums up Blake's attitude admirably:

To sum. Blake does not think England the place of primitive humanity, or of the original wisdom because they were before the
flood of time and space—the historical druids he thought degenerate
man—"rocky druidism." He spoke of England and its past because
he lived there. In the same way the folklore of the Echte hills in
Galway says that the last judgment will be among those hills. Blake
seeks the near and the particular always.[41]

Blake himself wrote that the last judgment "is seen by the [Im-
aginative Eye, *del.*] of Every one according to the situation he

holds." [42] And he explained his own particular vision in this way: "The Last Judgment is one of those Stupendous Visions. I have represented it as I saw it; to different People it appears differently as every thing else does." [43]

The guiding principle which led Blake to organize a British topographical symbolism is, as Yeats saw, clearly a logical extension of the Blakean metaphysics of vision, an extremely complex principle arising from the idea of macrocosm and microcosm. Blake's perceptions of England were microcosms of more vast mythical projections. His identification of himself with Los and his reduction of the world-form to England, the rock surrounded by the great sea of time and space, most certainly run together to form a single consistent unit of vision. We are not surprised to find Los standing in London building Golgonooza and shouting:

> I must Create a System or be enslav'd by another Man's.
> I will not Reason & Compare: my business is to Create.[44]

The system to which Los-Blake refers is a highly ambitious one. Its creation would be a reaffirmation of the Poetic Genius. His own perseverance would indicate that man is something more than Urizen.

One of the important lessons Yeats could have learned from Blake (though one doubts that poets learn lessons in this fashion) was the lesson of Blake's failure to work out his microcosmic symbolism satisfactorily. Blake often made veiled references to English politics and attempted to mythicize contemporary figures, both famous and obscure. In this he often failed conspicuously. Yeats's cast of characters includes actual people under no disguise; his plot concerns actual things. And yet these people and things *take on* symbolical proportions, while Blake's figures, at first symbolical, *suggest* actual people.

There are, of course, exceptions in both cases. Blake mentions actual people in *The French Revolution* and *America*. George

III is so thinly disguised in the Lambeth books that we cannot think of Blake's treatment of him as allegory. But even in these poems the actual names seem not to represent actual people but instead the broader aspects of the actions of these people. Thus the words of Washington spoken in *America* are hardly those of Washington as he spoke but those representing the acts in which Washington was involved. Yeats's characters are often mythical constructions, but they live in a world acceptable to a materialist as real, not in "a timeless and spaceless community of spirits," as Yeats describes reality.[45] When he creates a world which seems not to be actual, as in some of his plays, he does not allegorize.* His usual practice, especially with poems on political or Irish subjects, is to write about actual people and show how these characters enlarge their significance in his eyes, transcend their material surroundings to become mythical figures. Thus Maud Gonne shows herself to be a Helen of Troy caught in an age which frustrates the kind of action proper to her mythical reality. The leaders of the Easter Rebellion renew the legendary spirit of Cuchulain in Ireland. Major Robert Gregory becomes an image of the archetypal courtier.

Yeats's success in treating these people as particulars who advance to the status of archetypes is, I think, undeniable. It stems from considerable power of technique and from two other sources. First, Yeats usually works out the analogy between the minute particular and the mythical figure in the context of the poem, and he builds a pattern of these images in the larger context of his whole work. Actually Yeats's poems can be thought of as the manipulation of a limited number of particular symbols, observed and reobserved so that they interlock, poem to poem, to create "bright sculptures." Second, time and place favored Yeats as it most certainly did not favor Blake. In some respects the quirks of history decide the fates of poets. Yeats appeared on the scene in Ireland at a dramatic time. He lived in a

* There are exceptions to this—*Cathleen Ni Houlihan*, for example.

true microcosm of history. He was, as W. H. Auden has recently said, one of the last political poets; for in Ireland politics was somehow still related to the individual, and Yeats knew the principal characters of the drama. Blake, who also lived in a violent time, was nevertheless more isolated from his political subject. His allegorical treatment of politics symbolizes this isolation even from the microcosm of his vision. But Blake's failure (it is only a partial failure within a far greater success) and Yeats's success in no way suggest that Yeats's method of approach is categorically the better. If Yeats learned anything from Blake's failure, it was not that to have Blake's particular kind of vision is bad for poetry but that to write what Blake himself disdained as "allegory" is bad, that the microcosm of the symbol must be able to carry all the weight of its macrocosmic counterpart, that purely arbitrary correspondences are "rattle traps of mythology." *

In comparing the work of Blake and Yeats, we return inevitably to the problem of point of view. Blake's failure was probably inevitable, given the ambitiousness of his attempt. The point of view of the seer is difficult to sustain and communicate. Yeats, we shall see, chose a more modest position. To say, as it appears one should, that Yeats probably felt he had no choice in this matter is to make a comment upon our century as damaging as

---

* Even now we are beginning to see that much of what has been thought arbitrary and nonsensical in Blake's work is in fact part of an organized criticism of the English political and social scene. The major work in the area has been done by David V. Erdman and published in his important book, *Blake: Prophet against Empire.* Mr. Erdman shows that in spite of the obscurity of many allegorical references Blake's allegory is not the product of automatic writing or otherworldly visions. If we come away from Mr. Erdman's book with a better understanding of what Blake was saying allegorically, it is doubtful that our estimation of Blake's poetry *as poetry* is raised quite in proportion to the increase in our understanding. But it *is* raised, and further researches will probably do much toward raising it even more, especially among those who still hide their failure to comprehend even the larger pattern of Blake's symbolism by passing him off as a mystic with incoherent visions or, worse yet, a madman.

any comment upon the inability of Blake's age to accept Blake. Blake's age did at least produce Blake.

In his lifetime Blake may have achieved that vortex of vision sought by Urizen. He was in some degree successful in communicating that vision to his Urizenic modern audience if not to his contemporaries. The tragedy of Blake was this: he was peculiarly of his time, he was writing *at* the people of his time, and he was misunderstood by them. On the other hand, some modern interpretations of Blake present us with an unconscious irony in their attempts to fit Blake into systems not his own—Urizen is still with us, and Blake is glorified as an anticipator of truths later discovered and rationalized.

Surely Blake would not have been much interested in "anticipating" anything except the great day he envisioned. He would have argued that his prophecies were not *discoveries* of certain isolated truths of human life but *rediscoveries* of them. Nor would he have believed that any modern discipline—psychology, anthropology, history—could in its present state assimilate all that he had to offer. Nor would he have allowed that his work could be interpreted in terms of a single interest other than a religious interest. Even then the term "religious" would demand careful scrutiny.

Blake preached social equilibrium, not social compromise. That does not mean that he failed to recognize the necessity of perseverance—the obligation of all people, especially the poet, to the creation of social perfection. In Blake's day the cry was primarily "rights," with little immediate care for the question of "obligations." In *Attitudes toward History*, Kenneth Burke tells of an episode in the Assembly at the time of the French Revolution: "When a 'bill of rights' was being drawn, some members of the Assembly suggested that a 'bill of obligations' be included to match them. The proposal was voted down by an overwhelming majority." [46] When Blake began to write the early prophecies, he had formed a considerable attachment for those who were voting down "obligations," but later he accepted the necessary coexistence of "rights" and "obligations." The result for him was disillusion with the apocalyptic potentiality of eighteenth-century political revolution and the subsequent disappearance of Orc as the hero of his myth, for Orc is the state of revolt which is incapable of the self-imposed obligation. Concretely stated, his obligation is to the Poetic Genius. In order to shoulder that obligation, he must exercise his spirited "right" to imagination. The concept of Los transcends that of both Orc and Urizen. It is in the nature of man that obligation and right are intertwined. The artist-hero faces off against a tragi-comic vision of reality: "Without contraries is no progression." In Blake's apocalyptic poetry there is finally a human resolution of the contraries; and Los himself is the symbol of that resolution, although he is the *fallen* symbol of it.

An example of Blake's contraries as they have appeared in modern history is given by Kenneth Burke in the following paragraph:

The Church thought of man as a prospective citizen of heaven. In time, the critical inaccuracy that such transcendental emphasis brought to the gauging of material relationships became bureaucratically exploited to its limits. Out of this over-emphasis, a purely antithetical over-emphasis developed. Against man as a citizen of heaven, thinkers opposed man in nature; and with the progress of efficiency in reasoning, we got simply to *man in the jungle.*[47]

Burke attempts to bring us out of the dilemma by suggesting a "transcendent" emphasis upon "man in society." Blake's vision of his age would accept Burke's apt symbol of "man in the jungle" as a result of two previous contrary overemphases. He would bring man out of the jungle in the shape of the Eighth Eye of God, which emerges from the forests of Albion.

What we discover in Blake's mythology is the emergence of his idea of apocalypse, which includes the reasons for its occurrence and the way it can be brought about. The definition leads us back into the very sources of life and toward a fundamental emphasis in his work: that there is not only a Universal Poetic Genius, a form of imaginative thought, but that this form of thought leads us to an archetypal poetic theme. And, since poetry is prophecy, this theme is the receptacle of religious mystery. The term "mystery" of course is used, in the Blakean sense, to suggest that all religious truth is mystery to the "corporeal understanding." The single theme is cyclic in nature. "Visions of these eternal principles or characters of human life appear to poets, in all ages." [48] Blake's essay on Chaucer's Canterbury pilgrims discloses his belief that poetic creation is in one sense re-creation, just as he believed that there is a principle of re-creation operating at the foundation of the cyclic movement of life. Chaucer, like Milton and later Blake himself, is the "great poetical observer of men, who in every age is born to record and eternize its acts." [49]

For Blake the greatest of all prophetic statements of religious truth was the Bible, which portrays the cyclic drama from fall to redemption. This drama occurs on all of the so-called levels of life, from day to night, dark to full moon, spring to winter, birth to death, rise to fall of civilizations. For Blake the greatest English prophetic statements of religious truth were the great poems; the most ambitious of these statements was Blake's own work. "We do not want either Greek or Roman Models if we are but just & true to our own Imaginations, those Worlds of Eternity in which we shall live forever in Jesus Our Lord." [50]

CHAPTER VI

Toward a Yeatsian Aesthetic

> After Stephane Mallarmé, after Paul Verlaine, after
> Gustave Moreau, after Puvis de Chavannes, after our
> own verse, after all our subtle colour and nervous
> rhythm, after the faint mixed tints of Conder, what
> more is possible? After us the Savage God.
>
> —W. B. YEATS [1]

IN 1827, when William Blake died, three obituaries appeared, the
first in the *Literary Gazette* for August 18, 1827, the other two
in the *Gentleman's Magazine* and the *Annual Register*. None of
these magazines referred to Blake as a poet; he was in their eyes
an illustrator, a "designer," an "artist." The *Literary Gazette*
wrote, "He has left *nothing* except some pictures, copper-plates,
and his principal work of a series of a hundred large designs from
Dante." [2] The *Gentleman's Magazine* briefly mentioned some
plates called "Songs of Experience, with plates; America: A
Prophecy, folio, and Europe, a Prophecy, 1794, folio," but failed
to mention that in these folios a poetic text accompanied the en-
gravings. [3] As these obituaries show, Blake's reputation even as
a pictorial artist was indeed meager; yet meager as it was it saved
most of his poetry from oblivion. Blake's manuscript book, con-
taining many poems and early drafts of the *Songs of Innocence
and Experience*, was preserved by the artist Samuel Palmer and

passed on to the painter-poet Dante Gabriel Rossetti. Blake was taken up and glorified by the Pre-Raphaelite group. Both Rossetti and his friend, the poet Swinburne, wrote on Blake, Rossetti completing the *Life of Blake* begun by Alexander Gilchrist and Swinburne writing the first full-length critical study of Blake as a poet.[4] Although both writers spoke highly of Blake's poetry, neither was greatly influenced by his poetic techniques. Swinburne held Blakean attitudes toward politics and social repression; Rossetti and other Pre-Raphaelite painters were influenced by Blake's pronouncements on painting, but their own work is far different from Blake's and does not seem to have followed important Blakean principles.

Rossetti and Pre-Raphaelitism influenced, in turn, John Butler Yeats, the poet's father, who, although he finally forsook Pre-Raphaelite style, passed on to his son a passionate interest in it. Yeats writes in his *Autobiography:* "I was in all things pre-Raphaelite. When I was fifteen or sixteen my father had told me about Rossetti and Blake and given me their poetry to read."[5] Thus Blake's influence played upon the young Yeats in two ways; one influence filtered itself through Pre-Raphaelitism, and the other came directly from Blake's own work.

INFLUENCES AND PROBLEMS

Pre-Raphaelitism held the germ of the movement often called English Aestheticism. The continental counterpart of English Aestheticism was the French Symbolist movement, and there is a link between them in Swinburne, himself. Unlike English Aestheticism, French Symbolist theory does not seem to have influenced Yeats directly.[6] Instead it came to him in more devious ways, for example, through a colleague in the English literary world, Arthur Symons, who recognized that the problems of poetry attacked by French Symbolist theory had much in common with problems Yeats had already become aware of. Symons'

influential book, *The Symbolist Movement in Literature* (1899),
is dedicated to Yeats:

May I dedicate to you this book on the Symbolist movement in
literature, both as an expression of a deep personal friendship and
because you, more than anyone else, will sympathise with what I
say in it, being yourself the chief representative of that movement
in our country? France is the country of movements, and it is
naturally in France that I have studied the development of a principle
which is spreading throughout other countries, perhaps not less
effectually, if with less definite outlines.[7]

For Yeats as well as for Symons symbolism was more than a
contemporary movement. It was, in fact, a kind of aesthetic
religion transcending all "schools" and countries and apprehensible as an element in any great art. Blake, for instance, was
in the eyes of both men a symbolist poet. It is properly symbolical that in 1907 Symons published his own study of Blake and
that in the same year a study of Blake as a poet and mystic appeared in France.[8] The thread of Blake's influence weaves itself
through the whole fabric of the aesthetic of symbolism.

And just as Blake's influence provides a thread in the fabric,
so does the tortured awareness of a single philosophical and psychological problem, epistemological in character. It is the problem brought to crisis since the Renaissance by the bifurcation
of nature into a perceiving subject and an outer object.[9] The so-
called "subject-object" problem appears not only on the highly
abstract level of science and philosophy but also on the highly
concrete level of personal emotion. It was first expressed directly,
as Edmund Wilson says in *Axël's Castle*, on both levels by the
Romantic poets:

The arena of literature [in the Romantic movement] has been trans-
ferred from the universe conceived as a machine, from society conceived as an organization, to the individual soul.
    What has really taken place, says Whitehead, is a philosophical
revolution. The scientists of the seventeenth century who presented
the universe as a mechanism had caused people to draw the conclu-

sion that man was something apart from nature, something introduced into the universe from the outside and remaining alien to all
that he found. But a Romantic poet like Wordsworth has come to
feel the falsity of this assumption.[10]

If Wordsworth, whom Blake suspected of a love for the delusion
"nature," had sought to deny the assumed gap between subject
and object, the Pre-Raphaelites and later poets had come simply
to regret the assumption (it was unfortunately a spectacularly
workable scientific hypothesis). And their regret was expressed
in the guise of many concrete experiences. They dramatized
physical and mental aloneness in verse, allegorizing the philosophical problem as they did so:

> A wayfarer by barren ways and chill,
> Steep ways and weary, without her thou art,
> Where the long cloud, the long wood's counterpart,
> Sheds doubled darkness up the labouring hill.[11]

These lines from Rossetti's sonnet "Without Her" might have
been spoken by the sorrowful Urizen to himself as he wandered
through his material world seeking Ahania and the vortex of
vision. To this modern consciousness, man was Melville's Ahab,
adrift on a wide sea, seeking completion of self in the distortion
called nature's "vegetable glass." For monomaniac Ahab there is
no resolution of the subject-object problem, no escape from
himself. In *Moby Dick* only Ishmael escapes through the vortex
to some understanding:

So, floating on the margin of the ensuing scene, and in full sight of
it, when the half-spent suction of the sunk ship reached me, I was
then, but slowly, drawn toward the closing vortex. When I reached
it, it had subsided to a creamy pool. Round and round, then, and
ever contracting towards the buttonlike black bubble at the axis of
that slowly wheeling circle, like another Ixion I did revolve. Till,
gaining that vital centre, the black bubble upward burst; and now,
liberated by reason of its cunning spring, and, owing to its great
buoyancy, rising with great force, the coffin life-buoy shot lengthwise
from the sea, fell over, and floated by my side.[12]

The Pre-Raphaelites and other nineteenth-century poets searched constantly for the vortex of vision achieved by Ishmael and by Los, but their searching led them in a direction strangely oblique to Blake's. Blake's symbolical system, at one and the same time the expression of an aesthetic ideal and an epistemology, obliterated the subject-object distinction by showing that the old philosophical questions were misplaced and led inevitably to irrelevant answers because they were enclosed within the circle of false assumptions. Blake is the foremost poet of "symbolic form," a symbolist poet belonging to no movement or school. Yeats wrote that Blake created a "religion of art," but it would be more accurate to say that he re-created an "art of religion" and an attitude making art and religion a single form of experience. For Blake everything is symbolical. We live in a world of symbolic forms. All of our experiences are vortical—infinite perceptions delineated by minute discrimination into symbols. For Blake there is no real world of being set off against a strange, subjective world of fantasy. In this view he is very near to the philosopher of "symbolic form," Ernst Cassirer, who writes:

[Mythical conceptions] are not culled from a ready-made world of Being, they are not mere products of fantasy which vapor off from fixed, empirical, realistic existence, to float above the actual world like a bright mist; to primitive consciousness they present the *totality* of Being. The mythical form of conception is not something super-added to definite *elements* of empirical existence; instead, the primary "experience" itself is steeped in the imagery of myth and saturated with its atmosphere. Man lives with *objects* only in so far as he lives with these *forms;* he reveals reality to himself, and himself to reality, in that he lets himself and the environment enter into this plastic medium, in which the two do not merely make contact, but fuse with each other.[13]

In Blake's cosmos "that thing as it really is" is no more than an expression of the perceiving consciousness, an image of mental infinitude, a world in a grain of sand. The experience is immediate simply because there is no transformation of material into idea. Here is Cassirer:

In mythic conception . . . things are not taken for what they mean indirectly, but for their immediate appearance; they are taken as pure presentations, and embodied in the imagination. It is easy to see that this sort of hypostatization must lead to an entirely different attitude toward the spoken word, toward its power and content, than the standpoint of discursive thought would produce.[14]

Certainly Blake's whole system militates against the chains of discursive language. Language is not a system of signs for thought; it is the very form of thought itself. With Blake perception and conception join to become one. The world is consciousness; the world is a single symbol. Again Cassirer:

Every part of the whole is the whole itself; every specimen is equivalent to the entire species. The part does not merely represent the whole or the specimen its class; they are identical with the totality to which they belong; not merely as mediating aids to reflective thought, but as genuine presences which actually contain the power, significance, and efficacy of the whole. Here one is reminded forcefully of the principle which might be called the basic principle of verbal as well as mythic "metaphor"—the principle of *pars pro toto*. It is a familiar fact that all mythic thinking is permeated by this principle.[15]

For Blake the language of symbolism, whether word or pictorial image, is the structure of the world, and each image is itself the world in microcosm expanding to its infinity in the mind which conceives it and joining in infinity to all other images and all other minds. When Blake speaks of the corporeal body—the body of Albion, for example—he speaks of symbols which contain the world. For Blake any imaginative act inevitably expresses itself in a certain pattern of images, archetypal and timelessly accessible to any human consciousness. His symbolic method follows logically from his theory of knowledge.

But between Blake and the contemporary "philosophy of symbolic form" there lies a great sea in which, as Matthew Arnold wrote, "mortal millions live *alone*"; and although Blake appealed strongly to such men as Rossetti and Swinburne, neither of them was able to write an adequate interpretation of the fearful symmetry of his vision. Blake's synthesis of religion and art by means of a new, yet almost primitive, method of experiencing did not communicate itself discursively to them, and they passed it on only in fragments. Dante Rossetti's comments on Blake's poems are often somewhat naïve:

Here again but little need be added to what has already been said in the *Life* respecting the *Songs of Innocence and Experience*. The first series is incomparably the more beautiful of the two, being indeed almost flawless in essential respects; while in the second series, the five years intervening between the two had proved sufficient for obscurity and the darker mental phases of Blake's writing to set in and greatly mar its poetic value.[16]

With this attitude surely Rossetti was mystified by the later prophecies. In truth, he had little if anything to say about them; and he admitted that "The Mental Traveller" was a hopeless riddle until his brother, William, offered an explanation of it.[17] William seems to have studied Blake with some care and thought about the possibility of actually explicating the prophecies. In one of his letters to Alexander Gilchrist's widow he wrote, "No doubt Jacob Behmen & Swedenborg wd. [*sic*] be in some degree elucidatory of Jerusalem: I know something of them both. But what one ought first to do, I think, is look up old mediaeval legends about 'the Giant Albion' &c." [18] He recognized that Blake sought to create a mythology simultaneously from the depths of his own mind and from past mythologies. His explanation of "The Mental Traveller" was the first intelligent word on that poem.[19]

Swinburne's critical study of Blake suggests that he understood more of Blake's system than he actually succeeded in communicating. He was especially interested in Blake's denial of what he called "the moral heresy," by which he meant the stultification of supposedly virtuous action by the tyranny of law. It is never clear whether or not Swinburne understood that Blake was really attempting to assert a higher morality based not on rules but on form. Blake thought that his higher morality (though he would never have used the word) would follow naturally from a cleansing of the doors of perception; no laws would really be necessary; intuition would overthrow coercion. Blake's morality would be the result of a communal theory of knowledge. Unlike Blake, Swinburne never articulated the form. Instead he battled the law and tended, like Blake's Orc, to invert the rules. Nevertheless, in his theoretical writing on Blake he often seems to be a new Blake speaking an ornate language:

The contingent result of having good art about you and living in a time of noble writing or painting may no doubt be this; that the spirit and mind of men then living will receive on some points a certain exaltation and insight caught from the influence of such forms and colours of verse or painting; will become for one thing incapable of tolerating bad work, and capable therefore of reasonably relishing the best; which of course implies and draws with it many other advantages of a sort you may call moral or spiritual. But if the artist does his work with an eye to such results or for the sake of bringing about such improvements, he will too probably fail even of them. Art for art's sake first of all, and afterwards we may suppose all the rest shall be added to her . . . , but from the man who falls to artistic work with a moral purpose, shall be taken away even that which he has.[20]

Although Swinburne seems to see here that there is a form of apprehension which must be attained not by coercion but by some other means and that art is a concrete and not an abstract form, he also seems willfully to overlook the stubborn fact that Blake consciously wrote with an eye toward revealing truth to people. Blake did "have an eye" for the didactic results of his art, and it could well be argued that the greatness of his art comes directly in part from his preoccupation with a unique message.

Swinburne's second error reveals more clearly a startling misconception of Blake's aims in developing a symbolical system:

Blake was not incapable of mixing the Hellenic, the Miltonic, and the Celtic mythologies into one drugged and adulterated compound. He had read much and blindly; he had no leaning to verbal accuracy, and never acquired any faculty of comparison.[21]

If Blake's attempt to restore the single great myth to its proper outline was sometimes unsuccessful, it was certainly worth attempting. Swinburne does not seem to have understood the force which drove Blake to create his "drugged and adulterated compound." The truth is that Blake's faculty of comparison may have been too subtle for Swinburne. Swinburne not only missed the point of central archetypal form but also overlooked the very point where religion and art, subject and object converge in Blake's thought.

Swinburne's own world of art is a fantasy world of long rhythms and dim outlines, a world consciously abstracted from a material reality; it is not Blake's world of symbolic reality beyond which lies nothing at all. Blake's "prayer is the study of art" is far different from Swinburne's "art for art's sake," for Blake's art is an intuition of the mental form for things, while Swinburne's is a conscious separation of the world of art from a vast, practical world of life. In much of Swinburne's poetry, as in, for example, "The Garden of Proserpine," incantatory rhythm closely interwoven with a controlled vagueness of image slides the reader magically toward some soft, easy resolution of conflict. Everything disperses to nothingness. The remarkable power of Swinburne's poetry is the commingling of movement and sound which lures the reader on to embrace something that in the cold light of day might repel him, as Blake was repelled by Rahab. But for Blake neither perception nor conception properly occurs in the form of Swinburnean "doubtful dreams." Images are not abstract and weary; only Orc-Urizen gives himself to Proserpine-Rahab. Swinburne's poetry is Orcian in its quality of revolt, but he did not recognize that the figure opposite him was really Urizen and therefore himself. Revolution is tied to law; inversion of symbols is circular without progression, emphasizing return.

Swinburne, who transvaluated values in order to show the absurdity of those commonly accepted, certainly found a precedent in Blake's *Marriage of Heaven and Hell*, but his long wavering rhythms and regressive symbolism are the antitheses of Blake's hard coldness and apocalyptic vision. Yet both Blake and Swinburne, in spite of these differences, influenced in thought, image, and rhythm the young poet Yeats; and it was some time before Yeats was able to sort out these influences and recognize that they were basically incompatible with each other in spite of their superficial similarities. Yeats did learn very soon that a blatantly Swinburnean poem was merely parody, and he wisely suppressed the following lines from his published works:

> Afar from our lawn and our leveé
> O sister of sorrowful gaze!
> Where the roses in scarlet are heavy
> And dream of the end of their days,
> You move in another dominion
> And hang o'er the historied stone,
> Unpruned is your beautiful pinion,
> Who wander and whisper alone.[22]

This is Yeats influenced not only by Swinburne and the Pre-Raphaelite image of woman but also by the English Aestheticism of Pater, Wilde, and others whose artistic pronouncements were strangely antithetical to Blake's in emphasis and influence. Wilde's own words symbolize the difference between Blake's "Prayer is the study of art" and the "art for art's sake" cliché: "All bad art comes from returning to Life and Nature and elevating them into ideals." [23] Blake would have corrected him by pointing out that all bad art comes from believing that there is a "nature" to return to and thus falling into death. Wilde, he would have said, admits to the reality of the delusion by fleeing from it.

Blake would have attacked Pater, who wrote, "Experience, already reduced to a group of impressions, is ringed round for each one of us by that thick wall of personality through which no real voice has ever pierced on its way to us, or from us to that which we can only conjecture to be without." [24] For Blake this man is simply Urizen speaking of his own circled self-enclosure. French Symbolist poets and Impressionist painters are similarly ringed round, sometimes by a jealously guarded private vision. In defending the arts against life, they adopt a tone which is the antithesis of Blake's. Villiers de l'Isle Adam's "As for living, our servants can do that for us" is not the Blakean mood. For the Symbolist poet Mallarmé, according to Arthur Symons, "To name is to destroy, to suggest is to create." [25] This view led too often to the expression of vague, undifferentiated emotion, mystical but vaporous. It was Blake's business to "name" things, to give them sharp outline, whether they were objective symbols or not. Los's "naming" of Rahab for what she is is an allegory of Blake's own theory of art.

Any poet, for all poets are really symbolists, runs the risk of creating nothing more than a chaos of private significance without any central form. To be successful he must create a communal significance out of a personal emotion. According to Blake's theory of knowledge the communal vision was at least possible. Other poets, ringed round by nature, began to accept delusion as reality and sought to make the best of a bad world by glorifying art over life, mind over matter, self over crowd. Still others dramatized the aloneness of man in a natural world growing more and more hostile to the soul. In the nineteenth century surely nature was growing more hostile. Man was now not only a congeries of peculiarly organized particles of matter; he was also no better than an animal. For Yeats, who began to write in the late nineteenth century, the great advances of a materialistic science made the harlot Rahab even more powerful than she was in Blake's time. The old Blakean triumvirate of "Bacon, Newton, Locke" was joined by the Yeatsian triumvirate of "Huxley, Tyndall, Bastien-Lepage."

A central defect in the world of Yeats's youth was the lack of spiritual community. Men, who had always found it necessary to form some direct relationship with something other than themselves, saw only Urizen across the circle. The world was "pragmatical, preposterous"; and Yeats, transvaluating all enlightenment values in a Swinburnean manner, took the side of dream in a false dream-reality dichotomy. Yet even in Yeats's early poems there is an embarrassing awareness that neither the taking of sides nor the Swinburnean inversion which turns dream into reality and life into death is an adequate answer to the problem of enclosure. Thus many early poems end in a wavering irresolution. The first poem of "Crossways" is illustrative. "The Song of the Happy Shepherd" begins with these words:

> The woods of Arcady are dead,
> And over is their antique joy;
> Of old the world on dreaming fed;
> Grey Truth is now her painted toy.[26]

The poem (we have it revised in the collected edition) first appeared as an epilogue to an early play entitled "The Island of Statues." Originally, then, "The woods of Arcady are dead" signifies among other things the end of the illusion on the stage; it is also evident from the last lines of the poem that the speaker will return to Arcady behind the curtain. But clearly Arcady is not dead in any figurative sense. The truth is that life is death, death is life. The real death, or life transvaluated, is the sick world of "grey truth," the "dreary dancing" of an atomic world of multiplicity to the "cracked tune" of Chronos. This truth is called grey because the world it describes is really colorless or, more specifically, a world of sheer material—what Whitehead calls a "dull affair, soundless, scentless, colourless; merely the hurrying of material, endlessly meaninglessly." [27] The image, "painted toy," dominates the opening lines. The toy is "truth," the world of science. It is a world to be played with, a selected world, a hypothesis, painted the most dull and colorless of all colors by a science according to which the world is bright and alive only by means of the "hallucination" of the secondary qualities of perception.

But Yeats has turned things upside down. The real hallucination is the scientific "dream" which has "hungered fiercely" after a "grey truth" and reduced the world to illness:

> But O, sick children of the world,
> Of all the many changing things
> In dreary dancing past us whirled,
> To the cracked tune that Chronos sings,
> Words alone are certain good.

The Happy Shepherd goes on to tell us that there are two kinds of dreams: first, the more real word-dreams of the poet, and, second, the distorting, less real dreams of science:

> Then nowise worship dusty deeds,
> Nor seek, for this is also sooth,
> To hunger fiercely after truth,
> Lest all thy toiling only breeds
> New dreams, new dreams; there is no truth
> Saving in thine own heart. Seek, then,
> No learning from the starry men,
> Who follow with the optic glass
> The whirling ways of stars that pass—
> Seek, then, for this is also sooth,
> No word of theirs—the cold star-bane
> Has cloven and rent their hearts in twain,
> And dead is all their human truth.
> Go gather by the humming sea
> Some twisted echo-harbouring shell,
> And to its lips thy story tell,
> And they thy comforters will be,

Rewording in melodious guile
Thy fretful words a little while,
Till they shall singing fade in ruth
And die a pearly brotherhood.

Compared to the divided Urizenic dream of science, the poetic dream is pleasant, but it is also ephemeral. For the poet to hear his *own* words in the shell may have some vague emotional effect, but the suggestion that from such self-enclosure comes truth of the heart is somewhat weak and in itself woefully suggestive of decadence. Finally even the echoes dissolve themselves in an essentially irrational death image, suggesting some communal brotherhood but failing to state just what the nature of it is. There is evidently no possibility of attaining to any reality, if there is a reality; there is only a choice of dreams, the one workable, the other pleasant but vague.

At one point in the poem Yeats seems to be moving toward a new and transcendent conception of reality, but he puts it forth only tentatively:

The wandering earth herself may be
Only a sudden flaming word,
In clanging space a moment heard
Troubling the endless reverie.

Here is a suggestion of symbolic form, but only a suggestion, a hypothesis advanced and withdrawn before it is explored. Maybe the word itself is our reality, the vehicle for our conceptions beyond which lies no material; but no, we have only the dream of Arcady to cling to—the vague, harmless dream of an unreality called the heart. The Happy Shepherd admits that the only escape brings one into a land of "melodious guile," and that escape is only temporary before a return to the ravages of the workable and practical unrealities of science.

In another poem, "The Sad Shepherd" (1886), similar imagery and the same frustrated search for reality appear. The shepherd cries out his aloneness to star, sea, and dew drop:

And he called loudly to the stars to bend
From their pale thrones and comfort him, but they
Among themselves laugh and sing alway:
And then the man whom Sorrow named his friend
Cried out, *Dim sea hear my most piteous story!*
The sea swept on and cried her old cry still,
Rolling along in dreams from hill to hill.
He fled the persecution of her glory
And, in a far-off, gentle valley stopping,
Cried all his story to the dew drops glistening.
But naught they heard, for they are always listening,
The dew drops, for the sound of their own dropping.[28]

Urizenic heaven gives no comfort to the shepherd; the stars, like
Blake's chain of stars created by Urizen, are symbols of multiplicity, bodily separation, and enclosure. Nor is there any hope
for communion with things of the earth, which are every bit as
enclosed in ego as the shepherd who seeks to break the bonds of
his selfhood. The sea gives him no opportunity to maintain anything of himself at all; it conquers everything, and the shepherd
seeks communion without passive surrender. So finally he is
caught between two contending powers, his egoism and his desire for "unity of being." The final attempt to overcome this
tragic condition of life is also a failure:

And then the man whom Sorrow named his friend
Sought once again the shore, and found a shell,
And thought, *I will my heavy story tell*
Till my own words, re-echoing, shall send
Their sadness through a hollow, pearly heart;
And my own tale again for me shall sing,
And my own whispering words be comforting,
And lo! my ancient burden may depart.
Then he sang softly nigh the pearly rim;
But the sad dweller by the sea-ways lone
Changed all he sang to inarticulate moan
Among her wildering whirls, forgetting him.

The conclusion in frustration, following the shepherd's appeal
to the music of words, is itself a comment upon the style of the

poem. The powerful incantatory rhythm suggests some magical resolution of contraries, but the statement of the poem gives no resolution. The ego remains enclosed in a natural world. The evocation of indefinite emotion is not enough.

There is a traditional never-never land where one is supposed to be able to escape from the shell dilemma—the oasis-island—but such an image is charged with hopeless nostalgia. In Yeats's "The Indian to His Love" all motion is curiously halted by the juxtaposition of static ("enamelled") and violent ("raging") images; nothing but artifice remains:

> The island dreams under the dawn
> And great boughs drop tranquillity;
> The peahens dance on a smooth lawn,
> A parrot sways upon a tree,
> Raging at his own image in the enamelled sea.[29]

Time is no longer a factor in life. Life becomes death, death becomes life:

> Here we will moor our lonely ship
> And wander ever with woven hands,
> Murmuring softly lip to lip,
> Along the grass, along the sands,
> Murmuring how far away are the unquiet lands.

But again the whole issue of reality is clouded. There is no intuition, only a symbolic inversion of values and an escape into controlled nirvana where problems are not solved but do seem to become irrelevant. Even there the parrot rages at himself, breaking the spell, and the lovers know that there is another world somewhere. They are even driven to murmur its name to each other. One of the great myths of the hero tells of his dissatisfaction with the "Bowre of Bliss" and his willingness to return like Ulysses to the world of battle. The enchanted island, no matter how attractive, is false because it is a dream; the goddess with whom man joins is thus a false temptress. Yeats looks, and seems to know that he is doing so, in the direction of delusion.

The land of Irish faery is also a land of delusion and escape, just as uninhabitable to the hero as the enchanted island. In "The Stolen Child" the faery entice the human being into an apparently lovely enchantment which is really no better than the schizoid dreams of the Yeatsian shepherds. The faery sing:

> Away with us he's going
> The solemn-eyed.[30]

There is a kind of irony here—a note of exuberance in the faery victory, of ridicule because the solemn face does not for all its solemnity comprehend, because the face has no gaiety. There is also, perhaps, a counterfeeling of ineffable sympathy for his plight, but the faery are capriciously demonic and do not succumb to sympathy. The poem leaves the reader trapped between two worlds, neither satisfactory. Yeats resorts to exploitation of rhythm and sound in order to make the irresolution of the problem seem irrelevant to the pleasantly vague and nostalgic feeling evoked. But this poetry, if it is escapist, is also a poetry in which escape clearly does not solve the problem of experience. In these early poems of Yeats the subject-object problem remains unsolved in a conflict between tone and statement.

The same plangency is evident in Yeats's early love poetry, where Villiers de l'Isle Adam's famous phrase seems to be the text. The theme of withdrawal and negation can be followed through "Ephemera," "To the Rose upon the Rood of Time," "The White Birds," to "He Wishes His Beloved Were Dead," beyond which nothing more can be done:

> Were you but lying cold and dead,
> And lights were paling out of the West,
> You would come hither, and bend your head,
> And I would lay my head on your breast;
> And you would murmur tender words,
> Forgiving me, because you were dead:
> Nor would you rise and hasten away,
> Though you have the will of the wild birds,

> But know your hair was bound and wound
> About the stars and moon and sun:
> O would, beloved, that you lay
> Under the dock-leaves in the ground,
> While lights were paling one by one.[31]

Love and death join symbolically in the love poems. The women are languid-lipped Pre-Raphaelite creations, passionate yet unapproachable.

When the early Yeats writes of apocalypse he writes of something which is also safely unattainable. The intimation of apocalypse in the last lines of "The Secret Rose" is phrased as a rhetorical question:

> . . . I, too, await
> The hour of thy great wind of love and hate.
> When shall the stars be blown about the sky
> Like the sparks blown out of the smithy, and die? *
> Surely thine hour has come, thy great wind blows,
> Far-off, most secret, and inviolate Rose? [32]

These are, of course, hopes for Irish freedom, stated allegorically and wrapped, perhaps without intention, in a pseudo-Blakean imagery. The great blacksmith will obliterate the materialistic heavens of Urizen; all will be spiritual:

> Far-off, most secret, and inviolate Rose,
> Enfold me in my hour of hours; where those
> Who sought thee in the Holy Sepulchre,
> Or in the wine-vat, dwell beyond the stir
> And tumult of defeated dreams; and deep

---

* Compare Erdman's comment (*Blake: Prophet against Empire*, 180) on Blake's lines from "The Tyger" which describe the blacksmith creating the tiger: "The creative blacksmith who seizes the molten stuff of terror and shapes it into living form on the cosmic anvil must employ dread power as well as daring and art, but the dread, Blake hopes, will be sufficient unto the day. The climax of the forging is a mighty hammering which drives out the impurities in a shower of sparks, like the falling stars children call angels' tears." Blake's poem probably influenced Yeats's lines here, but the difference in tone between the two poems is so great that the similarity seems superficial.

> Among pale eyelids, heavy with the sleep
> Men have named beauty. . . .

After emphasis on return to a mythological age projected as dream, the possibility of violence seems remote indeed. Yeats hopefully awaits; the symbol of danger is safely "far-off."

This allegorical poem of intimation and passivity is, despite the appearance of images used also by Blake, really anti-Blakean in tone. Instead of obliterating the gap between men, it plays totally on the subjective side of the epistemological dichotomy. It deals with private sensation and emotion, lamenting a sorry state of affairs.

In later years Yeats detected in his early work "a slight, sentimental sensuality which is disagreeable." [33] He characterized this aura as a "lingering between sense and spirit." He castigated the early stories of *The Celtic Twilight* as bits of "ornamental trivial needlework sown on a prophetic fury got by Blake and Boehme." [34] In his *Autobiography* he described his new quest for style:

Years afterwards when I had finished *The Wanderings of Oisin*, dissatisfied with its yellow and its dull green, with all that overcharged colour inherited from the romantic movement, I deliberately reshaped my style, deliberately sought out an impression as of cold light and tumbling clouds. I cast off traditional metaphors and loosened my rhythm, and recognising that all the criticism of life known to me was alien and English, became as emotional as possible but with an emotion which I described to myself as cold.[35]

He briefly summarized his desires in an essay on Synge written in 1910, when he had made significant strides in the quest: "Great art chills us at first by its coldness or its strangeness, by what seems capricious, and yet it is from these qualities it has authority, as though it had fed on locust and wild honey." [36] The style and the attitude implicit in a poem cannot be separated from each other. Yeats deliberately reshaped his style and projected new emotion: "As I look backward upon my own writing, I take pleasure alone in those verses where it seems to me I have found something hard and cold." [37] Yeats's change from celebrating regression and death to celebrating fury and life brought with it stylistic hard coldness. Sloughing off the imagery of withdrawal and the rhythm of dream, Yeats began to champion Blakean action. Along with a new style came a concept of the hero very much like Blake's. Yeats saw the heroic personality facing the wheel of history, forced to achieve some psychological balance or perish. If he came to believe that conflict was inevitable in life, he also believed it to be the paradoxical principle of harmony in the universe, expressible only by the dramatic structure of myth. Blake's great symbolical system served Yeats as a mythological school, a "corpus of poetic reference" which related itself to his other interests—magic, esoteric philosophy—through what seemed to be a world-wide, communal symbolism, perhaps a new religion.

SKEPTICISM AND MAGIC

According to Yeats, Blake believed that "we perceive the world through countless little reflections of our own image." The natural question is, "How?" And it is the question that Yeats asked throughout his life. He tells us in the *Autobiography* that an early skepticism fostered by environment frustrated his desire for faith. Yeats's father, John Butler Yeats, a skeptic and free thinker, greatly influenced his son. For many years a Pre-Raphaelite painter, he gradually lost faith in Pre-Raphaelite principles and never gave his allegiance to another school. The son remembered that his father had been frustrated by the movement of time:

My father was painting the first big pond that you come to if you have driven from Slough through Farnham Royal. He began it in spring and painted all through the year, the picture changing with the seasons, and gave it up unfinished when he had painted the snow upon the heath-covered banks. [38]

The father was suspicious of organized religion—Blake's "natural religion"—and of law. He made a distinction between religious and poetic belief, meaning by poetic belief exactly what Blake meant by true religion.

There are two kinds of belief; the poetical and the religious. That of the poet comes when the man within has found some method or manner of thinking or arrangement of fact (such as is only possible in dreams) by which to express and embody an absolute freedom, such that his whole inner and outer self can expand in full satisfaction.

In religious belief there is absent the consciousness of liberty. Religion is the denial of liberty. An enforced peace is set up among the warring feelings. By the help of something quite external, as for instance the fear of hell, some feelings are chained up and thrust into dungeons that some other feelings may hold sway; and all the ethical systems yet invented are a similar denial of liberty, that is why the true poet is neither moral nor religious.[39]

He hated the stultifying tendency of rigid morality and saw only too clearly the necessity for a form of belief independent of it. He thought that belief could come only through a new form of knowledge. This form was the form of symbolism, the breaker of ego barriers:

The poet's seriousness is his quest for what I may call the poetic omniscience; a continual progress in identifying himself with everything that lives, and that does not live, not merely men and women or animals and birds but even trees and plants and rocks and stones. This adventurous thirst and appetite for more life, sought through the power of poetical omniscience, is the poet's demon which he will follow into hell itself. Because of his demon he will break all laws and face all perils; that is the fascination of poets and poetry. And that is his seriousness, that is his devil.[40]

Like Blake's, his view was gnostic. In the passage above we see a link between Blake and John Butler Yeats's son. The image and idea are Blake's; the dramatic battle between the poet's Demon and his Beast is the subject of the son's poetry.

The father's view of the relation between morality and art was also the son's. In defending Synge and the Abbey Theatre plays, Yeats attacked superficial morality; earlier in *Samhain* he had written:

A writer in *The Leader* has said that I told my audience after the performance of *The Hour-Glass* that I did not care whether a play was moral or immoral. . . . I have always been of Verhaeren's opinion that a masterpiece is a portion of the conscience of mankind. My objection was to the rough-and-ready conscience of the newspaper and the pulpit in a matter so delicate and so difficult as literature. Every generation of men of letters has been called immoral by the pulpit or the newspaper, and it has been precisely when that generation has been illuminating some obscure corner of the conscience that the cry against it has been more confident.[41]

According to Yeats, the "rough-and-ready conscience" of the moralist substitutes "certain generalizations . . . personified averages, partisan fictions" for the universal particularity found deep in "secret thoughts." [42] Like Blake, he attacked abstraction and defended the form of experience which dictates nondiscursively its own higher morality and comprehension, its gnosis.

We lose our freedom more and more as we get away from ourselves, and not merely because our minds are overthrown by abstract phrases and generalisations, reflections in a mirror that seem living, but because we have turned the table of value upside down, and believe that the root of reality is not in the centre but somewhere in that whirling circumference.[43]

Even the imagery is Blake's: One achieves unity at the center, not at the edge of the circle of abstraction:

Every argument carries us backwards to some religious conception, and in the end the creative energy of men depends upon their believing that they have, within themselves, something immortal and imperishable, and that all else is but as an image in a looking-glass. So long as that belief is not a formal thing, a man will create out of a joyful energy, seeking little for any external test of an impulse that may be sacred, and looking for no foundation outside life it-self.[44]

Following Blake again, Yeats insisted that reality lies in expansion inward to freedom, not outward to the "vegetable glass" or mirror of nature.

As a boy, Yeats was "in all things Pre-Raphaelite":

When alone and uninfluenced, I longed for pattern, for pre-Raphaelitism, for an art allied to poetry, and returned again and again to our National Gallery to gaze at Turner's "Golden Bough." . . . I was always hoping that my father would return to the style of his youth.[45]

The chaos of his father's unfinished picture mirrored the philosophic and religious anarchy of his time, to which the young Yeats was peculiarly sensitive. In one of his last prose writings Yeats recalled that in his youth he could find no acceptable dominant opinion.[46] Elsewhere he wrote that he sought for a tradition of poetic belief among artists:

I was unlike others of my generation in one thing only. I am very religious, and deprived by Huxley and Tyndall, whom I detested, of the simple-minded religion of my childhood, I had made a new religion, almost an infallible church of poetic tradition, of a fardel of stories, and of personages, and of emotions, inseparable from their first expression, passed on from generation to generation by poets and painters with some help from philosophers and theologians. I wished for a world, where I could discover this tradition perpetually.[47]

Looking toward poetry for a religion, he found that he was looking also toward symbolism, for in the evocation of the symbol something more than the literal was communicated. He would come to believe with Arthur Symons that "symbolism, as seen in the writers of our day, would have no value if it were not seen also, under one disguise or another, in every imaginative writer." [48] That is, the traditional form of poetry is symbolic, and the symbol is a vehicle for knowledge beyond that discursive knowledge which becomes abstract and literal.

Yeats went not only to the poets for his beliefs but also to occult lore, psychical research, and mystical philosophy. He helped to found the "Dublin Hermetic Society" and at an early meeting proposed "that whatever the great poets had affirmed in their finest moments was the nearest we could come to an authoritative religion, and that their mythology, their spirits of water and wind were but literal truth." [49] He added to this provisional faith based on a study of occult and poetic symbols a belief in the powers of comparative religion and mythology to get at the truth: "I began occasionally telling people that one should believe whatever had been believed in all countries and periods." [50]

To Yeats magical practices were not assertions of personal power over nature; instead they were assertions of a new communal human power which tends to transform nature:

I believe in the practice and philosophy of what we have agreed to call magic, in what I must call the evocation of spirits, though I do not know what they are, in the power of creating magical illusions, in the visions of truth in the depths of the mind when the eyes are closed; and I believe in three doctrines, which have, as I think, been handed down from early times, and been the foundations of nearly all magical practices. These doctrines are—

(1) That the borders of our mind are ever shifting, and that many minds can flow into one another, as it were, and create or reveal a single mind, a single energy.

(2) That the borders of our memories are as shifting, and that our memories are a part of one great memory, the memory of Nature herself.

(3) That this great mind and great memory can be evoked by symbols.[51]

He experimented constantly with the transmission of images between minds, and with the sudden appearance of traditional mythological images to the minds of people unacquainted with them. In his 1901 essay entitled "Magic" and later in his *Auto-*

biography he tells the story of some of these evocations. Often several people in a room saw similar or identical images in a kind of trance. At other times people had been visited by symbols which Yeats later discovered in his own occult reading. Those visions seen simultaneously by people at great distances from each other were, Yeats thought, "symbolical histories of . . . moods and events, or rather symbolical shadows of the impulses that have made them, messages as it were out of the ancestral being of the questioner." [52] He was convinced that these visions were evidence of the power of many minds to become one mind or single energy, which itself is supernaturally the great store-house of human imagination, timeless and archetypal.

Almost every one who has ever busied himself with such matters has come, in trance or dream, upon some new and strange symbol or event, which he has afterwards found in some work he had never read or heard of. Examples like this are as yet too little classified, too little analyzed, to convince the stranger, but some of them are proof enough for those they have happened to, proof that there is a memory of nature that reveals events and symbols of distant centuries. Mystics of many countries and many centuries have spoken of this memory; and the honest men and charlatans, who keep the magical traditions which will some day be studied as a part of folk-lore, base most that is of importance in their claims upon this memory . . . I have found it in the prophetic books of William Blake, who calls its images "the bright sculptures of Los's Halls"; and says that all events, "all love stories," renew themselves from those images.[53]

He found these "bright sculptures" in that other great influence upon his work, the poetry of Shelley. Defending Shelley against those who called him a fuzzy metaphysician writing in verse, Yeats tried to show that Shelley was employing an archetypal symbolism which differed from the discursive form of philosophy. According to Yeats, the great symbols of Shelley's poems display the "glowing forms of his mind when freed from all impulse not out of itself or out of supersensual power." [54]

Yeats learned that poetry must be an expression of the individual, not "the deliberate creation of a kind of Holy City in the imagination." [55] But he also thought that a certain objectivity is necessary in such an expression. Myths created by the poet "must be 'objective' rather than 'subjective,' an inner way of looking at things assumed by a single mind." [56] The single mind must become the communal mind in poetry, and Yeats thought he was uncovering a lost tradition as he frequented out-of-the-way places, affected strange poses, and studied magical evocation. If the poetic symbol does arise out of some common substratum, then perhaps the poetic symbol is the real spiritual language of man which transcends his simple location in space and time.

Elaborate modern psychology sounds egotistical, I thought, when it speaks in the first person, but not those simple emotions which resemble the more, the more powerful they are, everybody's emotion, and I was soon to write many poems where an always personal emotion was woven into a general pattern of myth and symbol.[57]

His great problem was, of course, the creation of that general pattern. Like Blake, Yeats could not accept myths distorted by time and reason, and his attempt to appropriate an Irish mythology which had been dispelled to shadows through the Celtic Twilight and the Pre-Raphaelite haze was a failure. His early work expresses neither the individual nor the central form of myth, for the Irish myths, like the Greek myths for Blake, had been too greatly distorted. When Yeats wrote the following words in his essay on Shelley, he had apprehended portions of his later theory of individual objectivity, but he was not yet writing poetry which made a success of the theory:

It is only by ancient symbols, by symbols that have numberless meanings beside the one or two the writer lays an emphasis upon, or the half-score he knows of, that any highly subjective art can escape from the barrenness and shallowness of a too conscious arrangement, into the abundance and depth of nature. The poet of essences and pure ideas must seek in the half-lights that glimmer from symbol to symbol as if to the ends of the earth, all that the epic and dramatic poet finds of mystery and shadow in the accidental circumstance of life.[58]

Here the description of the symbol is still vague and clouded. Later Yeats decided that to be the poet of "pure ideas" is not really enough, that some of life's "accidental circumstances" are the stuff of poetry. The distinction between two types of poetry is really false. The accidents become symbolical microcosms of the central form. Everything has its significance. He would agree with Blake's words, "Every thing that lives is Holy."

Whatever the passions of man have gathered about, becomes a symbol in the great memory, and in the hands of him who has the secret, it is a worker of wonders, a caller-up of angels or of devils. The symbols are of all kinds, for everything in heaven or earth has its association, momentous or trivial, in the great memory.[59]

And strangely enough, according to his magical studies, our symbols seem to come to us from some source beyond conscious control. This force is probably the communal mind or memory which Yeats later called "Spiritus Mundi" or "Anima Mundi": "When a man writes any work of genius, or invents some creative action, is it not because some knowledge or power has come into his mind from beyond his mind? . . . Our images must be given to us, we cannot choose them deliberately." [60] One must seek to create out of that strange communal mind; one cannot willfully appropriate a mythology. One of Yeats's last poems, "The Circus Animals' Desertion," has as its theme this very point.

While he studied magic, Yeats vacillated in his attitude toward the nature of the symbol. He could not decide whether the symbol as an object itself is powerful or whether symbols are simply vehicles for the transmission of ideas from one mind to another:

It was long before I myself would admit an inherent power in symbols, for it long seemed to me that one could account for everything by the power of one imagination over another, telepathy, as it is called with that separation of knowledge and life, of word and emotion, which is the sterility of scientific speech. The symbol seemed powerful, I thought, merely because we thought it powerful, and we would do just as well without it. In those days I used symbols made with some ingenuity instead of merely imagining them. I used to give them to the person I was experimenting with, and tell him to hold them to his forehead without looking at them; and sometimes I made a mistake. I learned from these mistakes that if I did not myself imagine the symbol, in which case he would have a mixed vision, it was the symbol I gave by mistake that produced the vision.[61]

This amateur experimentation in extrasensory perception seems partially to have convinced him that the material object can influence the mind even though it cannot be perceived by the five known senses. Here a complicated epistemological problem rears its head. In what form does the symbol transfer itself from mind to mind and object to mind? Where in space is this form? Is there a material existence at all?

Many years after he had written the essay called "Magic," Yeats carried on by letter an epistemological argument with the poet and illustrator, T. Sturge Moore, brother of the Cambridge philosopher, G. E. Moore. In that correspondence Yeats tried to show that certain visions usually called "hallucinations" should be honorifically referred to as "real." Throughout the correspondence he vacillated between what he conceived certain idealist and realist positions to be. The discussion began after Yeats had read a refutation of idealism by G. E. Moore. He wrote to Sturge Moore about a vision seen by a friend:

The night of the day I left you I made an old friend see a vision. For about a minute she sat turning the pages of a missal invisible to me and describing the pictures. Hitherto I have always taken the idealistic view of such visions but now, thanks to your brother's *Refutation of Idealism*, I am permitted to think they exist outside the human mind.[62]

Moore replied that Yeats had obviously misinterpreted his brother's thought, for his brother had never meant to assert that "hallucinations" existed outside of the mind. Here Yeats, perhaps ironically as he later asserted, was holding to the same position taken provisionally in "Magic." Symbols are powerful in themselves, independent of mind. He replied to Moore's criticism with the story of Ruskin's cat:

John Ruskin, while talking with Frank Harris, ran suddenly to the other end of the room, picked up, or seemed to pick up, some object which he threw out of the window. He then explained that it was a tempting demon in the form of a cat. Now if the house cat had come in both cats would have looked alike to Ruskin. (I know this for I once saw a phantom picture and a real picture side by side.) Neither your brother nor Russell [Bertrand] gives any criterion by which Ruskin could have told one cat from the other. No doubt if pressed they would have said that if Ruskin's cat was real Harris would have seen it. But that argument amounts to nothing. Dr. Smyllie, a well-known Dublin doctor, made his class see the Indian rope trick by hypnotic suggestion a few years ago. All saw it: whether the suggestion was mental merely or visual makes no difference. Perhaps Russell would say "a real object" persists, a phantom does not. Shelley pointed out once that the same dream recurs again and again. It is because of these arguments that Eddington, who is a greater mathematician than Russell, and, I think, a sounder philosopher, said lately that all we have a right to say of the external world is that it is a "shared experience." . . .
Things are more or less "real" according to the extent to which they are capable of being shared with others or ourselves, at a different date, but there is no hard and fast line.[63]

Here Yeats was still trying to hold to some objective, non-idealistic position. But later, as Moore observed, he shifted his ground and tried to take up a position of objective idealism. In a long letter he stated three possible epistemological positions and then criticized each:

The *Times Literary Supplement* this week (page 27 column 2) divides possible beliefs about the nature of the external world as follows:—
(1) Everything we perceive "including so-called illusions exists

in the external world." (Ruskin's cat and the house cat are real.)

(2) Nothing can exist that is not in the mind as "an element of experience." (Neither Ruskin's cat nor the house cat is real.)

(3) There is a physical world which is independent of our minds —"real"—but we can only know it through "representations" that are a part of our mind and quite unlike it.[64]

He characterized Bertrand Russell's view—he had been reading Russell's little book, *Problems of Philosophy*—as a compromise between views one and three. He refused to accept the compromise because "Russell and his school cannot escape from the belief that each man is a sealed bottle." He added that view number one was driven from his mind by Blake at an early age (though this contradicts his opening argument). This left view number two, which he tended then to accept. In a later letter Moore characterized this view as the belief that "there may be no object but only the appearance, like an image in a looking-glass." [65] But Moore foresaw difficulties, because once one begins to call all experience mental one ceases to make the useful distinction between what are obviously two qualitatively different forms of experience. Even Berkeley, he pointed out, resorted to calling objective reality the thoughts of God, and therefore merely substituted a new name for outer materiality.

Yeats now complicated the argument by submitting new evidence: Ideas had been photographed; people had seen double images; the Society for Psychical Research had succeeded in transferring mental images from one person to another in different rooms and even different towns:

The present realist argument breaks down because we have no longer the right to say that there is any image of the mind peculiar to one person: something of it is peculiar, as something of the images we call physical is peculiar, and that is all we can say. It becomes necessary to consider that all minds may make under certain circumstances a single mind.[66]

He believed that any philosophy based on the isolation of the individual, "sense-corked" mind had become obsolete. Images of mind and sense have a common root, which (he used White-head's term) "is not fixed at one spot in space." [67] The suggestion is perhaps that man has certain sense powers undeveloped in all but a few people.

The great difference between Yeats and a systematic philosopher like G. E. Moore, as Sturge Moore now pointed out, was that Yeats was seeking an "imagined hypothesis" into which certain strange facts would fit, while G. E. Moore refused to make the hypothesis until the strange facts had been studied and controlled.[68] Yeats's own "philosophy" as expressed in *A Vision* systematized images on the Blakean principle of the literal unity of metaphors. Yeats sought to bring philosophy into the realm of the poetically symbolical by creating a statement which, as he described Blake's system, could be read on any level, any region of nature or thought. His distinction between symbol and allegory is the same as Blake's distinction between vision and allegory:

A symbol is indeed the only possible expression of some invisible essence, a transparent lamp about a spiritual flame; while allegory is one of the many possible representations of an embodied thing, or familiar principle, and belongs to fancy.[69]

In his introductory essay to *The Poems of Spenser* he wrote that he was "for the most part bored by allegory" and its air of unreality when it is "used to describe things which can be described as well in ordinary words." [70] Of Spenser himself he wrote:

One is persuaded that his morality is official and impersonal—a system of life which it was his duty to support—and it is perhaps a half understanding of this that has made so many generations believe that he was the first poet laureate, the first salaried moralist among the poets.[71]

Yet for all his study of the Blakean epistemology and the Blakean aesthetic, Yeats vacillated and continued to search, the one-eyed man among the blind, for that fourfold Blakean vision of reality. His theory of symbolism, if often expressed ephemerally and with implications of the existence of a world Blake would deny, was provocative and essentially Blakean from the beginning:

If people were to accept the theory that poetry moves us because of its symbolism, what change should one look for in the manner of our poetry? A return to the way of our fathers, a casting out of the descriptions of nature for the sake of nature, of the moral law for the sake of the moral law, a casting out of all anecdotes and of that brooding over scientific opinion that so often extinguished the central flame in Tennyson, and of that vehemence that would make us do or not do certain things.[72]

His early prose implies the Blakean belief in vision, but it also often makes a somewhat objectionable (Blake would have considered it false) distinction between two worlds. It then assigns validity by connotation to the less acceptable of the two:

So I think that in the making and in the understanding of a work of art, and the more easily if it is full of patterns and symbols and music, we are lured to the threshold of sleep, and it may be far beyond it, without knowing that we have ever set our feet upon the steps of horn or ivory.[73]

Nevertheless, Yeats was searching to pull the cork of the senses from the bottle; and though he may never have achieved what he vaguely called Blake's "mystical" vision, he most certainly did succeed in dramatizing his struggle for it from within the enclosure. He discovered that even to create the drama it was necessary to create his own imaginative "hypothesis," a structure of archetypal symbolism like Blake's, in which the objective tradition would be represented and in which the subjective experience would serve as a microcosm.

CHAPTER VII

The Symbology:
Dramatic Explication

We have come to give you metaphors for poetry.
　　　　　　　—The "instructors" in *A Vision* [1]

I send you the introduction of a book which will, when
finished, proclaim a new divinity. —W. B. YEATS [2]

YEATS'S strange book, *A Vision*, presents a paradox, for to
Yeats experience itself is a paradox. *A Vision* both explains
human experience and pulls the props from beneath its own explanation, leaving all great questions antinomially unresolved in
a dramatic, nondiscursive structure. The reason for the frustrating paradox is that in seeking for the central form of things Yeats
began to suspect that, as he suggests in the Moore correspondence, the form was itself expressible only in paradoxes in the
terms available to human beings—a single symbol representing
conflict on all levels of experience. Any attempt to explain the
symbol involves one in the conflict itself. That is what Yeats
meant when he said to John Sparrow: "Philosophers have tried
to deny the antinomy and give a complete account of existence
either as unity (as in the case of Spinoza and Hegel) or as plural-

ity (as in the case of Leibnitz), but the antinomy is there and can be represented only by a myth." [3] Yeats was creating a symbolism of conflict between reason and poetic inspiration—by Urizenic laws irrational:

If Kant is right the antinomy is in our method of reasoning; but if the Platonists are right may one not think that the antinomy is itself "constitutive," that the consciousness by which we know ourselves and exist is itself irrational? I do not yet put this forward as certainly the thought of my instructors, but at present it seems the natural interpretation of their symbols.[4]

He was referring here to his famous image of the gyres, which symbolizes in *A Vision* and in many of his poems a perpetual conflict of opposites; he believes in a Blakean "central form" of which all other things are microcosmic identities.

The conflict symbol in its full complexity represents all levels of human experience from the mass history of the world to the phases of individual life. Man's life is a struggle with himself and with his age.

I think that two conceptions, that of reality as a congeries of beings, that of reality as a single being, alternate in our emotion and in history, and must always remain something that human reason, because subject always to one or the other, cannot reconcile. I am always, in all I do, driven to a moment which is the realization of myself as unique and free, or to a moment which is the surrender to God of all that I am. I think there are historical cycles wherein one or the other predominates. . . .[5]

The irresolution symbolized by the Sad Shepherd of Yeats's early poems becomes a conscious symbol of conflict in his later poems. It becomes the pattern of things and the paradox—a higher rationality expressed by a symbolism which is relevant, as Yeats says in the Blake volumes, to "any region of nature and thought."

In Chapters VIII and IX of this book I have arbitrarily divided my investigation of the symbolism of conflict into "history" and "personality." These are roughly the divisions made by Yeats himself in *A Vision*, and they are helpful for the study of many poems in which Yeats's theme is either objectively philosophical and historical or personal or both at once. First, however, it is important to see the central form developing in Yeats's work and to examine hitherto-neglected aspects of *A Vision*.

THE SYMBOLISM OF CONFLICT

The strands of *A Vision* reach back into Yeats's early prose where the symbolical characters, Michael Robartes and Owen Aherne, first appear. They represent the twofold element of conflict in every man—the Orc and Urizen perhaps. Michael Robartes and Owen Aherne are together Yeats himself, but in the early stories and in *A Vision* Yeats appears not only as Robartes-Aherne but also as a separate character. "Rosa Alchemica" and "The Tables of the Law" dramatize unresolved conflict, with Robartes, Aherne, and Yeats as actors.

In the early pages of "Rosa Alchemica," Yeats sits alone in his Dublin rooms:

I had just published *Rosa Alchemica*, a little work on the Alchemists. . . . I had discovered, early in my researches, that their doctrine was no merely chemical phantasy, but a philosophy they applied to the world, to the elements and to man himself; and that they sought to fashion gold out of common metals merely as part of an universal transmutation of all things into some divine and imperishable substance; and this enabled me to make my book a fanciful reverie over the transmutation of life into art, and a cry of measureless desire for a world made wholly of essences.

I was sitting dreaming of what I had written. . . .[6]

These early prose lines reveal a dissatisfaction with reverie corresponding to the irresolution of the Sad Shepherd. Here the dissatisfaction appears as a veiled and somewhat mild self-satire. Yeats has placed himself in a slightly ridiculous position by the very fantasy of his outlandish hopes and doddering dreaminess.

Years later in the *Autobiography* he spoke of his early tendency toward self-satire: "I was always ready to deny or turn into a joke what was for all that my secret fanaticism." [7] Behind one face lies another, below the derision lies half-hope. Later, in *A Vision*, Yeats wrote a more decisive and complex self-satire, in which he plays the dual role of sage and fool.

His reverie is broken by the appearance of the fabulous Michael Robartes, "whom I had not seen in years, and whose wild red hair, fierce eyes, sensitive tremulous lips . . . made him look now, just as they used to do fifteen years before, something between a debauchée, a saint, and a peasant." [8] Robartes is determined to persuade Yeats that he should become an initiate of the mystical Order of the Alchemical Rose; but Yeats, who had refused to join years ago, wants no part of the venture. Nevertheless, Robartes insists:

You have changed greatly since then. . . . I have read your books, and now I see you among all these images, and I understand you better than you do yourself, for I have been with many and many dreamers at the same cross-ways. You have shut away the world and gathered the gods about you, and if you do not throw yourself at their feet, you will be always full of lassitude and wavering purpose. . . .[9]

An enchantingly persuasive speaker, Robartes has that same incantatory power which may be detected in the rhythms of Yeats's own early poems. Yeats, somewhat suspicious of Robartes' paganism, asks him why he should not make his pilgrimage to Calvary rather than to Eleusis; and Robartes answers with a "slightly rhythmical intonation":

There is no one who communes with only one god . . . and the more a man lives in imagination and in refined understanding, the more gods does he meet with and talk with, and the more does he come under the power of Roland, who sounded in the valley of Roncesvalles the last trumpet of the body's will and pleasure; and of Hamlet, who saw them perishing away and sighed; and of Faust, who looked for them up and down the world and could not find them; and under the power of all those countless divinities who have taken upon themselves spiritual bodies in the minds of the modern poets and romance writers, and under the power of the old divinities, who since the Renaissance have won everything of their ancient worship except the sacrifice of birds and fishes, the fragrance of garlands and the smoke of incense. The many think humanity made these divinities, and that it can unmake them again; but we who have seen them pass in rattling harness, and in soft robes, and heard them speak with articulate voices while we lay in deathlike trance, know that they are always making and unmaking humanity, which is indeed but the trembling of their lips.[10]

Angered at what seems a hideous Satanism, Yeats struggles for his self-control; but Robartes' peculiarly magical rhetoric has already won out. In a speech suggesting images from later poems he melodramatically intones:

They have come to us; they have come to us; . . . all that have ever been in your reverie, all that you have met with in books. There is Lear, his head still wet with the thunder-storm, and he laughs because you thought yourself an existence who are but a shadow and him a shadow who is an eternal god; and there is Beatrice, with her lips half parted in a smile, as though all the stars were about to pass away in a sigh of love; and there is the mother of the God of humility who cast so great a spell over men that they have tried to unpeople their hearts that he might reign alone.[11]

Having fallen under the spell, Yeats passively agrees to accompany Robartes to the temple of the mystical order so that they may join in an important ritual. They travel many miles to the western sea coast of Ireland where the temple is situated. As they come to the door, an old peasant curses them as idolators, but to Yeats's surprise Robartes is unconcerned, fearing no violence from such neighbors. He confidently says that eventually these peasants too "will sacrifice a mullet to Artemis, or some other fish to some new divinity" unless perhaps their own ancient gods and goddesses are revived. Robartes predicts an impending cataclysm, "perhaps even that long-foretold battle in the Valley of the Black Pig," which according to legend would mark the turning point in Ireland's fortunes. His words express some vague apocalyptic thought, typical of Yeats's intimations of return to a soft and beautiful golden age. Later, when Yeats was writing drafts for *A Vision*, he put new prophetic words in Robartes' mouth. One draft called "Michael Robartes Foretells" predicts historical events according to the historical system of *A Vision*.[12] Another, actually printed in the first version of *A Vision* but deleted from the second, is not spoken by Robartes, but the prediction is made on the basis of Robartes' theory. Later I shall present a possible reason for Yeats's decision to delete the material.

Neither draft for *A Vision* prophesies Blakean apocalypse. By this time Yeats saw only the turning wheel. He began his career by hopefully intimating a regressive apocalypse; later he predicted the future yet questioned his own prediction, as in "The Second Coming"; finally he affirmed cyclic pattern and sought to delineate man's proper attitude toward it. The development of Yeatsian prediction tells much about the development of his attitudes.

In the strange library of the temple (it contains, we are told, a complete facsimile set of Blake's prophetic books) Yeats is prepared for the ritual. Robartes invites him to read from a large book the secret story of the society's founding. Then,

a couple of hours after sunset Michael Robartes returned and told me that I would have to learn the steps of an exceedingly antique dance, because before my initiation could be perfected I had to join three times in a magical dance, for rhythm was the wheel of eternity, on which alone the transient and accidental could be broken, and the spirit set free.[13]

It is not clear just how seriously we should take the poet when he tells us that, being an excellent dancer, he had no trouble mastering the intricate steps. Perhaps it really was easy for him, for having entered the great hall where the dance has already begun, he is swept at once into the movement by a voice which

cried to me from the crimson figures: "Into the dance! there is none
that can be spared out of the dance! into the dance! into the dance!
that the gods may make them bodies out of the substance of our
hearts"; and before I could answer a mysterious wave of passion that
seemed like the soul of the dance moving within our souls, took hold
of me, and I was swept, neither consenting nor refusing, into the
midst.[14]

Once in the dance he has no control over body or mind, and
the next thing he fully remembers is waking suddenly to strange
noises and seeing all of the crimson dancers lying about the hall
asleep. Peasants, who in righteous indignation have come to destroy this house of the devil, are beating at the doors. Yeats tries
unsuccessfully to arouse Robartes and then at the last possible
moment flees the temple through an unguarded exit, eluding
the howling mob.

As the story ends, Yeats tells the reader that he has now assumed orthodoxy. He attributes his experience to the work of
Satan and wears the rosary about his neck to ward off future
temptation. Badly frightened by Robartes, he tends to assume the
personality of Robartes' symbolical opposite, Owen Aherne. By
means of their endless conflict Robartes and Aherne represent
the mind of Yeats and of all men in varying degrees. Though
"Rosa Alchemica" ends with Yeats protesting against Robartes, it
is not a final protest. He has simply vacillated from Orc to Urizen in the whirling gyre of his own life.

Yeats criticizes the personality of Owen Aherne in "The
Tables of the Law":

When he and I had been students in Paris, we had belonged to a
little group which devoted itself to speculations about alchemy and
mysticism. More orthodox in most of his beliefs than Michael Robartes, he had surpassed him in a fanciful hatred of all life, and this
hatred had found expression in the curious paradox—half borrowed
from some fanatical monk, half invented by himself—that the beautiful arts were sent into the world to overthrow nations and finally

life herself, by sowing everywhere unlimited desires, like torches thrown into a burning city.[15]

Aherne represents all Robartesian values inverted. The Robartes in Yeats would welcome such an apocalyptic conflagration set off by art, but Aherne knows that this is not an answer. As Yeats sees him now, many years after their student days, Aherne has begun to collect paintings of French Symbolists and English Pre-Raphaelites: "I have changed my taste. I am fascinated a little against my will by these faces, where I find the pallor of souls trembling between the excitement of the flesh and the excitement of the spirit." [16] He no longer collects the ethereal art of Siena, which he once praised so greatly for its spirituality. In his private chapel he now keeps a long-forgotten secret book, thought to have been destroyed by Pope Alexander IV, called *Expositio in Apocalypsin,* by a twelfth-century abbott named Joachim de Flora. According to Aherne, Joachim presented a heretical cyclic theory of history: "The Kingdom of the Father was passed, the Kingdom of the Son passing, and the Kingdom of the Spirit yet to come." In the first section of the work, entitled "Fractura Tabularum," Joachim speaks of those famous men and women of history who defied the commandments and created a greater spirituality.

The second book is called *Lex Secreta,* and describes the true inspiration of action, the only Eternal Evangel; and ends with a vision, which he saw among the mountains of La Sila, of his disciples sitting throned in the blue deep of the air, and laughing aloud, with a laughter that was like the rustling of the wings of Time.[17]

Convinced of the efficacy of "supreme art which is to win us from life and gather us into eternity like doves in their dove cotes," Aherne now decides to travel the world, searching for the new laws of a higher spirituality. Yeats, seeing that he will merely substitute a new set of laws for the old, attempts to dissuade him from his search; but Aherne is fired with enthusiasm. It is many years before the two meet again. Yeats sees Aherne on a Dublin street, lifeless and defeated. He has rationalized his dilemma. For a time, he says, he had been happy in his quest:

Then all changed and I was full of misery, and I said to myself that I was caught in the glittering folds of an enormous serpent [compare plate 6 of Blake's *Urizen*], and was falling with him through a fathomless abyss, and that henceforth the glittering folds were my world; and in my misery it was revealed to me that man can only come to that Heart through the sense of . . . sin, and I understood that I could not sin, because I had discovered the law of my being, and could only express or fail to express my being, and I understood that God has made a simple and an arbitrary rule that we may sin and repent! [18]

If Robartes provides the impetus toward new forms of thought, Aherne regulates and systematizes. Alone each of them is somewhat inadequate. Together as Blakean contraries they symbolize the tension without which there is no progression. Their equilibrium is the balance of personality which Yeats wished to achieve for himself and to create as the heroic image of his poetry. If Yeats himself often leaned toward Robartes, it was Aherne who made control possible. There is some truth to the idea that Yeats in the company of Robartes is Aherne and in the company of Aherne is Robartes, the conflict never dropped for fear of losing the balance. The red-haired, fierce-eyed Robartes resembles Blake's red Orc; the old and rationalistic Aherne with his arbitrary law resembles Blake's grey Urizen. Yeats's two characters can be thought of as symbolical particulars of Blake's archetypes.

In an unfinished manuscript novel called *The Speckled Bird*, Yeats dramatized a search similar to those upon which both Aherne and Robartes embarked and from which Robartes, as we shall see, returned bringing with him the system described in *A Vision*. At the conclusion of the novel Yeats's hero, according to Joseph Hone, now believes that the symbols of Christianity must be the central expression of his ideas, but the Christian mysteries must inhabit every land equally, and above all they must be reconciled to the natural emotions. He is going to the East, to Arabia and Persia, to find wisdom among the common people, as he had found it in Ireland, and perhaps discover from them this doctrine of reconciliation between religion and that bodily law from which all the arts had sprung.[19]

Owen Aherne, Michael Robartes, and the hero of *The Speckled Bird* agree on one principle of action, the search for a cultural tradition. To Yeats a tradition was a necessity. He tells us that when he studied Swedenborg late in life he discovered certain early thoughts of his own which he "had not set on paper because they seemed fantastic from the lack of some traditional foundation." [20] He sought "traditional statement" in symbolism and the assertion of a continuity in experience.

In the early stories Yeats introduced certain symbols which he developed more fully in his later poetry and in *A Vision*. Hints of the later symbolical system appear in the ritual dance of "Rosa Alchemica," the rhythm of life regulated to the dance of the heavens, of sun and moon. The dance was to represent the paradoxical order of life—a somewhat grim order as Yeats finally conceived it, an ordered conflict. For conflict was the condition of reality, a paradoxical expression of the harmony of the universe. In Yeats's plays, for example, the battles and duels are really dances which symbolically represent conflict but maintain at the same time the formal structure. Yeats's attitude permeates even his stage directions. In 1910, some time before he began to write *A Vision*, he declared that all things have conflicting central form: "I think that all noble things are the result of warfare; great nations and classes, of warfare in the visible world, great poetry and philosophy, of invisible warfare, the division of the mind within itself, a victory, the sacrifice of a man to himself." [21] Later, when those mysterious instructors of *A Vision* also presented a symbolism of conflict, Yeats was assured that he had found the tradition in the symbolic form of myth. In his introduction to the first edition of *A Vision* he stated that what he had found "is indeed nothing new." Blake and Swedenborg, to name only two, had used similar symbolical systems. The great myth was really a statement of a single great central form by means of shifting minute particulars, "a system of thought that would leave my imagination free to create as it chose and yet make all that it created or could create, part of the one history, and that of the soul's." [22] The minute particulars of existence resolved themselves not into a chain of being or any hierarchical system of degrees, but into one symbol representing all so-called degrees of existence simultaneously.

Yeats's "symbolical system displaying the conflict in all its forms" is an extremely complex yet coherent mass of interlocking images based upon a single archetypal pattern or, as Yeats puts it in *A Vision*, "a single geometrical conception." [23] Yet the conception is geometrical in only a very limited sense. For this reason the reader of *A Vision* is likely to throw up his hands when the logic of geometry somehow ceases to function and Yeats, as if he were following Blake, calls upon the metaphorical unity of symbolism. Blake asserted that this unity is the only higher logic—the form of imagination, which eventually through literal belief in the metaphorical rather than the material structure of the world leads to the resolution of all things in apocalyptic vision. Indeed, *A Vision* has been a murky quagmire for those who have sought to pursue Yeats's elusive geometric conception to its Euclidean conclusions. Taken as a structure of poetic symbols Yeats's paradoxical system overcomes the inherent contradictions of his geometry and formalizes conflict.

The "single geometrical conception" is actually composed of two symbols, one superimposed upon the other. The first is the Great Wheel, upon which history and individual life revolve. Yeats found it a central image of Blake's prophecies, where the Circle of Destiny symbolizes all movement from birth back to death. He also found it a central image in ancient astrology, a kind of dance like that of "Rosa Alchemica," generated by conflict, like Urizen and Orc facing each other in a perpetual whirl:

It was perhaps obvious when Plotinus substituted the archetypes of individual men in all their possible incarnations for a limited number of Platonic ideas, that a Greatest Year for whale and gudgeon alike must exhaust the multiplication table. Whatever its length, it divided, and so did every unit whose multiple it was, into waxing and waning, day and night, or summer and winter. There was everywhere a conflict like that of my play ["The Resurrection"] between two principles or "elemental forms of the mind" each "living the other's life dying the other's death." [Probably a misprint: read "living the other's death, dying the other's life."] I have a Chinese painting of three old sages sitting together, one with a deer at his side, one with a scroll open at the symbol of yen [*sic*] and yin, those two forms that whirl perpetually creating and re-creating all things.[24]

The principal characters of Yeats's circular cosmic dance are moon and sun, traditional images symbolizing the antinomies of the fallen world:

Perhaps some early Christian—Bardaison had speculations about the sun and moon nobody seems to have investigated—thought as I do, saw in the changes of the moon all the cycles; the soul realizing its separate being in the full moon, then, as the moon seems to approach the sun and dwindle away, all but realizing its absorption in God, only to whirl away once more: the mind of man separating itself from the common matrix, through childish imaginations, through struggle—then Vico's heroic age—to roundness, completeness, and then externalizing, intellectualizing, systematizing, until at last it lies dead, a spider smothered by its own web [the Urizen symbol]: the choice offered by the sages, either with the soul from myth to union with the source of all, the breaking of the circle, or from the myth to reflection and the circle renewed for better or for worse.[25]

To Yeats the scientific inaccuracy of astrology was irrelevant. Like any art, ancient astrology dealt in formal relationships: "Astrology does not rely as is generally supposed upon the direct influence of the stars but upon that of certain mathematical relations among the stars." [26] In the correspondence with Sturge Moore he wrote:

[Bertrand Russell] now thinks that physical objects are merely appearances and that nothing is real but space-time (the event or date and place) and this pleases me because it is in the most exact way the doctrine of ancient astrology. It was never, as modern astrologists think, the "influence" of this or that star that mattered but always date and place. The stars were figures on a clock-face.[27]

Astrology in its pristine state was thus really a symbolic form of expression like poetry, but like many mythologies it had been debased: "Probably the Great Year grew less symbolical as astrology spread through the Graeco-Roman world." [28] In *A Vision*, Yeats wrote:

Perhaps at the start a mere magnification of the natural year, it grew more complicated with the spread of Greek astronomy, but it is always the simpler, more symbolic form, with its conflict of light and dark, heat and cold, that concerns me most.[29]

Further development of the astrological system may be found in the section of *A Vision* entitled "The Great Year of the Ancients."

Always seeking traditional precedent, Yeats found the circular moon-sun conflict in the Upanishads. In his introduction to the translation of Bhagwan Shri Hamsa's *The Holy Mountain* he showed how it applies to individual lives as well as to historical periods:

Man is born into "a mortal birth of twelve months or thirteen months," into the lunar year that sometimes requires an extra month that it may keep the proper seasons, from which it is plain that every incarnation is divided into twelve or thirteen cycles. As the first and last crescents are nearest the Sun, the visionary must have seen in those cycles a conflict between Moon and Sun, or when Greek astronomy had reached India, between a Moon that has taken the Sun's light into itself. "I am yourself," and the Moon lost in the Sun's light, between Sun in Moon and Moon in Sun. The Eastern poet saw the Moon as the Sun's bride; now in solitude; now offered to her Bridegroom in a self-abandonment unknown to our poetry. A European would think perhaps of the moonlit and moonless nights alone, call the increasing moon man's personality, as it fills into the round and becomes perfect, overthrowing the black night of oblivion. Am I not justified in discovering there the conflict between subjectivity and objectivity, between self and not self, between waking life and dreamless sleep? [30]

In *A Vision*, Yeats explained that the form of a single life is in microcosm the form of all historical periods and of reality itself.

The year of twelve or thirteen months that constitutes a single life-time was thought of as a day or night in a still greater year, and that year divided in its turn into months until we reach some greatest year. One must imagine everywhere enclosed one within another, circles of Sun in Moon, Moon in Sun. Mixed with these mythological or symbolic periods were others founded upon the astronomical phantasy of Greece. Certain cycles must have begun when all the planets stood toeing a line like young athletes.[31]

The most perfect of geometrical symbols, the circle, represents, as in Boehme and in Blake, the truth about time. Within the Circle of Destiny, according to Yeats, there are symbolical dials, all of which come around to completion of their personal cycles at the same moment—at which point a new Great Year or Great Wheel begins.[32] Yeats's description of such a reality from within the circles seems to recall these lines from *The Four Zoas*, Blake's description of Urizen's world:

Travelling in silent majesty along their order'd ways
In right lined paths outmeasur'd by proportions of number,
    weight,
And measure, mathematic motion wondrous along the deep . . .
. . . Such the periods of many worlds.[33]

The "completed symbol" represents "complete integrity." [34] In a rejected typescript for *A Vision*, Yeats wrote:

My instructors compare it to a work of art because in a work of art each separate line, colour or thought is related to the whole as if it were their multiplex. It is the sphere or multiple of all gyres. The gyres until this multiple is reached lead to new gyres like the over-lapping members and so typify the suffering of man.[35]

In another typescript Robartes tells Aherne that "a work of art is any piece of life that has been completely expounded." Finally, in *A Vision*, Yeats wrote:

My instructors offer for a symbol the lesser unities that combine into a work of art and leave no remainder, but we may substitute if we will the lesser movements which combine into the circle that in Hegel's *Logic* unites not summer solstice to summer solstice but absolute to absolute.[36]

The second symbol of the "single geometric conception" is that of two interlocking cones or gyres which whirl perpetually one against another (see drawing). Yeats discovered allusions to

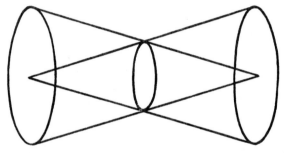

this symbol of conflict in *Timaeus*, Alcemon, Aquinas, and Macrobius. Swedenborg, too, knew of gyres:

Gyres are occasionally alluded to, but left unexplored in Sweden-borg's mystical writings. In the *Principia*, a vast scientific work writ-ten before his mystical life, he describes the double cone. All physical reality, the universe as a whole, every solar system, every atom, is a double cone.[37]

There was Blake's vortex, the whirling travels of Urizen, the spectre and emanation, all of which created the central form of Blake's symbolical system:

I had never read Hegel, but my mind had been full of Blake from boyhood up and I saw the world as a conflict—Spectre and Emana-tion—and could distinguish between a contrary and a negation.

"Contraries are positive," wrote Blake, "a negation is not a contrary," "How great the gulph between simplicity and insipidity," and again, "There is a place at the bottom of the graves where contraries are equally true."

I had never put the conflict in logical form.[38]

Yeats inserts a note here: "Though reality is not logical it becomes so in our minds if we discover logical refutations of the writer or movement that is going out of fashion. There is always error, which has nothing to do with 'the conflict' which creates all life."

The appropriation of this apparently simple expression of duality led to new poetic achievements. Yeats had not transcended the problem of duality, but he had symbolized the problem and organized his experience in symbolical form. In a note on "The Only Jealousy of Emer" he intimated that his system was basically complete: "I have now found all the mythology and philosophy I need." [39] All minute particulars are reflections of the single archetype, all life is a drama of warring contraries: "I am satisfied, the Platonic year in my head, to find but drama. I prefer that the defeated cause should be more vividly described than that which has the advertisement of victory." [40] All things fall and are built again, for destiny is really a circle, progress a "counter-myth." [41] The heroic personality must have a fearless attitude toward circularity. The common aim of poetry should be "traditional statement of certain heroic and religious truths, passed on from age to age, modified by individual genius, but never abandoned." [42]

Several poems written while Yeats was developing his symbolical structure employ the sun-moon imagery. One, "Under the Round Tower," expresses the sun-moon relationship as a dance, which dramatically symbolizes the order of conflict. In this poem the dream of the beggar, Billy Byrne, relates dance and conflict imagery to images of sexuality, predicting the sages of Yeats's later poetry: Crazy Jane, Old Tom, Ribh, and the "Wild Old Wicked Man." Here are three stanzas:

Upon a grey old battered tombstone
In Glendalough beside the stream,
Where the O'Byrnes and Byrnes are buried,
He stretched his bones and fell in a dream
Of sun and moon that a good hour
Bellowed and pranced in the round tower;

Of golden king and silver lady,
Bellowing up and bellowing round,
Till toes mastered a sweet measure,
Mouth mastered a sweet sound,
Prancing round and prancing up
Until they pranced upon the top.

That golden king and that wild lady
Sang till stars began to fade,
Hands gripped in hands, toes close together,
Hair spread on the wind they made;
That lady and that golden king
Could like a brace of blackbirds sing.[43]

The imagery of sexuality traditionally suggests conflict super-imposed upon unity. With the building up of a mass of meta-phorical suggestion, Yeats's multiverse, like Blake's, becomes a single macrocosmic metaphor, a universe. All things finally re-late themselves to all other things in a unified vision. The dif-ference from Blake lies in the fact that conflict becomes the form of the only world Yeats knows, not simply, as in Blake, the delusion to be transcended.

Another poem, "The Cat and the Moon," dramatizes the re-lation between the dance of the organic world and the dance of the moon itself. Yeats commented on the poem:

I wrote a little poem where a cat is disturbed by the moon, and in the changing pupils of its eyes seems to repeat the movement of the moon's changes, and allowed myself to think of the cat as the normal man and of the moon as the opposite he seeks perpetually, or as having any meaning I have conferred upon the moon else-where.[44]

The dance of the cat and the moon is stately, delicate, and formal
—a dance fit to honor the queen who controls it:

> The cat went here and there
> And the moon spun round like a top,
> And the nearest kin of the moon,
> The creeping cat looked up.
> Black Minnaloushe stared at the moon,
> For, wander and wail as he would,
> The pure cold light in the sky
> Troubled his animal blood.
> Minnaloushe runs in the grass
> Lifting his delicate feet.
> Do you dance, Minnaloushe, do you dance?
> When two close kindred meet,
> What better than call a dance?
> Maybe the moon may learn,
> Tired of that courtly fashion,
> A new dance turn.
> Minnaloushe creeps through the grass
> From moonlit place to place,
> The sacred moon overhead
> Has taken a new phase.
> Does Minnaloushe know that his pupils
> Will pass from change to change,
> And that from round to crescent,
> From crescent to round they range?
> Minnaloushe creeps through the grass
> Alone, important and wise,
> And lifts to the changing moon
> His changing eyes.[45]

Dissonance, alliteration, and intricate rhythm suggest the noc-
turnal planetary movement in traditional order. The initiates of
the Order of the Alchemical Rose sought in their dance to attain
to the rhythm of eternity. The cat dances to the stately rhythm
of the known world. The sound structure of these lines suggests
both harmony and antithesis:

> For wander and wail as he would,
> The pure cold light in the sky
> Troubled his animal blood.

The lines move initially in alliteration and drop into a slight dissonance from "wail" to "would" and thence to "pure," "troubled," and finally "blood." The key word, "troubled," ruffles the rhythm enough to intensify the paradoxical effect of formal conflict.

Movement through the Great Year is properly a dance. All things are driven to seek the equilibrium achieved by the dance of sun and moon in Billy Byrne's dream. But Billy Byrne, like all men, is a victim of internal conflict, which creates in the fallen world a tension of opposites. Yeats's poems, though they suggest that the tension is really a unity broken into conflicting pieces by limited human perceptions, do not fully resolve the conflict in apocalyptic vision. The Great Year itself is a kind of work of art, "which leaves no remainder." [46] If the two major images of Yeats's system—the circle or wheel and the gyres—are apparently geometrical, they are not conventionally rational, for they represent an ineradicable antinomy in what is really a single symbol.

In any work of art the manner of expression cannot be divorced from the so-called "message." For this reason, the system which Yeats explicates in *A Vision* cannot be abstracted totally from the work as a whole. Just as important as the strange geometry of circle and cone are those sections of *A Vision* in which Yeats creates the legend of its genesis. In the remainder of this chapter I shall investigate the spoofery of *A Vision*, its serious undertone, and the reasons for the existence of a geometry which is not a geometry at all.

THE REAPPEARANCE OF MICHAEL ROBARTES

In a letter to Yeats printed in the final version of *A Vision*, Owen's brother, John Aherne, wrote:

You ask if Robartes and my brother are as hot as ever about that old quarrel and exactly what is the quarrel. This is what I found after questioning various people. Some thirty years ago you made "Rosa Alchemica," "The Tables of the Law" and "The Adoration of the Magi," out of a "slight incident." Robartes, then a young man, had founded a society, with the unwilling help of my brother Owen, for the study of the *Kabbala Denudata* and similar books, invented some kind of ritual and hired an old shed on Howth Pier for its meetings. A foolish rumour got out among the herring or mackerel sorters, and some girls (from Glasgow, my brother says, for they come from all parts) broke the window. You hatched out of this the murder of Robartes and his friends.[47]

Yeats revived the symbolical characters of the early stories for *A Vision* in order to create a wild and humorous legend which would account for the sources of his symbolical system. Yeats made several false starts before he decided upon the form which his book should take. One first draft took the form of a dialogue between Robartes and Aherne, but it proved laborious and too long. All early drafts suggest that the reappearance of Michael Robartes was a part of the structure as Yeats originally conceived it.

Early in the section of *A Vision* entitled "Stories of Michael Robartes and His Friends: An Extract from a Record Made by One of His Pupils," Robartes tells of his strange adventures in the Near East, where he had decided to go after the failure of his Dublin society. There he learned the esoteric philosophy which he has now asked Yeats to expound in book form. Robartes' story, somewhat revised for the 1938 version, is essentially this: After leaving Dublin, Robartes went to Rome, where in squalid surroundings he found by sheer chance a strange dilapidated volume called *Speculum Angelorum et Hominum*, written by a man named Giraldus and printed in 1594, at Cracow. Between the covers he discovered

a series of allegorical pictures, a man torn in two by an eagle, and some sort of wild beast, a man whipping his shadow, a man between a hunchback and a fool in cap and bells, and so on to the number of eight and twenty, a portrait of Giraldus, a unicorn several times repeated, a large diagram in the shape of a wheel where the phases of the moon were mixed up with an apple, an acorn, a cup, and what looked like a sceptre or wand.[48]

Robartes' interest was aroused, and he unsuccessfully sought information about Giraldus, attempting to identify him first with a Giraldus of Bologna and then Giraldus Cambrensis. In the two versions of *A Vision* somewhat different stories are told of what occurred after the discovery. In the first version Robartes states:

I had decided to continue my prayers at Mecca, and hoped to get there in disguise. I had gone the greater portion of the way when I saw certain markings upon the sands which corresponded almost exactly to a diagram in the "Speculum." Nobody could explain them or say who made them, but when I discovered that an unknown tribe of Arabs had camped nearby a couple of nights before . . . I took the first opportunity of plunging into the desert in pursuit.[49]

According to the second version, having come to pray at the Holy Sepulchre, he decided, "Jesus does not understand my despair, He belongs to order and reason."

The day after, an old Arab walked unannounced into my room. He said that he had been sent, stood where the *Speculum* lay open at the wheel marked with the phases of the moon, described it as the doctrine of his tribe, drew two whorls working one against the other, the narrow end of one in the broad end of the other, showed that my single wheel and his two whorls had the same meaning. He belonged to a tribe of Arabs who called themselves Judwalis or Diagrammatists because their children are taught dances which leave upon the sand traces full of symbolical meaning.[50]

Robartes joined the tribe and studied its orally perpetuated doctrines, said to have come from a book, since lost, by Kusta ben Luka, a philosopher at the court of Harun Al-Raschid; but Robartes did not believe that ben Luka was the founder of the system:

Certain terms and forms of expression suggest some remote syraic origin. I once told an old Judwali of my conviction on this point but he merely said that Kusta ben Luka had doubtless been taught by the desert djinns who lived to a great age and remembered ancient languages.[51]

These words recall Blake's myth of the original language, the Universal Poetic Genius. Yeats insisted that his system have the authority of tradition.

When Robartes returns from Arabia, Aherne also appears. Fascinated by Robartes' new theories, he is unable to accept all of their implications. From the very beginning he causes trouble, for he disagrees with Yeats himself over the manner in which Yeats seems to be writing the explication of Robartes' system. In the first edition of *A Vision*, Yeats dramatizes this disagreement by allowing Aherne to add certain footnotes. In one of them Aherne discloses that he has argued with Robartes over the advisability of permitting Yeats, an undisciplined poet, to arrange and present the "Robartes papers." Robartes, who found it difficult to express anything in writing, did not wish to do the job himself:

"You will give them to a man," I [Aherne] said, "who has thought more of the love of woman than of the love of God." "Yes," he replied, "I want a lyric poet, and if he cares for nothing but expression, so much the better, my desert geometry will take care of the truth." [52]

Both men had carried grudges against Yeats since last they had been on intimate terms with him. Aherne strongly resented the story of his involvement with pagan gods, "The Tables of the Law," which Yeats had circulated. On the other hand, according to Owen's brother, Robartes was bitter about another matter:

Robartes makes no complaint about your description of his death and says nobody would have thought the Aherne and Robartes of such fantastic stories real men but for Owen's outcry. He is, however (and this I confirm from my own knowledge), bitter about your style in those stories and says that you substituted sound for sense and ornament for thought. What happened immediately before his separation from Europe must stand out with an unnatural distinction. I wrote once to remonstrate. I said that you wrote in those tales as many good writers wrote at the time over half Europe, that such prose was the equivalent of what somebody had called "absolute poetry" and somebody else "pure poetry"; that though it lacked speed and variety, it would have acquired both, as Elizabethan prose did after the *Arcadia*, but for the surrender everywhere to the sensational and the topical; that romance driven to its last ditch had a right to swagger. He answered that when the candle was burnt out an honest man did not pretend that grease was flame.[53]

In the dialogue poem "The Phases of the Moon," which appears in both versions of *A Vision* as a kind of prologue dramatizing the return of Robartes and explaining the moon symbolism, Robartes and Aherne walk past the Galway tower where Yeats reads late into the night. Robartes again airs his animosity over Yeats's early prose style:

> He wrote of me in that extravagant style
> He had learnt from Pater, and to round his tale
> Said I was dead; and dead I choose to be.[54]

Finally, of course, Robartes does turn his papers over to Yeats, despite his belief that the "hard gem-like flame" is now no more than grease. But Aherne does not forgive so easily. He takes diabolic pleasure when he sees the lamp in the tower window, for it signifies that Yeats still vainly seeks the great philosophic secret that Robartes now owns:

> Were not our beds far off I'd ring the bell,
> Stand under the rough roof-timbers of the hall
> Beside the castle door, where all is stark
> Austerity, a place set out for wisdom
> That he will never find; I'd play a part;
> He would never know me after all these years
> But take me for some drunken countryman;
> I'd stand and mutter there until he caught
> "Hunchback and Saint and Fool," and that they came
> Under the last three crescents of the moon,
> And then I'd stagger out. He'd crack his wits
> Day after day, yet never find the meaning.[55]

Aherne is partially fooling himself here, since it is doubtful whether he fully comprehends Robartes' meaning himself. A further and more profound irony is the picture of Yeats "cracking his wits" and the mockery of both himself and his early style. Such self-mockery is perhaps a clever defensive strategy against the derision of others, for Yeats's interest in the occult learning of the world is susceptible to derision. But it is difficult to accuse someone who has already made fun of himself. The dual animosity of Aherne and Robartes is a tool for sharpening a satire. And Yeats lays around himself with it, not sparing his own idiosyncrasies.

Yeats and all men, as the symbolism of Robartes and Aherne shows, are more than one man. At least, they change their masks over and over again; and Yeats as self-critic is Yeats commenting upon himself masked. The Yeats of the lonely tower, who struggles with learning like the fly in the vase, the searcher for elusive gnostic power, who searches for the solution to antinomies beyond human understanding, falls victim in life to those very Ahernean or Urizenic powers which enable him to cope with life. The Yeats of the tower is the victim of his own pen, the self-satirized dolt, striving and failing, an intellectual Everyman. As a hero, he is Cuchulain battling the bitter tide; as a fool, he is a naïve rationalist who puts all his faith in a false myth called progress; and to the practical fool, Cuchulain is a fool.

In his most important comment upon Yeats's treatment of the Robartes material, Aherne is quick to criticize Yeats's one-sidedness; but it appears that he may be arguing more vehemently against Robartes' paganism than against Yeats's incapacity:

Mr. Yeats's completed manuscript now lies before me. The system itself has grown clearer for his concrete expression of it, but I notice that if I made too little of the *antithetical* phases he has done no better by the *primary*. I think too that Mr. Yeats himself must feel that the abstract foundation needs some such exploration as I myself had attempted. The twelve rotations associated with the lunar and solar months of the Great Year first arose, as Mr. Yeats understands, from the meeting and separation of certain spheres. I consider that the form should be called elliptoid, and that rotation as we know it is not the movement that corresponds most closely to reality. At any rate I can remember Robartes saying in one of his paradoxical figurative moods that he pictured reality as a number of great eggs, laid by the Phoenix and that these eggs turn inside out perpetually without breaking the shell.

O.A.

London, May, 1925 [56]

Some of the terminology here is beyond the point of the present discussion and will be dealt with later. Aherne is confused by the rational impossibility of Robartes' inside-out egg image—a paradox from Blake's place at the bottom of the grave where "contraries are equally true." His approach to the "Robartes papers" is often one of a rather unimaginative textual scholar, who though impressed by the prestige of his subject is at a loss to understand its real importance. Yeats, though he had great respect for scholarship and learning, could attack with vehemence:

> All shuffle there; all cough in ink;
> All wear the carpet with their shoes;
> All think what other people think;
> All know the man their neighbour knows.
> Lord, what would they say
> Did their Catullus walk that way? [57]

It may be that Aherne's criticisms are a form of Yeatsian self-satirization. Yeats-Robartes lacks the organizational ability of Aherne. But the top level of satire is directed at the Ahernean mind, bogged down in minutiae. Yeats could never satisfy Aherne, whose quibbles have a tone familiar to readers of scholarly journals. Nevertheless, Aherne is a valuable man; he preserves important details (and sometimes recognizes their importance) such as Michael Robartes' story of the Great Wheel symbol, which appeared in the first edition of *A Vision* as "The Dance of the Four Royal Persons." It was deleted from the 1938 version:

Michael Robartes gives the following account of the diagram called "The Great Wheel" in Giraldus. A Caliph who reigned after the death of Harun Al-Raschid discovered one of his companions climbing the wall that encircled the garden of his favourite slave, and because he had believed this companion entirely devoted to his interests, gave himself up to astonishment. After much consideration he offered a large sum of money to any man who could explain human nature so completely that he should never be astonished again. Kusta ben Luka, now a very old man, went to the palace with his book of geometrical figures, but the Caliph, after he had explained them for an hour, banished him from the palace, and declared that all unintelligible visitors were to be put to death. A few days later four black but splendidly dressed persons stood at the city gate and announced that they had come from a most distant country to explain human nature, but that the Caliph must meet them on the edge of the desert. He came attended by his Vizir, and asked their country. "We are," said the eldest of the four, "the King, the Queen, the Prince and the Princess of the Country of Wisdom. It has reached our ears that a certain man has pretended that wisdom is difficult, but it is our intention to reveal all in a dance." After they had danced for several minutes the Caliph said: "Their dance is dull, and they dance without accompaniment, and I consider that nobody has ever been more unintelligible." The Vizir gave the order for their execution, and while waiting the tightening of the bowstrings, each dancer said to the executioner: "In the Name of Allah, smooth out the mark of my footfall on the sand." And the executioner replied, "If the Caliph permit." When the Caliph heard what the dancers had said, he thought, "there is certainly some great secret in the marks of their feet." He went at once to the dancing place, and, having stood for a long time looking at the marks, he said: "Send us Kusta ben Luka, and tell him that he shall not die." Kusta ben Luka was sent for, and from sunrise to sunset of the day after, and for many days, he explained the markings of the sand. At last the Caliph said: "I now understand human nature; I can never be surprised again: I will put the amount of the reward into a tomb for the four dancers." Kusta ben Luka answered: "No, Sire, for the reward belongs to me." "How can that be?" said the other, "for you have but explained the marks upon the sand, and those marks were not made by your feet." "They were made by the feet of my pupils," said ben Luka. "When you banished me from the Palace they gathered in my house to console me, and the wisest among them said, 'He that dies is the chief person in the story,' and he and the three others offered to dance what I chose." "The reward is yours," said the Caliph, "and henceforth let the figure marked by their feet be called the Dance of the Four Royal Persons, for it is right that your pupils be rewarded for dying."

According to the Robartes MSS, the Dance of the Four Royal Persons is one of the names for the first figure drawn by the Judwali elders for the instruction of youth and is identical with the "Great Wheel of Giraldus."

I am inclined to see in the story of its origin a later embodiment of a story that it was the first diagram drawn upon the sand by the wife of Kusta ben Luka, and that its connection with the lunar phases, the movements and the nature of the Four Faculties and their general application to the facts of human life, were fully explained before its geometrical composition was touched upon. The Judwali doctor of Bagdad, who is mentioned elsewhere in this book, said that the whole philosophy was expounded in a series of fragments which only displayed their meaning, like one of those child's pictures which are made up out of separate cubes, when all were put together. The object of this was, it seems, to prevent the intellect from forming its own conclusions, and so thwarting the Djinn who could only speak to curiosity and passivity. I cannot, however, let this pass without saying that I doubt the authenticity of this story, which Mr. Yeats has expanded into the poem "Desert Geometry or The Gift of Harun Al-Raschid," at least in its present form, and that an almost similar adventure is attributed in one of the Robartes documents to a Mahometan grammarian of a much later date. I will, however, discuss all these matters at length in my own book upon the philosophy and its sources.

O.A.

May, 1925 [58]

This selection and the poem "The Gift of Harun Al-Raschid" contain the first veiled references to the collaboration of Yeats and his wife in automatic writing, which Yeats later described as the true source of the system. Aherne is correct in doubting "the authenticity of this story . . . at least in its present form," for it is Yeatsian allegory. As a critic of poets Aherne represents one gyre of the explication of Yeats's system. He is a controlling factor in any expression; he must be heard, but occasionally he must be put down.

Among the rejected typescripts of *A Vision*, written when Yeats was still attempting to make the work a dialogue between Robartes and Aherne, there is this statement by Robartes:

It will be understood that just as a man can investigate the laws by which the ocean moves in a cup of water we can investigate by studying our own minds the final destination of the soul. In that day the system of Aquinas will be weighed and that of Ben Luki [Yeats is inconsistent in his spelling of ben Luka] who thinks not more inaccurately because he thinks in pictures.[59]

Several possible reasons for the deletion of this passage come to mind. The most interesting speculation is that Yeats was probably less afraid of his own daring attack on orthodoxy than of the violent words he would feel compelled to put in the mouth of the orthodox Owen Aherne as a reply to such an heretical conclusion. Nor did Robartes have time now to explain to Aherne the accuracy of "picture thinking."

THE INSTRUCTORS AND THE GREAT EGG

"When supernatural events begin, a man first doubts his own testimony, but when they repeat themselves again and again, he doubts all human testimony." [60] So wrote Yeats in his *Autobiography*, and so must he have doubted when on October 24, 1917, shortly after his marriage, he discovered that Mrs. Yeats was apparently a medium through whom creatures from another world sought to communicate to him. From trance she had begun to write down automatically the rudiments of the symbolism described in *A Vision*, and this peculiar phenomenon continued for several years. Yeats never finally decided whether the mysterious instructors were "certain dead men" or subconscious manifestations of his own and his wife's minds:

Much that has happened, much that has been said, suggests that the communicators are the personalities of a dream shared by my wife, by myself, occasionally by others—they have, as I must someday prove, spoken through others without change of knowledge or loss of power—a dream that can take objective form in sounds, in hallucinations, in scents, in flashes of light, in movements of external objects.[61]

Since he had no real proof, he discarded from the final draft of *A Vision* the following statement which assumed that the instructors were dead men: "This book would be different if it had not come from certain dead men who in all they say assume their own existence. In this it resembles no philosophical book since Descartes taught the living to assume theirs." [62] At first Yeats offered to spend his life as human explicator of the automatic script, but the mysterious instructors would not have it. " 'No,' was the answer, 'we have come to give you metaphors for poetry.' " [63] These words suggest that the thought expounded in *A Vision* is inextricably related to poetry and that the proper form of that thought is poetry. The instructors had come to present a structure of symbolic form, a pattern of archetypes; and this structure was to be communicated *for* poetry, not for philosophy or for science. The instructors had come to organize all that Yeats had sought from Blake, from Mme. Blavatsky and psychical research, from dreams, and from mythology. The instructors had come to organize his poetic mind.

A Vision is an attempt to discuss the nature of symbolic form, from which any poetry gains its coherence and power. It is, in a sense, a book of poetic interpretation. Since the symbolic form is deep in Yeats's mind—Yeats sometimes thought it was from the subconscious—*A Vision* is also about Yeats himself, and thus it has a drama of its own. *A Vision* is sometimes satirical, sometimes comical, and in the end tragic. In the story of the automatic writing of Mrs. Yeats, seriousness masks comedy and comedy masks seriousness like the two interlocking gyres themselves.

The unknown writer took his theme at first from my just published *Per Amica Silentia Lunae*. I had made a distinction between the perfection that is from a man's combat with himself and that which is from a combat with circumstance, and upon this simple distinction he built up an elaborate classification of men according to their more or less complete expression of one type or the other. He supported his classification by a series of geometrical symbols and put these symbols in an order that answered the question in my essay as to whether some prophet could not prick upon the calendar the birth of a Napoleon or a Christ. A system of symbolism, strange to my wife and to myself, certainly awaited expression, and when I asked how long that would take I was told years.[64]

Yeats, as he tells us, read and absorbed much philosophy in the time between the appearances of the two editions of *A Vision*. When he revised, he was better prepared to strengthen his defense of symbolic form and to satirize the positivistic temper so foreign to the Robartesian aspect of his nature. In his 1930 diary he had been dramatically critical: "Science separated from philosophy is the opium of the suburbs." [65] *A Vision*, 1938, satirizes such a science and the materialist philosophy upon which it is based. Yeats's account of his experience with the instructors in the introduction to *A Vision* comically sharpens the satire. His own offer to give up poetry in order to become an explicator of the system mocks his lack of understanding, for the instructors answer that the system is "for poetry." His tendency to exaggerate the eccentricity of his system suggests that a poetic structure of experience is foreign to modern man even when it is directly communicated to him in terms of mathematic design. In *A Vision*, Yeats casts himself as modern man—a naïve rationalist unable to deal with symbolism:

I was constantly reproved for vague or confused questions, yet I could do no better, because though it was plain from the first that their exposition was based upon a single geometrical conception, they kept me from mastering that conception. They shifted ground whenever my interest was at its height, whenever it seemed that the next day must reveal what, as I soon discovered, they were determined to withhold until all was upon paper.[66]

The communicators chose this method, as Owen Aherne points out, in order to "prevent the intellect from forming its own conclusions," to prevent the partial view of life. The structure depended upon a grasp of the whole, not the summarization of its parts. Yeats was forced to move beyond apparently simple mathematics from the very beginning, just as the reader of Blake must be willing to forego map plans if he wishes to understand the strange geography of Golgonooza.

His difficulties were multiplied by the confusing actions of his instructors:

They seemed ignorant of our surroundings and might have done so [put Mrs. Yeats to sleep] at some inconvenient time or place; once when they had given their signal in a restaurant they explained that because we had spoken of a garden they had thought we were in it.[67]

We see him as the Yeats of the tower, the human fool in search of wisdom, at the mercy of capricious powers in a sometimes raucous, sometimes bitter comedy. He was beset by "frustrators," who seemed capable of blotting out the coherence of the script for prolonged periods:

The automatic script would deteriorate, grow sentimental or confused, and when I pointed this out the communicator would say, "From such and such an hour, on such and such a day, all is frustration." I would spread out the script and he would cross all out back to the answer that began it, but had I not divined frustration he would have said nothing. Was he constrained by a drama which was part of the conditions that made communication possible, was that drama itself part of the communication . . . ?[68]

If these instructors and frustrators formed unknown areas of the mind of his wife and himself, the battle was another aspect of eternal conflict in the human world. If they did not, it followed that the conflict extended far beyond our own common experience into hidden realms.

Only once did he [an instructor] break the rule and without waiting for a question declare some three or four days' work frustration. A predecessor of his had described the geometrical symbolism as created for my assistance and had seemed to dislike it, another had complained that I used it to make their thought mechanical, and a Frustrator doubtless played upon my weakness when he described a geometrical model of the soul's state after death, which could be turned upon a lathe.[69]

Yeats's weakness was Urizen's weakness, the inability to escape the mechanics of reason, of literal interpretation. The mechanical aspects of the symbolism are clearly a simplification, merely a beginning. *A Vision* itself dramatizes the difficulty of making a discursive study of the nondiscursive. To accept the gyres, cones, and other geometrical models as final is to be trapped in nets and gins. Early in *A Vision*, Yeats wrote of Ezra Pound's *Cantos:* "I may, now that I have recovered leisure, find that the mathematical structure, when taken up into imagination, is more than mathematical, that seemingly irrelevant details fit together into a single theme." [70] The Yeatsian geometry is similar to what Yeats is describing here. It is a geometry beyond geometry; his gyres and cones are a simplified, abstract design for a whole structure, a design "disliked" by the instructors themselves and probably adopted as the result of their own frustrations in the human world of space-time:

It was part of their purpose to affirm that all the gains of man come from conflict with the opposite of his true being. Was communication itself such a conflict? One said, as though it rested with me to decide what part I should play in their dream, "Remember we will deceive you if we can." Upon the other hand they seem like living men, are interested in all that interest living men, as when at Oxford, where we spent our winters, one asked upon hearing an owl hoot in the garden, if he might be silent for a while. "Sounds like that," he said, "give us great pleasure." [71]

Their strangely human qualities, comically recorded by Yeats the writer, often absurdly puzzled Yeats the rationalist; for although the instructors might stop to hear the cry of a bird, they sometimes appeared demonical. Often he could not distinguish between "instructor" and "frustrator" and wondered whether the frustration was not mere caprice:

Some frustrations found us helpless. Some six months before the communications came to an end, a communicator announced that he was about to explain a new branch of the philosophy and seemed to add, "But please do not write anything down, for when all is finished I will dictate a summary." He spoke almost nightly for I think three months, and at last I said, "Let me make notes, I cannot keep it all in my head". He was disturbed to find that I had written nothing down, and when I told him of the voice, said it was frustration and that he could not summarise.[72]

Here the ridiculous comedy, like the shouting of two people who cannot understand each other's language, verges on the tragic. Yeats is both the fool, the dolt, and the hero, the searcher after power. His striving toward knowledge is blocked by hopelessly capricious demons, his ability frustrated by human limits, his mind extended to the breaking point by intellectual desire.

But the comic view often, in its own turn, rends the veil of tragedy. It is true that man strives against the limits of experience, but it is also true that some men labor under an unnecessary burden. The rationalistic incapacity, for which Yeats satirizes himself, is an unnecessary naïveté of many men, leading toward a false worldly optimism. One must understand, like Plato, that there are limits of understanding and that these limits must be mythically represented. The rationalist fails to achieve this balance of attitude because he fails to understand paradox. Here the break between Blake and Yeats is most extreme, for Blake saw only the unnecessary, eradicable stupidity, not the necessity of tragedy. Blake would never have cast himself in the role of Urizen, even for dramatic effect. In a short poem Yeats characterizes Blake as "[beating] upon the wall/Till truth obeyed his call," but actually Blake beat on no walls. Such frantic action symbolizes the hopeless journeys of Urizen. Yeats consciously sees himself as the Urizen figure.

The instructors wished to avoid any confusion which might result from the intrusion of another vocabulary or another orientation upon their material. They therefore forbade Yeats to talk of the system to others and for a while to read philosophy. One day after the ban on philosophy had been lifted a communicator became very irritated over some terms Yeats was employing in his conversation:

He had no more than tolerated my philosophical study and was enraged by the intrusion, not so much into what I had written as into the questions I put, of a terminology not his. This led to one of those quarrels which I have noticed almost always precede the clearest statements, and seem to arise from an independence excited to injustice because kept with difficulty. "I am always afraid," he said in apology, "that when not at our best we may accept from you false reasoning." [73]

The instructors sought to present to Yeats a myth beyond the hindrances of "this pragmatical, preposterous pig of a world," but their attempt to get into the glass vase was often as difficult as it was for Yeats to escape it. Thus the communication was only partially successful. Each gain in the human world, as the instructors seemed to recognize, is from "conflict with the opposite." As long as Yeats felt that he could not disclose the secret of *A Vision*, it was consistent for him to attempt to express its message in the form of a collaboration between Robartes and Aherne, for any collaboration between them was itself a conflict. Even after the secret of the strange communication was out he did not give up the Robartes-Aherne drama, although he made excuses for what now appeared to be a useless tale:

The first version of this book, *A Vision*, except the section on the twenty-eight phases, and that called "Dove or Swan" which I repeat without change, fills me with shame. I had misinterpreted the geometry, and in my ignorance of philosophy failed to understand distinctions upon which the coherence of the whole depended, and as my wife was unwilling that her share should be known, and I to seem sole author, I had invented an unnatural story of an Arabian traveller which I must amend and find a place for some day because I was fool enough to write half a dozen poems that are unintelligible without it.[74]

Yet what the story of the "Arabian traveller," Robartes, signifies in the new version of *A Vision* belies Yeats's scorn of it. He enlarged the story so that it might contribute to an explication of the structure of symbolism, especially as it applies to history.

The newly revised Robartes-Aherne tale, told by Robartes' pupil John Duddon, begins at a house in Regent's Park. Duddon is talking to two people, Peter Huddon and a young woman "who insists on calling herself Denise de L'Isle Adam." They are expecting Owen Aherne, but before he appears a young man named Daniel O'Leary comes to the door. Duddon speaks first:

"Where is Mr. Owen Aherne?" "Owen," said he, "is with Michael Robartes making his report." Said I, "Why should there be a report?" Said he, "Oh, there is always a report. Meanwhile I am to tell you my story and to hear yours. There will be plenty of time, for as I left the study Michael Robartes called the universe a great egg that turns inside-out perpetually without breaking its shell, and a thing like that always sets Owen off. . . ."[75]

When Aherne and Robartes finally show up, an egg becomes the central symbol of the whole story. As in the original tale Robartes speaks of his discovery of Giraldus' "sacred book" and of his experiences with the Judwali tribesmen in Arabia. At a second meeting three weeks later Michael Robartes presents two people called Mary Bell and John Bond to the assembled group.* Bond then relates a fantastic symbolical story of an

---

* It is probable that Yeats appropriated these names from Blake and that part of the joke relates to Blake's poems. See Blake's "Long John Brown & Little Mary Bell" and "William Bond." I am indebted to Professor E. E. Bostetter for this suggestion. Both poems are examples of Blake's Rabelaisian humor. In *A Vision*, Yeats places Blake and Rabelais in the same phase of personality and himself in an adjoining phase.

adulterous love affair between Mary Bell and himself, which led to his involvement with Mary Bell's eccentric husband, who had dedicated the last years of his life to teaching various breeds of cuckoos to build nests. Just before his death Mary Bell made an authentic nest with her own hands and convinced her husband that one of his charges had succeeded in manufacturing a nest.

For some reason this story appealed strongly to Robartes, who had been having strong extrasensory visions of the whole drama. He decided to choose Mary Bell for a certain task to be undertaken soon by Aherne and himself.

When Bond has completed his tale, Robartes produces an ivory box. Mary Bell opens it and lifts out "an egg the size of a swan's egg":

"Hyacinthine blue, according to the Greek lyric poet," said Robartes. "I bought it from an old man in a green turban at Teheran; it had come down from eldest son to eldest son for many generations." "No," said Aherne, "you never were in Teheran." "Perhaps Aherne is right," said Robartes. "Sometimes my dreams discover facts, and sometimes lose them, but it does not matter. I bought this egg from an old man in a green turban in Arabia, or Persia, or India. He told me its history, partly handed down by word of mouth, partly as he had discovered it in ancient manuscripts. It was for a time in the treasury of Harun Al-Raschid and had come there from Byzantium, as ransom for a prince of the imperial house. Its history before that is unimportant for some centuries. During the reign of the Antonines, tourists saw it hanging by a golden chain from the roof of a Spartan temple. Those of you who are learned in the classics will have recognised the lost egg of Leda, its miraculous life still unquenched. I return to the desert in a few days with Owen Aherne and this lady chosen by divine wisdom for its guardian and bearer. When I have found the appointed place, then Aherne and I will dig a shallow hole where she must lay it and leave it to be hatched by the sun's heat." He then spoke of the two eggs already hatched, how Castor and Clytemnestra broke the one shell, Helen and Pollux the other, of the tragedy that followed, wondered what would break the third shell.[76]

From this story the symbolic structure of Yeats's theory of history gathers its impetus. Yeats's view of history begins with Leda and ends with "The Second Coming," in which the slouching "rough beast" of a future era breaks the shell of the third egg. Yeats's discussion of history is bound at either end by two of his most famous poems.

The question of what *A Vision* is may now be partially answered. The story of the genesis of the system is a statement of Yeats's belief in some strange relation between dream and consciousness. If he could not determine whether the strange voices which spoke through his wife were supernatural or not, he was at least able to affirm out of his own experience the beliefs set down in his early essay on magic. The mind passes beyond the body into other minds:

I have heard my wife in the broken speech of some quite ordinary dream use tricks of speech characteristic of the philosophic voices. Sometimes the philosophic voices themselves have become vague and trivial or have in some other way reminded me of dreams. Furthermore their doctrine supports the resemblance, for one said in the first month of communication, "We are often but created forms," and another, that spirits do not tell a man what is true but create such conditions, such a crisis of fate, that the man is compelled to listen to his Daimon. And again and again they have insisted that the whole system is the creation of my wife's Daimon and of mine, and that it is as startling to them as to us. Mere "spirits," my teachers say, are the "objective," a reflection and distortion; reality itself is found by the Daimon in what they call, in commemoration of the Third Person of the Trinity, the ghostly Self. The Blessed spirits must be sought within the self which is common to all.[77]

This is Yeats's "Spiritus Mundi," Blake's Poetic Genius, a common ground for the "sleeping and waking minds."

But *A Vision* is more than this. It is a synthesis of tradition and personality by means of a synthetic study of magic, myth, dream, and consciousness, resulting in a complex archetypal system of symbolism, "metaphors for poetry." It is a statement of belief in a dramatic universe where conflict is the dance-form of life. It is also a comic satire on modern day Urizens, a spoof on "science separated from philosophy," dramatically heightened by a cast of fantastic characters, one of which is Yeats himself wearing Urizen's mask. Yet *A Vision* is still more, for though Yeats assumes a doltish mask he also performs the heroic and perhaps inevitably tragic task of intellectual search. As *A Vision* reaches toward its climax—and this is yet to be fully demonstrated—it dramatically presents a tragi-comic vision of life.

CHAPTER VIII

History

All the stream that's roaring by
Came out of a needle's eye;
Things unborn, things that are gone,
From needle's eye still goad it on.
—W. B. YEATS [1]

YEATS'S attitude toward time permeates his work. Much of this attitude is embodied in his treatment of history, which is similar to Blake's, though again he looks at history from a different point of view. Several key poems disclose, when considered together, the central form of Yeats's view of history.

LEDA

According to ancient legend, Leda, the daughter of Thestius, was the wife of Tyndareus, by whom she became the mother of Timandra and Philonae. One night she was embraced both by her husband and by Zeus. By the former she was the mother of Castor and Clytemnestra and by the latter Helen and Pollux. Variant traditions reverse the father roles. A popular variation supposes that Zeus visited Leda disguised as a swan and that she produced two eggs, from the one of which issued Helen and from the other Castor and Pollux.

Working his own variation on the myth, Yeats wrote the first version of "Leda and the Swan" on September 18, 1923, first choosing "Annunciation" as its title, but discarding it in the final draft. In the years which just preceded and followed the writing of this poem, Yeats was busy writing his essay on history, the section of *A Vision* entitled "Dove or Swan." An early discussion, rejected from the essay, comments upon the historico-symbolical significance of Leda:

In the midst or upon the edge of the Mediterranean Civilization all that world whose fall is symbolized by the burning of Troy, there occurred somewhere among the obscure northern tribes a multitudinous supernatural event which my poem "Leda" represents as the begetting of Love and War, for from the eggs of Leda came no Helen only but Castor and Pollux. Then for some 1000 years I imagine these tribes each stirred at moments to heroic frenzy by Daimon or Hero struggling one against another and with the old Mediterranean civilization grown inert and vague. At a time of which I am ignorant and even of which the latest research has discovered little my symbols [given to him by the instructors as the key to history] compel me to pose them not only with the predecessors among whom I imagine incomplete monotheistic ideas like those we associate with the famous hymn of Aknaton, but also against a *primary* Asiatic world which shares nothing of their western nature but a complementary dream.[2]

In *A Vision* the poem "Leda and the Swan" serves as an introduction to Yeats's discussion of history. Though it symbolizes the first act of human history, it symbolizes also a constantly recurring act, man's realization that he is something more than an animal and something less than divine. Thus, to anchor the poem somewhere in history is to look at history in the wrong way. History is not linear but cyclic. The act of "Leda and the Swan" is a "bright sculpture," constantly renewed in microcosmic everyday acts, released from the ravages of delusory time.

In this supernatural incarnation man is granted a partial divinity; afterward he constantly aspires toward its totality. He is

caught in the juggle of opposites. Paradoxically, divinity comes
to him in animal guise, and the eggs of supernatural union release
contrary powers:

I imagine the annunciation that founded Greece as made to Leda,
remembering that they showed in a Spartan temple, strung up to
the roof as a holy relic, an unhatched egg of hers; and that from one
of her eggs came Love and from the other War. But all things are
from antithesis, and when in my ignorance I try to imagine what
older civilisation that annunciation rejected I can but see bird and
woman blotting out some corner of the Babylonian mathematical
starlight.[3]

The Leda-swan image is the image of miracle. It represents the
founding of Greece; but more than that, it blots out all else; it
returns us to beginnings—the joining of primitive humanity and
God, the initial manifestation of man's peculiar spiritual make-
up. As such it symbolizes the creation of conflict, born of itself,
of "love and hate and all the shades between." [4]

> A sudden blow: the great wings beating still
> Above the staggering girl, her thighs caressed
> By the dark webs, her nape caught in his bill,
> He holds her helpless breast upon his breast.
>
> How can those terrified vague fingers push
> The feathered glory from her loosening thighs?
> And how can body, laid in that white rush,
> But feel the strange heart beating where it lies?
>
> A shudder in the loins engenders there
> The broken wall, the burning roof and tower
> And Agamemnon dead.
>   Being so caught up,
> So mastered by the brute blood of the air,
> Did she put on his knowledge with his power
> Before the indifferent beak could let her drop? [5]

The sudden violence ("sudden" itself, a word whose two
syllables are dominated by heavy consonants, suggests violent

change, cataclysm, like the impact of a nearby dynamite blast
on the country quiet), and then the rhythmic, sustained excitement of beating wings, staggering girl, and shuddering loins: the
blow sets off a reaction of terror. The fingers are both "terrified"
and "vague" from lack of understanding, from unpreparedness.
The human mind, caught in the fantasy of experience, cannot
immediately cope with miracle, reacts physically and weakly in
terror. The girl is shaken, helpless. The question of lines 5–6 is
rhetorical, the answer obvious: She cannot possibly repel the
supernatural. The question is also a dramatic description of her
own reaction; it embodies a thought on her part which, though
not articulated, comes vaguely expressed through the finger tips
from a mind in panic, too weak to cope with the situation in any
positive way. The lines are a statement by someone contemplating the problem of the human being's relation to the supernatural.
They also act to bring the reader into the frightened mind of the
girl herself and describe without detachment her physical and
psychological reaction.

As the poem progresses, rhythm sustains the excitement, although we gradually move outside the girl's experience—her
own flustered attempts at self-control—toward the final, more
detached metaphysical question of the poem's conclusion. Leda
herself no longer asks or expresses the question even vaguely,
having been subdued or "mastered" by the supernatural "brute
blood." With Yeats we now contemplate what this event portends. The question is again rhetorical, but the implied answer
is indefinite: Surely she must have felt that "strange heart beating." And if she did, may we not ask another question, the question of the poem's conclusion?

> Did she put on his knowledge with his power
> Before the indifferent beak could let her drop?

Even if she cannot repel the God-bird, has she not gained a
knowledge of the principle of his own existence? Clothed in his

power, is she not now able to feel his heart; and after she has
lain with God, after she has felt the "brute blood of the air," the
procreative power of heaven, the animal power of God, has not
some new possibility in mankind been released through her and
through her offspring? Can the solitary swan, despite its "indif-
ference" and its perfect singularity, "let her drop" soon enough
to remain perfectly solitary and unknown?

The poem, like Blakean prophecy, brings opposites into some
kind of relationship; but, unlike Blakean prophecy, it does not
reconcile them. There is no resolution, only the gyring away
of history to a new falling apart. Vision is momentary, personal,
and inarticulate. Leda's vision comes as raw experience and is
gone almost as soon as it appears; the strange residue of a new
life remains. This is the experience of the thinker too. After it is
all over, what is there left of it?

> Where got I that truth?
> Out of a medium's mouth,
> Out of nothing it came,
> Out of the forest loam.[6]

It is the question one asks about history:

> . . . Whence had they come,
> The hand and lash that beat down frigid Rome?
> What sacred drama through her body heaved
> When world-transforming Charlemagne was conceived? [7]

But something *is* left, born of contraries. From the intercourse of
Godhead and primitive humanity comes the love goddess Helen,
who "engenders" the violent fall of Troy—love, hate, and war.
Castor and Clytemnestra break Leda's second egg. Castor becomes a Spartan war god, and Clytemnestra is involved in the
murder of the great Agamemnon. The meeting of opposites
brings into the world a race of beings in which contraries are
continually warring, the animal blood against the spiritual. Each
of us is figuratively a son of Zeus, a son of Leda; and to complete

the paradox, Zeus himself came into the world in animal cloth-ing. What is the extent of man's God-power, and what is the ex-tent of his animal weakness, and is God in this world necessarily an animal?

Conflict is born microcosmically, on the Leda-swan analogy, in the mind of any thinker; for the perfect circularity of eternal thought becomes two warring opposites in the time world:

> "The stallion Eternity
> Mounted the mare of Time,
> 'Gat the foal of the world." [8]

The momentary inarticulate vision which must have come to Leda destroys animal peace, frustrates man because it seems capable of expression only in cryptic symbolism, creators of which are heretics or fools—Yeats's Old Tom, who speaks the lines above; Crazy Jane, who argues with bishops; and "wild old wicked men" approaching the end of life. The essential irra-tionality of man's visionary experience, represented by Yeats's heretics and fools, is tragic in the light of man's pride in the power of his reason to control nature.

Leda and swan stand at the initial vortex of history, before which is only God solitary and a human being not yet human as we know him because he is without the half-knowledge created by the swan's act. Afterward he has been provided with some nondiscursive, frustrating image which leads him to aspiration: "Nations, races, and individual men are unified by an image, or bundle of related images, symbolical or evocative of a state of mind, which is of all states of mind not impossible, the most difficult to that man, race, or nation." [9] This image is the Daimon, born of the paradox of swan and Leda, who therefore symbolize not only the great initial vortex of human history, but later microcosms of it and also vortexes of individual experience.

The questions raised in "Leda and the Swan" haunted Yeats not only because they stood at the beginnings of history in his myth and there was no cause beyond them in time, but also because they suggested a relationship between man and God which had been suggested time and again in mythology: Man is a microcosm of God and is therefore God himself, God enclosed, if only in a partial sense. This is very much a Blakean "theology." Ribh, Yeats's aged heretic or Blakean "devil," criticizes St. Patrick and corrects some mistaken dogma:

Ribh Denounces Patrick

An abstract Greek absurdity has crazed the man—
Recall that masculine Trinity. Man, woman, and child (a daughter or a son),
That's how all natural or supernatural stories run.

Natural and supernatural with the self-same ring are wed.
As man, as beast, as ephemeral fly begets, Godhead begets Godhead.
For things below are copies, the Great Smaragdine Tablet said.

Yet all must copy copies, all increase their kind;
When conflagration of their passion sinks, damped by the body or the mind,
That juggling nature mounts, her coil in their embraces twined.

The mirror-scalèd serpent is multiplicity,
But all that run in couples, on earth, in flood or air, share God that is but three,
And could beget or bear themselves could they but love as He.[10]

Ribh believes that the basic religious error in the western world has been its foolish acceptance of a masculine trinity when all the human impulses demand the man, woman, and child trinity of all natural and supernatural stories. The important thing to affirm is the similarity between the natural and the supernatural, not the delusory differences which plague us. Western religion has affirmed the feminine principle only surreptitiously in a virgin woman undefiled by the masculine Godhead. The result has been a comedy of lip service and, as Blake pointed out, a false code of chastity. According to all traditions, "things below are copies." Therefore:

As man, as beast, as an ephemeral fly begets, Godhead begets Godhead.

Ribh goes beyond castigation of Patrick and affirms that this sexual coupling of all things from Godhead to fly is the basic principle of nature and of all existence. The gyre or "coil" of "juggling nature," or of the illusion called time, Yeats's symbol of all action, is twined in all of these embraces and guided by their passion. All whirl on in this particular spatial and temporal order. Nature oscillates between extremities, juggles opposites. God, however, begets self. He is the circle symbolized by the initial coil of nature, the wedding ring, which is not a circle at all but a single point or vortex. He is joined to himself.

The last stanza presents a Blakean image and a metaphysical conceit:

The mirror-scalèd serpent is multiplicity.

The serpent is Blake's Orc-Urizen likened to the multiverse of Henry Adams. The mirror scales of the serpent deceive us into seeing a multiverse of images rather than a vortex of vision. Yeats wrote in *A Vision*, "Only one symbol exists, though the reflecting mirrors make many appear and all different," and *A Vision* was meant to illustrate this very point.

The conceit follows from acceptance of the single image as reality. We all share God, but in our peculiar world of time and space we do not seem to beget ourselves. God, like the swan of Leda, is the greatest lover, but even He in the time world seemed not to beget himself. Instead He begat us. If this world is a world of mirrors, our multiplicity is His unity, and we may in truth be one with Him, a part of the single image which is reality. We are, however, trapped in the crazy house of nature, stumbling into reflecting walls and searching for hidden doors. In time, we are like Yeats in his comedy of errors with his instructors,

who were not in time, who lived and thought in a different form
beyond the unsolved antinomies which make the mirrors appear
as reality. We are back to Plato's cave, but we have affirmed the
ancient theory of macrocosm and microcosm, restated by Blake.

We need no longer wonder at the tremendous importance,
increasing as he grew older, which Yeats gave to sexual imagery.
The Great Smaragdine Tablet states that the human sexual act
is the copy below and that the greatest lover, both spiritual and
sexual, is God himself. In our world we are made tragically
aware that we see only reflections. Michael Robartes' words bear
repetition: "The marriage bed is the symbol of the solved antinomy, and were more than symbol could a man there lose and
keep his identity, but he falls asleep. That sleep is the sleep of
death." [11]

Yeats once said to John Sparrow:

"The tragedy of sexual intercourse is the perpetual virginity of
the soul." Sexual intercourse is an attempt to solve the eternal antinomy, doomed to failure because it takes place only on one side of
the gulf. The gulf is that which separates the one and the many, or
if you like, God and man.[12]

This continual affirmation of the tragic gulf, the attitude which
appears to border on despair, paradoxically gives rise to a short,
terse poem shot through with irony and a peculiar tragi-comic
attitude.

For Anne Gregory

"Never shall a young man,
Thrown into despair
By those great honey-coloured
Ramparts at your ear,
Love you for yourself alone
And not your yellow hair."

"But I can get a hair-dye
And set such colour there,
Brown or black, or carrot,

> That young men in despair
> May love me for myself alone
> And not my yellow hair."

> "I heard an old religious man
> But yesternight declare
> That he had found a text to prove
> That only God, my dear,
> Could love you for yourself alone
> And not your yellow hair." [13]

Here Yeats ironically denies what he sets out to affirm in "Ribh Denounces Patrick." For here the thing below, if it is a copy of the thing above, is surely a fallen, imperfect copy of it. Man is a clownish, doltish copy, a tragi-comic figure; for the coupling of man and woman is not the creation of self, or at least does not seem to be. Innocence dies into experience, spirituality into sensuality. Experience is a kind of acceptance of the multiverse of mirrors.

With Blake's active passion but without his faith in his own vision, Ribh returns and attempts to bridge the paradox in one of Yeats's most important poems, "Ribh at the Tomb of Baile and Aillin." Therein two legendary lovers, "purified" by tragedy and death, lose the virginity of their souls in an embrace unknown to our own lives:

> The miracle that gave them such a death
> Transfigured to pure substance what had once
> Been bone and sinew; when such bodies join
> There is no touching here, nor touching there,
> Nor straining joy, but whole is joined to whole;
> For the intercourse of angels is a light
> Where for a moment both seem lost, consumed.[14]

And Ribh reads his holy book in the light, though "somewhat" obscured, of their union:

> Here in the pitch-dark atmosphere above
> The trembling of the apple and the yew,

> Here on the anniversary of their death,
> The anniversary of their first embrace,
> Those lovers purified by tragedy,
> Hurry into each others arms; these eyes,
> By water, herb and solitary prayer
> Made aquiline, are open to that light.
> Though somewhat broken by the leaves, that light
> Lies in a circle on the grass; therein
> I turn the pages of my holy book.*

A "somewhat broken" picture of the reflection of light upon the book is as close as we come to a bridging of the paradox. In spite of himself Ribh becomes Urizen here, his holy book locked in the circle. The book is Ribh's time-bound, space-bound philosophy, wrapped in the coil of that "juggling nature," born of contraries, and forced to vacillate between theories of unity and multiplicity. The Leda-swan image is a macrocosmic historical representation of Ribh's inarticulate struggle with vision. The words we use seem to assume the existence of space, time, and material; so do the images of our minds. Leda's "terrified vague fingers" symbolize man's mind in the face of delusory nature. "The antinomy is there and can be represented only as a myth."

There is more to the paradox of man's nature. The flow of the swan's blood in man's veins tends to explain the whole range of human aspirations. For man is now partially God:

> Some moralist or mythological poet
> Compares the solitary soul to a swan;
> I am satisfied with that,
> Satisfied if a troubled mirror show it,

* Compare, from *Per Amica Silentia Lunae*, p. 69: "The dead, as the passionate necessity wears out, come into a measure of freedom and may turn the impulse of events, started while living, in some new direction, but they cannot originate except through living. Then gradually they perceive, although they are still but living in their memories, harmonies, symbols, and patterns, as though all were being refashioned by an artist, and they are moved by emotions, sweet for no imagined good but in themselves; like those of children dancing in a ring; and I do not doubt that they make love in that union which Swedenborg has said is of the whole body and seems from far off an incandescence."

Before that brief gleam of its life be gone,
An image of its state;
The wings half spread for flight,
The breast thrust out in pride
Whether to play, or to ride
Those winds that clamour of approaching night.[15]

This to Yeats is the heroic mood, made possible by the swan or
bird in man as it faces off against the beast. The swan is, of
course, man's Godhead, and since it is most often uncontrollable
it is sometimes called man's Daimon. The beast in man corresponds roughly to Blake's spectre, the swan to Blake's emanation:

My Spectre around me night & day
Like a Wild beast guards my way.
My Emanation far within
Weeps incessantly for my Sin.[16]

These are the contrary images of man's vacillation, always, or
almost always, at war: "That crafty demon and that loud beast/
That plague me day and night." [17] In spite of momentary cessation of conflict, or, to put it another way, the appearance of
personal vortexes, man is most often whirled "between extremities." The heroic man as part swan—almost like Los when he
faces Rahab—casts derision upon his own situation, laughs at
adversity, attains to aristocratic disdain. In a short poem Yeats
describes this psychological achievement and at the same time
seems to show that in these moments of intense passion Blake's
theory of the creative imagination is correct.

Nor dread nor hope attend
A dying animal;
A man awaits his end
Dreading and hoping all;
Many times he died,
Many times rose again.
A great man in his pride
Confronting murderous men
Casts derision upon

> Supersession of breath;
> He knows death to the bone—
> Man has created death.[18]

After the swan comes to Leda, man is no longer an animal. When God comes into the fallen world he gives himself to man, and man becomes his protector, harboring Godhead in his own soul—Blake's "spiritual form."

In a poem of March 1929, "Lullaby," Leda protects the swan.

> Such a sleep and sound as fell
> Upon Eurota's grassy bank
> When the holy bird, that there
> Accomplished his predestined will,
> From the limbs of Leda sank
> But not from her protecting care.[19]

After incarnation, God, in both a mythical and theological sense, becomes the ward of mankind, under whose protection he either prospers or suffers. The same idea appears in a poem addressed to Christ, "A Prayer for My Son" (1922).

> And when through all the town there ran
> The servants of Your enemy,
> A woman and a man,
> Unless the Holy Writings lie,
> Hurried through the smooth and rough
> And through the fertile and waste,
> Protecting, till the danger past,
> With human love.[20]

There is, then, a kind of communion between man's world and eternity, imperfect and mysterious though it is; and the hero rises to strange equilibrium in which he may assert his dignity and half-assert his immortality. The time-born human being seeks to express this antinomial relationship by means of a myth which affirms pattern and unity. He seeks a pattern in history, an outward circumference for time. He also attempts to show, with man's own actions as evidence, that the form of his myth is the form of the world, the single image created by himself:

> Whatever flames upon the night
> Man's own resinous heart has fed.[21]

ANNUNCIATION

Yeats's instructors applied both symbols of the "single geometrical conception" to the movement of history:

November 1917 had been given to an exposition of the twenty-eight typical incarnations or phases and to the movements of their *Four Faculties*, and then on December 6th a cone or gyre had been drawn and related to the soul's judgment after death; and then just as I was about to discover that incarnations and judgment alike implied cones or gyres, one within the other, turning in opposite directions, two such cones were drawn and related neither to judgment nor to incarnations but to European history.[22]

The Great Wheel, produced by Yeats on page eighty-one of *A Vision*, represents the twenty-eight phases of the moon, which in turn symbolize the twenty-eight historical phases in the Great Year. There are, as in the Blakean historical system, wheels within wheels. The second symbol, that of dance and conflict, the double cone or gyre, may be superimposed upon the wheel and the "single geometrical conception" thereby achieved.

The diagram on the following page represents history at phase 3 and the personality of a man of phase 3, whose other attributes may be determined by the conflict of the two interlocking gyres, their corner positions at phase numbers 13, 17, 27. Man is categorized in this system according to the position of his Will (at phase 3), which Yeats defines as " 'the first matter' of the personality." It is man's controlling force, his Blakean Los. Numbers 13, 17, 27 represent respectively the positions of "Body of Fate, Mask, and Creative Mind." The Body of Fate represents man's physical and mental environment, "the stream of Phenomena as this affects a particular individual, all that is forced upon us from without. Time as it affects sensation. If any reality exists outside us, it lies in the Body of Fate." For Yeats, part of man's reality is paradoxically what he is a part of. The Mask (to be discussed later) represents all that man strives to be. Creative Mind is intellect "as intellect was understood before the close of

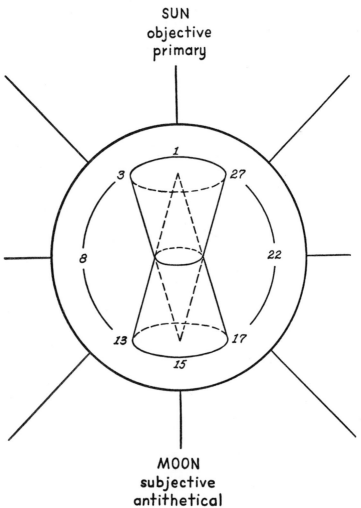

SUN
objective
primary

MOON
subjective
antithetical

The Great Wheel and the Gyres

the seventeenth century—all the mind that is consciously constructive, that part of the mind which acts on external events." [23]

When Will reaches phases 1 or 15, the two cones collapse into nothing. That is, Will and Creative Mind—imagination and intellect—become unified; and, opposite on the wheel, Mask and Body of Fate—man's environment and what he strives to become—become unified. At phases 8 and 22 (when Will appears at these points) the cones pass through one another like an egg turning inside out. That is, the cone whose base was originally in the upper half of the wheel now finds its base in the lower half, and vice versa. Although the cones again disappear at phases 8 and 22, this is a flattening out of the bases rather than a unification in a single point. Here the four elements are falsely unified in conflict, Will with Body of Fate, and Mask with Creative Mind. Phase 1 represents the dark of the moon, phase 15 the full moon; phases 23–7 (counterclockwise) are the phases in which sun or "primary" civilization predominates, phases 9–21 those in which an "antithetical" world exists, dominated by moon.

The important points for our examination of history are these:

1. Each civilization moves from its inception at phase 1 into the full moon and back to its impending collapse at phase 28.

2. Conflict exists except at phases 1 and 15, where there is no life, both being "perfect phases."

3. Phases 1 and 15 are phases of a supernatural quality, in which the usual gyre conflict (the breath of life) is stilled by some revelation.

4. Each wheel is part of a larger wheel, so that phase 1 of a millennium may be phase 15 of a greater era. Yeats's system moves beyond any conception possible in geometric logic. Contrary phases exist simultaneously, one within another *ad infinitum*. The system resolves itself, or rather remains unresolved, in perpetual conflict.

5. Furthermore, "every phase is in itself a wheel; the individual

soul is awakened by a violent oscillation . . . until it sinks in on that Whole where the contraries are united, the antinomies re-solved." [24] The conflict moves not only toward infinity but also toward the smallest of microcosms. Here Yeats's symbolism re-calls his own remarks on Blake's:

All these complex symbols contain the others in miniature within them. All is within all, and every one of the twenty-seven churches [Blake's symbols for eras] contains the whole twenty-sevenfold sym-bols in miniature. Thus, too, this great circle of day and night con-tains also many days and nights, many winters and many summers.[25]

Wheel within wheel within wheel allows for complete possibility, but possibility born always of conflict. According to Yeats, com-plete possibility is twofold in nature. There is God's predestined will—he calls it "God's Choice," the form of any single wheel. And there is also "God's Chance," the multiplied, conflicting wheels within wheels. In a note to the play "Calvary," Yeats asserts that Michael Robartes has told him that a famous old Arab poet had explained these ideas:

Kusta ben Luki has taught us to divide all things into Chance and Choice; one can think about the world and about man, or anything else until all has vanished but these two things, for they are indeed the first cause of the animate and inanimate world. They exist in God, for if they did not He would not have freedom, He would be bound by His own Choice. In God alone, indeed, can they be united, yet each be perfect and without limit or hindrance. If I should throw from the dice-box there would be but six possible sides on each of the dice, but when God throws He uses dice that have all numbers and sides. Some worship His Choice; that is easy; to know that He has willed for some unknown purpose all that happened is pleasant; but I have spent my life worshipping His Chance, and that moment when I understand the immensity of His Chance is the moment when I am nearest Him. Because it is very difficult and because I have put my understanding into three songs I am famous among my people.[26]

The old Arab poet knew that it is God's Chance which pre-vents man from predicting minute events, from breaking through that final outer circle of time; for beyond it lies that further circle representing another side of the dice. According to Yeats, "explanations of the world lie one inside another"; [27] each one in itself represents God's Choice, but each one alone fails to allow for the many-sided dice of God's Chance and thus represents only Urizen returning to himself. All theories which conceive of history as a single pattern without paradox are limited visions.

In Yeats's paradoxical system the annunciation made to Leda marks the first phase of a two-thousand-year cycle which ends with the birth of Christ. At phase 22 of this period the Ledaean civilization (at the interchange of the cones) moves from moonlight to sunlight:

Even before Plato that collective image of man dear to Stoic and Epicurean alike, the moral double of bronze or marble athlete, had been evoked by Anaxagoras when he declared that thought and not the warring opposites created the world. At that sentence the heroic life, passionate fragmentary man, all that had been imagined by great poets and sculptors began to pass away, and instead of seeking noble antagonists, imagination moved towards divine man and the ridiculous devil.[28]

The movement toward a new wheel, revelation, a new annunciation gathers strength as the sun symbolically rules all things.

Then finally:

> The threefold terror of love; a fallen flare
> Through the hollow of an ear;
> Wings beating about the room;
> The terror of all terrors that I bore
> The Heavens in my womb.
>
> Had I not found content among the shows
> Every common woman knows,
> Chimney corner, garden walk,
> Or rocky cistern where we tread the clothes
> And gather all the talk?
>
> What is this flesh I purchased with my pains,
> This fallen star my milk sustains,

This love that makes my heart's blood stop
Or strikes a sudden chill into my bones
And bids my hair stand up? [29]

There is a subtle distinction of tone between this poem and
"Leda and the Swan." The swan is a primitive image of power, a
totem deity; but the angel of the traditional Christian annunciation is a messenger *from* power. "Threefold terror" itself suggests abstract, irrational force. The message comes, once removed,
from a being conceived (in human dimensions) as trinity, not
palpable in its totality in the way that the swan's attack is palpable. "The fallen star" is born of an act of God—made visible
only by the mediary angel—upon a human being, but the eggs
of Leda are the result of the visible attack of brute, animal force,
against which there is at least the animal reaction. "The Mother
of God" is the traditional annunciation picture, perhaps after a
Botticelli—the emotional violence secondary to the formalized
posture of the figures, in positions which have made a tradition
out of miracle. The angel comes from beyond the antinomies,
the swan from the stream.

According to Yeats, from A.D. 1 onward, "God is now conceived as something outside man and man's handiwork." [30] "The
Mother of God" reflects this idea by symbolizing a shrinking
fear of seeing self create divinity. The unthinking terror of Leda
is now complicated by man's feeling of simple unworthiness and
by a terror born of the breaking of an accepted natural order.

Yeats dramatizes the approach of the new historical cycle
elsewhere by the image of Salome and her dance with the severed
head of John the Baptist. In *A Vision*, Yeats writes:

When I think of the moment before revelation I think of Salome—
she, too, delicately tinted or maybe mahogany dark—dancing before
Herod and receiving the Prophet's head in her indifferent hands, and
wonder if what seems to us decadence was not in reality the exaltation of the muscular flesh and of civilisation perfectly achieved. [31]

Her dance takes place upon the verge of phase 1 of the Christian millennium. At the moment of phase 1, which is the moment

of the moon's dark and a phase of supernatural incarnation, there is no bodily life; and the phase passes so quickly that there is no human awareness of its appearance in time except what it leaves behind. In *A Vision*, Yeats describes the phase:

Now body is completely absorbed in its supernatural environment. . . . Mind has become indifferent to good and evil, to truth and falsehood; body has become undifferentiated, dough-like; the more perfect be the soul, the more indifferent the mind, the more dough-like the body; and mind and body take whatever shape, accept whatever image is imprinted upon them, transact whatever purpose is imposed upon them, are indeed the instruments of supernatural manifestation, the final link between the living and more powerful beings. There may be great joy; but it is the joy of a conscious plasticity; and it is this plasticity, this liquefaction, or pounding up, whereby all that has been knowledge becomes instinct and faculty. All plasticities do not obey all masters, and when we have considered cycle and horoscope it will be seen how those that are the instruments of subtle supernatural will differ from the instruments of cruder energy; but all, highest and lowest, are alike in being automatic.[32]

The virgin body of the Mother of God is this very "instrument of supernatural will." She provides the human link between "living and more powerful beings." Her posture is so formalized as to become "automatic," the product of artistic instinct; her attitude of acceptance is combined with a sense of unworthiness. The dancer, whose movements are prophetic of the moon's dark and the appearance of a new civilization, suggests the paradox of "exaltation of the muscular flesh" and "plasticity," "joy," "where all that has been knowledge becomes instinct." She represents the movement out of body into "liquefaction." She sends the new civilization on its way.

Yeats points out the ritualistic significance of Salome's dance in his preface to "A Full Moon in March":

The dance with the severed head suggests the central idea of Wilde's "Salome." Wilde took it from Heine, who has somewhere described Salome in Hell throwing into the air the head of John the Baptist. Heine may have found it in some old Jewish religious legend, for it is part of the old ritual of the year, the mother goddess and the slain god.[33]

Ledaean goddess, epiphanic Mother of God, and ritualistic danc-ing girl are related images of prophecy, intimations of a new historical period. The Ledaean goddess and Mother of God also symbolize partial attainment to Godhead—"Did she put on his knowledge with his power"—and the dancing girl is the temporal image of complete spiritual and bodily equilibrium. As arche-types, all are related to Blake's "eternal female." They represent man's goal, the base of the cone opposite to his own.

Yeats thus moves toward the sharp delineation of various "minute particulars" of this single archetypal figure. The great central form of experience naturally resolves itself into a pattern of traditional symbols—"a complete corpus of poetic reference." This female image is, according to Robert Graves, who coined the "complete corpus" phrase, the "white goddess," central im-age of a "single poetic theme" seen over and over again in "cer-tain ancient poetic myths which though manipulated to conform with each epoch of religious change . . . yet remain constant in general outline." [34]

The Theme, briefly, is the antique story, which falls into thirteen chapters and an epilogue, of the birth, life, death and resurrection of the God of the Waxing Year; the central chapters concern the God's losing battle with the God of the Waning Year for love of the capri-cious and all-powerful Threefold Goddess, their mother, bride, and layer-out. The poet identifies himself with the God of the Waxing Year and his Muse with the Goddess; the rival is his blood-brother, his other self, his weird. All true poetry—true by Housman's prac-tical test—celebrates some incident or scene in this very ancient story, and the three main characters are so much a part of our racial inheritance that they not only assert themselves in poetry but recur on occasions of emotional stress in the form of dreams, paranoiac visions and delusions. . . .

The Goddess is a lovely, slender woman with a hooked nose, deathly pale face, lips red as rowan-berries, startlingly blue eyes and long fair hair; she will suddenly transform herself into sow, mare, bitch, vixen, she-ass, weasel, serpent, owl, she-wolf, tigress, mermaid, or loathsome hag. Her names and titles are innumberable. . . . I cannot think of any true poet from Homer onwards who has not independently recorded his experience of her.

As Goddess of the Underworld she was concerned with Birth, Procreation, and Death. As Goddess of the Earth she was concerned with the three seasons of Spring, Summer, and Winter: she animated trees and plants and ruled all living creatures. As Goddess of the Sky she was the Moon, in her three phases of New Moon, Full Moon, and Waning Moon. This explains why from a triad she was so often enlarged to an ennead. But it must never be forgotten that the Triple Goddess, as worshipped for example at Stymphalus, was a personification of primitive woman—woman the creatress and destructress. As the New Moon or Spring she was girl; as the Full Moon or Summer she was woman; as the Old Moon or Winter she was hag.[35]

Although one may disagree with Graves's statement of the central form in terms of specific symbols, it is instructive that this modern poet has found a continuity, applicable to both Blake and Yeats and to himself, which he can verify with literary evidence.

The meeting of the hero with the goddess, in one of her several forms, is the subject of several Yeatsian poems and plays. One story, based upon an old Gaelic legend, fascinated Yeats. He superimposed it upon the Salome image and used it in an early edition of "The Secret Rose," in "The King of the Great Clock Tower," "The Death of Cuchulain," and "A Full Moon in March."

In "A Full Moon in March" a swineherd, hearing of a queen's offer of marriage to anyone who can move her heart, decides to risk failure and death in order to win her. The queen has stipulated that if the lover is unsuccessful he must lose his head. The terms of the agreement are harsh, but the swineherd disregards all warnings which the queen, Blake's Rahab figure, addresses to him:

> Remember through what perils you have come;
> That I am crueller than solitude,
> Forest or beast. Some I have killed or maimed
> Because their singing put me in a rage,
> And some because they came at all. Men hold
> That woman's beauty is a kindly thing,
> But they that call me cruel speak the truth,
> Cruel as the winter of virginity.[36]

The swineherd, like Cuchulain of "The Green Helmet," who heroically offers his head to the mysterious red man, gaily "transfigures dread."

Swineherd:	My mind is running on our marriage night,
	Imagining all from the first touch and kiss.
Queen:	What gives you that strange confidence? What makes
	You think that you can move my heart and me?
Swineherd:	Because I look upon you without fear.
Queen:	A Lover in railing or in flattery said
	God only looks upon me without fear.
Swineherd:	Desiring cruelty, he made you cruel.
	I shall embrace body and cruelty. . . .[37]

The queen orders him beheaded, but his head continues to sing, and she embraces it in a Salome-like dance ritual which ends the play.

The swineherd is the heroic personality in the face of history—the high, solitary, disdainful hero. He gaily mocks the wheel, accepting God's Chance:

> I picked a number on the roulette wheel.
> I trust the wheel, as every lover must [38]

The goddess, though she is always most particularly woman, symbolizes the primal motivating force of the wheel of history, the vortex of the gyre. She symbolizes what Yeats calls "the needle's eye" to which all things come and from which all things emerge. She is that moment of vision sought by sages; she is that supernatural occurrence in history bringing swan to Leda, and

angel to Virgin. She is Blake's Jerusalem flashing momentarily
in ecstatic vision in the time world; she is Los's Enitharmon
metamorphosed into the destructress Rahab by the material
world.

It has always seemed to me that all great literature at its greatest intensity displays the sage, the lover, or some image of despair, and
that these are traditional attitudes.[39]

The "eternal female" provides the motivation for the traditional
attitudes of traditional heroes. In "At the Hawk's Well" the cry
of the hawk-woman, the beckon of the deceiving goddess who
guards the well of immortality and offers only death, signifies
all that man desires. Her deceit is again the deceit of Yeats's
"frustrators" in *A Vision* who tell him only enough to bring
him to the test at the brink of despair.

The annunciations of history are then complex images of
peculiar visions which gyre away on the mundane wheel of
time. Yeats calls civilization "a struggle to keep self-control."
The initial power of every idea, every vision, recedes rapidly in
larger spirals like the falcon of "The Second Coming." This
movement has been the form of history since Christ, beginning
with annunciation and Salome's dance, ending with some mysterious new vortex, antithetical in character to Christ because
opposite on the next larger wheel of time.

In Yeats's poem "The Crazed Moon" the moon's own dance
represents the birth and death of various goddesses: Leda, the
Virgin, and others. All are aspects of the one formally repeated
movement. But there is variation within similarity; the poem reveals the difference between modern and primitive reaction to
the rule of the moon:

> Crazed through much child-bearing
> The moon is staggering in the sky;
> Moon-struck by the despairing
> Glances of her wandering eye
> We grope, and grope in vain,
> For children born of her pain.

Children dazed or dead!
When she in all her virginal pride
First trod on the mountain's head
What stir ran through the countryside
Where every foot obeyed her glance!
What manhood led the dance!

Fly-catchers of the moon,
Our hands are blenched, our fingers seem
But slender needles of bone;
Blenched by that malicious dream
They are spread wide that each
May rend what comes in reach.[40]

This is the picture of an aging, waning moon, the burdened woman of "much child-bearing" set against the virginal moon of a recently revealed civilization. The first stanza symbolizes the anarchy depicted in "The Second Coming," the cosmic violence of the growing primary materialism. The third stanza is prophetic of the state of humanity at the moment of that anarchy. The image of virgin moon represents the early phases, the growth of a civilization, a ritual dance of communion; but these things are lost in a period of destruction, where men become, like Urizen, skeletons, where dance seems—only *seems*—no longer to function. We have advanced to this very moment on the wheel in Yeats's lifetime:

Things fall apart; the centre cannot hold.

The paradox, of course, is that the falling apart is the order of things. The dance really continues, increasing in violence to dissonant music.

The moon, it must be remembered, is always woman and may symbolize for the poet any particular woman; or to reverse the idea, any particular woman may symbolize the archetype. In order to describe a personal experience, in "A Man Young and Old," Yeats thus employs imagery identical to that of poems involving a macrocosmic theme. The man, upon meeting a woman, is transfigured by vision but then confused by it as his experience gyres on like the larger wheel of history:

> She smiled and that transfigured me
> And left me but a lout
> Maundering here, and maundering there,
> Emptier of thought
> Than the heavenly circuit of its stars
> When the moon sails out.[41]

The cold impersonality of the moon-goddess is dramatized:

> Like the moon her kindness is,
> If kindness I may call
> What has no comprehension in't,
> But is the same for all.

This is the curse of Rahab, the law of Urizen.

The moon as temptress regulates and frustrates man's lives. The movement of youth to age in "A Man Young and Old" is consistent with the phases of the moon's journey, the seasonal characteristics of birth and old age, the craze of love, the craze of aged impotence, and the shades between:

> A crazy man that found a cup,
> When all but dead of thirst,
> Hardly dared to wet his mouth
> Imagining, moon-accursed,
> That another mouthful
> And his beating heart would burst.
> October last I found it too
> But found it dry as bone,
> And for that reason I am crazed
> And my sleep is gone.[42]

Woman, moon, and old age appear in the poem "On Woman," and the imagery moves in the same cyclic turn:

> Though pedantry denies,
> It's plain the Bible means
> That Solomon grew wise

> While talking with his queens,
> Yet never could, although
> They say he counted grass,
> Count all the praises due
> When Sheba was his lass.[43]

Then Yeats invokes a phallic image:

> When she the iron wrought, or
> When from the smithy fire
> It shuddered in the water:
> Harshness of their desire
> That made them stretch and yawn,
> Pleasure that comes with sleep,
> Shudder that made them one.

Now, to the personal experience of Yeats and his slavery to the moon:

> What else He give or keep
> God grant me—no, not here,
> For I am not so bold
> To hope a thing so dear
> Now I am growing old,
> But when, if the tale's true,
> The Pestle of the moon
> That pounds up all anew
> Brings me to birth again—
> To find what I once had
> And know what once I have known,
> Until I am driven mad,
> Sleep driven from my bed,
> By tenderness and care,
> Pity, an aching head,
> Gnashing of teeth, despair.

To this point the relationship has been that between Yeats and an archetypal moon-goddess who governs all life. In the last lines the changeover to "minute particulars" occurs. Like Cuchulain at the hawk's well, he has been led astray by some real temptress:

And all because of some one
Perverse creature of chance,
And live like Solomon
That Sheba led a dance.

Such are the "accidents of life" which Yeats brings into the pattern of his myth by relating them imagistically to the greater archetypes, the "central form" of history.

PROPHECY

In its own strange way the future is a part of present history; if, as both Blake and Yeats asserted, the real or symbolical form of time is circular, then that future should maintain the pattern of things already known. With God's Chance multiplying the sides of the dice, the possibility of accurate prediction of events by means of some mathematical system is slim indeed. A visionary like Blake might prophesy the form of all reality, rolling past, present, and future up into one golden ball; but Yeats, "thrown upon this filthy modern tide," would struggle in his assumed role as modern man and dramatize his frustrating search for knowledge of the future.

Yeats's view of history is consistent with his idea of mysterious momentary personal visions. Blake's golden ball wound from string leads to the final apocalyptic vision and the destruction of material delusion. Yeats's golden ball unravels back into time just as soon as it achieves perfect circularity: "Each age unwinds the thread another age had wound." [44] Progress in any of its conventional senses is unknown in Yeats's cosmos. Blake chose as images of philosophical delusion "Bacon, Newton, Locke"; Yeats named "Huxley, Tyndall, Carolus Duran, Bastien-Lepage," who symbolized to him the bitter fallacy or "counter-myth" of progress, now totally disproved by the instructors of *A Vision:*

Certainly my instructors have chosen a theme that has deeply stirred men's minds though the newspapers are silent about it; the newspapers have the happy counter-myth of progress; a theme perhaps as Henry Adams thought when he told the Boston Historical Association that were it turned into a science powerful interests would prevent its publication.[45]

Huxley, Tyndall and the others represent the materialism of "Bacon, Newton, Locke" compounded with the virulent positivism of nineteenth-century science. Early in his intellectual life Yeats had begun to seek out some answer to the "counter-myth":

> For years I have been preoccupied with a certain myth that was itself a reply to a myth. I do not mean a fiction, but one of those statements our nature is compelled to make and employ as a truth though there cannot be sufficient evidence. When I was a boy, everybody talked about progress, and rebellion against my elders took the form of aversion to that myth. I took satisfaction in certain public disasters, felt a sort of ecstasy at the contemplation of ruin.[46]

The cyclic theory of existence implied periods of change, reversal, even wholesale destruction, and led Yeats to certain nightmarish visions which he contemplated with a strange detachment:

> Our civilization was about to reverse itself, or some new civilization about to be born from all that our age had rejected. . . . Had I begun *On Baile's Strand* when I began to imagine, as always at my left side just out of sight, a brazen winged beast that I associated with laughing ecstatic destruction? (Afterwards described in my poem "The Second Coming.") [47]

In the Christian era the ebbing movement leading to such a reversal had begun in about 1050: "The stream set in motion by the Galilean Symbol has filled its basin, and seems motionless for an instant before it falls over the rim." [48] In 1050 Western Europe lay under the spell of a symbolical full moon; in our own time the symbolical sun with its abstract animal force should gain total predominance. The turn from moon to sun, at phase 22 of the modern era, is represented by a very Blakean poem entitled simply "Fragments," in which Yeats, closely following Blake,

considers Locke a symbol of the whole philosophical temper
of an age changing over from the subjective to the objective: "I
can see in a sort of nightmare vision the 'primary qualities' torn
from the side of Locke." [49]

> Locke sank into a swoon;
> The Garden died;
> God took the spinning-jenny
> Out of his side.[50]

This apparent distortion of the genesis myth is really a microcosm of the original. The world is again moving from the garden
of cultural unity to an age of abstract force which will culminate
in the creation of a new divinity. This is what Michael Robartes
foresees when, in *A Vision*, he says to his assembled disciples,
"We are here to consider the terror that is to come." [51] Yeats's
poem "The Double Vision of Michael Robartes" more specifically delineates Robartes' prophecy. The poem is set in a dramatic
milieu. The vision comes to Robartes on the Rock of Cashel, the
ancient capital of Munster kings, a famous Irish shrine. Its own
history symbolizes Yeats's cyclic view. It has been the home of
Catholic, Protestant, and again Catholic archbishoprics. Now it
lies in ruins, symbolically fallow perhaps, high on a mass of rock,
the constant reminder of past ages. There on a dark night with
no moon, Robartes stands:

> On the grey rock of Cashel the mind's eye
> Has called up the cold spirits that are born
> When the old moon is vanished from the sky
> And the new still hides her horn.[52]

The moment is a microcosmic analogue of the moment of annunciation which set the now-dying era on its way, and as such
it puts Robartes strangely in tune with the forthcoming macrocosmic withdrawal of the old civilization and dominance of the
new. In the first edition of *A Vision*, Yeats illustrated his conception of the last phase of the Christian era with stanza three
of "The Double Vision":

Constrained, arraigned, baffled, bent, and unbent
By these wire-jointed jaws and limbs of wood
Themselves obedient,
Knowing not evil and good.[53]

He commented on the lines: "Then with the last gyre must come a desire to be ruled or rather, seeing that desire is all but dead, an adoration of force spiritual or physical, and society as mechanical force be complete at last." [54] The lines echo the imagery of "The Crazed Moon" ("Our hands are blenched, our fingers seem/But slender needles of bone"). Both poems symbolize a state of affairs put somewhat differently in "The Second Coming":

The best lack all conviction, while the worst
Are full of passionate intensity.[55]

Even in little Ireland, the new phase brings violence:

All changed, changed utterly:
A terrible beauty is born.[56]

The rebellion of Easter 1916 may have been a microcosmic assertion of the strange new force.

In Robartes' double vision two strange creatures appear balanced by a third familiar one:

On the grey Rock of Cashel I suddenly saw
A Sphinx with woman breast and lion paw,
A Buddha, hand at rest,
Hand lifted up that blest;

And right between these two a girl at play
That, it may be, had danced her life away,
For now being dead it seemed
That she of dancing dreamed.

Here the dancer, like Salome, symbolizes visionary experience, a strange balance between opposites caught momentarily by the mind's eye. She is the "needle's eye" drawing the antithetical Sphinx and Buddha into a single configuration. Her dance represents for Robartes a precarious balance between life and death, between the finite and the infinite, when the "doors of perception" are suddenly cleansed and the human being in the fallen world suddenly apprehends nondiscursively the truth of something beyond or deeply hidden within himself.

Her dance, like the dance of the woman with Cuchulain's severed head in "The Death of Cuchulain," or the dance of the queen with the swineherd's in "A Full Moon in March," or the dance of Salome with John the Baptist's, prophesies a new era, one hero dead, another ready to be born. The two symbols which the dancer draws into momentary unity, Sphinx and Buddha, reflect the light of Robartes' moon vision and represent "triumph of intellect" and "love." By incantation the dance provides the momentary, revelatory release from the moon's dark just before either Sphinx or Buddha overturns the balance of the scales. This balance is the release from antinomy, symbolized in the Byzantium poems as "death-in-life" and "life-in-death," "Hades' bobbin," the whirling sages who "may unwind the winding path" toward vision. Yeats's golden string is fouled and knotted by his "pragmatic pig of a world" and must be unraveled and then rewound.

The dancer brings the soul as well as the body into the dance and provides a symbol for Blake's assertion that no body really exists independent of the soul.

> O little did they care who danced between,
> And little she by whom her dance was seen
> So she had outdanced thought.
> Body perfection brought,
>
> For what but eye and ear silence the mind
> With the minute particulars of mankind?
> Mind moved yet seemed to stop
> As 'twere a spinning-top.
>
> In contemplation had those three so wrought
> Upon a moment, and so stretched it out

> That they, time overthrown,
> Were dead yet flesh and bone.

Yeats's dancer "overthrows time" in the same way that Blake's "eternal female" Eno "took a Moment of Time/And drew it out," causing it to flower into the mind of the visionary toward infinity, creating a Golgonooza or city of vision: "The Vegetative Universe opens like a flower from the Earth's center/In which is Eternity." [57] The dancer, like the mind wrapped in visionary contemplation spins down into herself, achieving the perfect commingling of motion and not-motion "as 'twere a spinning top." The image of the top is visual, the top spinning so rapidly that it seems actually not to spin at all—the opposites joined in equilibrium.

The Yeatsian vision is finally momentary. The visionary is removed suddenly from time and placed back in it with no moments lost, no fallen life destroyed. When Robartes returns to time, he knows that he has seen the archetypal goddess who comes to him when he passes over the brink of consciousness to that strange submerged sleep world. He feels as though he has been taken by Helen of Troy herself, and in a sense he has, for Helen is Homer's image of the goddess:

> I knew that I had seen, had seen at last,
> That girl my unremembering nights hold fast
> Or else my dreams that fly
> If I should rub an eye,
>
> And yet in flying fling into my meat
> A crazy juice that makes the pulses beat
> As though I had been undone
> By Homer's Paragon
>
> Who never gave the burning tower a thought;
> To such a pitch of folly I am brought,
> Being caught between the pull
> Of the dark moon and the full,
>
> The commonness of thought and image
> That have the frenzy of our western seas.

Robartes, who seeks perfect mystical annihilation, which he conceives to be the total vision, or not-vision, fails in the end to escape the common images of his own world and is thrust back among them. He reacts physically to the appearance of the eternal female. From Blake's point of view it is here that Robartes errs by failing to recognize the nonexistence of the material world to which he has returned. This world taken as an imaginative projection does exist. Annihilation through nirvana is not the answer.

The dancing body and spinning mind are really a unity creating a single mental state, a higher unity of all things. In "Among School Children" Yeats evokes this unity through image, but his method of statement, like Robartes' vision, is frustrating. He phrases his assertion as a question; and though the question implies a certain answer, the answer loses its visionary assurance.

> O chestnut-tree, great-rooted blossomer,
> Are you the leaf, the blossom or the bole?
> O body swayed to music, O brightening glance,
> How can we know the dancer from the dance? [58]

The drama of the poem is thus, as so often with Yeats, a searching battle with self.

But the lines do symbolize a complete equilibrium. In the movement or turn from death to birth there is no more soul than body, no more body than soul; both are one, one is both; thought is outdanced, "body perfection brought." Mind and body are caught in equilibrium like Robartes' image of the spinning top, where movement and not-movement seem to coincide. This is the mingled light of the intercourse of Ribh's angels. But for Ribh and for Robartes visions are phantoms. Time sweeps them away.

"The Double Vision" presents a kind of genealogy of the age to come, still a phantom because as yet unborn. "The Second Coming" presents the new age in its phantasmal form, a strange horrific image:

> Turning and turning in the widening gyre
> The falcon cannot hear the falconer;
> Things fall apart; the centre cannot hold;
> Mere anarchy is loosed upon the world,
> The blood-dimmed tide is loosed, and everywhere
> The ceremony of innocence is drowned;
> The best lack all conviction, while the worst
> Are full of passionate intensity.[59]

The opening lines create a hypnotic effect through rhythm—
"turning and turning in the widening"—and through visual
image. As we watch the falcon flying away in ever increasing
circles we tend to move in order to keep the falcon within our
visual field. An analogy is the movement of the top, suggested
in "The Double Vision." The top spins upright when it moves
at tremendous speed, but it wobbles when the speed decreases
so that to the eye it seems to fall apart. The falcon is no longer on
the falconer's wrist. This is the way of history too. The falcon on
the wrist is order, even revelation, like the whirling top in its
upright position or the dancer in mental and bodily equilibrium;
but the falcon circling in the sky is history moving toward some
new catastrophe. The falconer's wrist is thus the vortex of vision.
There the circling flight whirls to a center, the equilibrium of
the top itself when in its great speed it seems not to move at all.
But this moment of perfect balance, like Michael Robartes' re-
moval from time, is gone as soon as it comes, "the centre cannot
hold," anarchy and violence and war ensue.

In 1919, the date of the poem's composition, the falcon, according to Yeats, has moved out far beyond our control; and Yeats
comments briefly on man's political and spiritual state. Then suddenly it occurs to him that such violence and recklessness portends
some new revelation. What else but the Second Coming of Christ
predicted in the Bible? And yet when Yeats discloses exactly what
he sees in the mind's eye it is not the Second Coming at all. The
gap between expectation and actuality enforces the violence of
the image:

Surely some revelation is at hand;
Surely the Second Coming is at hand.
The Second Coming! Hardly are these words out
When a vast image out of *Spiritus Mundi*
Troubles my sight: somewhere in the sands of the desert
A shape with lion body and the head of a man,
A gaze blank and pitiless as the sun,
Is moving its slow thighs, while all about it
Reel shadows of the indignant desert birds.

The great beast emerges from that storehouse of images called "Spiritus Mundi," a sculpture from Los's Halls. Around it hover the carrion hunters, scavengers, vultures, the "passionless reasoners" of a dying civilization. These "indignant birds" are the apologists of an age at its nadir, where system has outlived passion and creation.* They bear the expression of the saint or angel in Byzantine ivory carving: "a look of some great bird staring at miracle." [60] In *A Vision,* Yeats writes:

My imagination was for a time haunted by figures that, muttering "The great systems," held out to me the sun-dried skeletons of birds, and it seemed to me that this image was meant to turn my thoughts to the living bird. That bird signifies truth when it eats, evacuates, builds its nest, engenders, feeds its young; do not all intelligible truths lie in its passage from egg to dust? [61]

The "indignant birds" are little different from the sun-dried skeletons, for they represent man become Urizen, man having succumbed to skeletal abstract thought. The living bird is the skeleton in its youth, and together the two form the cyclic pattern of history which "The Second Coming" dramatizes.

As the "darkness drops again" Yeats believes for a moment that he has attained to that same understanding of the pattern of past, present, and future, of which Blake's Ancient Bard boasts:

. . . but now I know
That twenty centuries of stony sleep

---

* Northrop Frye has suggested to me that the "horrible green birds" of Yeats's "On a Picture of a Black Centaur by Edmund Dulac" is related to these images. I shall discuss this in the section of Chapter IX entitled "Bird."

> Were vexed to nightmare by a rocking cradle,
> And what rough beast, its hour come round at last,
> Slouches towards Bethlehem to be born?

He has learned that we have been living in a cycle of twenty centuries during which the spiritual body of society has been asleep like Blake's Albion. Its activity has been suppressed rather than given the free rein of the waking spirit. This has lead to a violent revulsion in which the actual waking of the body seems gross and nightmarish, devoid of apocalyptic qualities. Suppression leads to its opposite, and the lion of violence devours the lamb of the cradle. In one respect, that which rocks in the cradle and that which slouches toward Bethlehem are different aspects of ourselves. In our stony sleep we have been rocked and tilted, swung like the tide between contraries and finally "vexed" to the creation of a new deity. But strangely this is all Yeats can tell us. The last two verses are phrased as a question. God's Chance intervenes before Yeats can make prediction. The rough beast is still a mystery.

"The Second Coming" creates a violence much like Blake's vision of the last day in *Europe:*

> The sun glow'd fiery red!
> The furious terrors flew around
> On golden chariots raging with red wheels dropping with blood!
> The Lions lash their wrathful tails!
> The Tigers couch upon the prey & suck the ruddy tide,
> And Enitharmon groans & cries in anguish and dismay.[62]

Yet there is an important difference. In Yeats's poem "the blood-dimmed tide is loosed" but not for any final battle, merely for the beginning of a new wheel. And though Yeats's poem suggests significant vision, that vision is strangely limited by the questioning of the poem's conclusion. Blake's major prophetic lyric, "The Tyger," ends with a question too, but that question is peculiarly rhetorical, the poem having provided the answer:

Tyger! Tyger! burning bright
In the forests of the night,
What immortal hand or eye
Could frame thy fearful symmetry?

In what distant deeps or skies
Burnt the fire of thine eyes?
On what wings dare he aspire?
What the hand dare sieze [*sic*] the fire?

And what shoulder, & what art,
Could twist the sinews of thy heart?
And when thy heart began to beat,
What dread hand? & what dread feet?

What the hammer? what the chain?
In what furnace was thy brain?
What the anvil? what dread grasp
Dare its deadly terrors clasp?

When the stars threw down their spears,
And water'd heaven with their tears,
Did he smile his work to see?
Did he who made the Lamb make thee?

Tyger! Tyger! burning bright
In the forests of the night,
What immortal hand or eye,
Dare frame thy fearful symmetry? [63]

The world of this poem is typically Blake's symbolical world. The tiger does not stand in the forests *in* the night. The forests belong *to* the night, the forces of darkness, the dream world of Albion. The tiger burns, suggesting simultaneously three visual images: the eyes of the tiger piercing through darkness like those of any cat; the tiger seen in the mind's eye in a glow of light, typical of symbolical religious art where the main figure seems to emerge from some vast supernatural glow; and the stripes of the tiger visualized as shooting flames, symbolical in Blake's painting of action, energy, purifying violence.

The tiger is a construction of the human imagination, a symbol, and Blake asks, "What immortal hand or eye" is capable of shaping such a form? The eye in Blake's thought is a shaping force symbolizing imagination; the preliminary answer to the question of the poem is that man himself shapes what he sees by means of his own powers of mental creation. But man, if he has created the tiger, is more than man as we usually think of him. If man's imagination has created the tiger, who has created the imagination? It is at this point that Yeats, dramatizing mystery, might have ended his poem: "Where got I that truth?" But Blake goes on to resolve his contraries. Does such a creature, he asks, come from "distant depths"—from some hell or underworld, from some hidden subconscious recess? Or does it come from the skies, from heaven, from somewhere out in space? Is the fire of the tiger's eyes some form of immediate truth, or is it a horrific image out of a collective unconscious, "the bright sculptures of Los's Halls"?

Blake asks what symbolical wings the person who created the tiger used in order to "aspire" to this terrible and violent understanding which the tiger itself signifies. Here he invokes by image a host of mythological heroes. He who seized the fire is, of course, Prometheus, who brings knowledge to man; and the tiger represents such knowledge or revelation. From stanzas three and four we learn that the creator and aspirant is evidently a blacksmith. And in stanza five, two obscure lines recall Blake's myth of the "wars of Eden," which he calls the fall. When the wars ended, did this creator smile upon his work? The creator referred to in this stanza is surely God, and we begin to see that the creation of the tiger, like Los's attempts to solidify and formalize the material world, is a movement toward apocalypse, that the blacksmith of "The Tyger" is equivalent to the Los of the prophetic books, and that both God and man are really one, just as the tiger and the lamb are really one in the world of eternity.

It is the Los in man—the worker, the aspirant, the imaginative power—that is capable of creating even in the delusory fallen world images like the tiger on the anvil of intuition. He creates an ideational reality where things may be seen as they really are. He is a fallen microcosm of God working in this world.

The tiger is itself a mirror image of man in his fallen state. He lives in a forest of darkness, a womb of nature. His identification and confrontation by Blake and Los is his symbolical leap from the forest into the light of day. In the prophetic books Blake says of man that he hides in the forests, and of the Eighth Eye of God that, "he came not, he hid in Albion's Forests." [64] When he is seen for what he is, he emerges into truth. The eye which frames the tiger is also the Eighth Eye of God—the symbol of apocalypse, the symbol of man's own visionary powers.

Blake's poem is a series of real questions only in a limited sense. If we take "The Tyger" as a poem spoken by a horrified Urizen, the questions betray Urizen's delusions. To Urizen, the apocalypse must be frightening and mysterious. Actually the answers to his questions are implicit in the formulations of the questions themselves. To the visionary, the poem is really a series of answers embodying Blake's whole apocalytic creed in one momentary experience. In it the poet strikes a tone of visionary frenzy and self-confidence. He, like Los facing Rahab, does not shrink from his task of confronting the terrifying delusion. In a letter, Blake once wrote: "I have travel'd thro' Perils & Darkness not unlike a Champion. I have Conquer'd, and shall Go on Conquering. Nothing can withstand the fury of my Course among the Stars of God & in the Abysses of the Accuser." [65]

The tiger stands as an image of apocalyptic light in a world of darkness; and although it is an awful light, it is the kind of light necessary in the battle with the forces of darkness, a light of energy and righteous wrath to be confronted without fear and even with a paradoxical joy.

In contrast to "The Tyger," Yeats's poem leaves us confront-

ing an unmistakable nameless terror which must be accepted un-
equivocally as terror to be endured. One must achieve a peculiar
psychological balance:

One of the sensations of my childhood was a description of a now
lost design of Nettleship's, "God Creating Evil," a vast terrifying
face, a woman and a tiger rising from the forehead. Why did it seem
so blasphemous and so profound? It was many years before I understood that we must not demand even the welfare of the human race.
nor traffic with divinity in our prayers. Divinity moves outside our
antinomies, it may be our lot to worship in terror: "Did He who
made the lamb make thee?" [66]

Though both Blake's and Yeats's view of history was cyclic, their
attitudes toward man's relation to the cycle were crucially different.

BLAKE, YEATS, AND HISTORY

In his lyrical prophecy "The Mental Traveller," Blake illustrated the central form of history and of all things by describing
what appears to be a never-ending cyclical conflict between an
archetypal male and female. Yeats also explained his wheel of
history in sexual terms:

A wheel of the Great Year must be thought of as the marriage of
symbolic Europe and symbolic Asia, the one begetting upon the
other. When it commenced at its symbolic full moon in March—
Christ or Christendom was begotten by the West upon the East.
This begetting has been followed by a spiritual predominance of
Asia. After it must come an age begotten by the East upon the West
that will take after its Mother in turn. [67]

The "completed symbol" of *A Vision* combined the gyres, or
joined opposites, and the circle:

All these symbols can be thought of as the symbols of the relations
of men and women and of the birth of children. . . . All the symbolism of the book applies to begetting birth, for all things are a
single form which has divided and multiplied in time and space. [68]

Yeats had in mind Blake's myth of division into spectre and emanation and especially "The Mental Traveller," a poem which had puzzled him for many years until the instructors had created similar metaphors for his own poetry.

Blake, in the Mental Traveller, describes a struggle, a struggle perpetually repeated between a man and a woman, and as the one ages, the other grows young. . . . When Edwin J. Ellis and I had finished our big book on the philosophy of William Blake, I felt we had no understanding of this poem: we had explained its details, for they occur elsewhere in his verse or his pictures, but not the poem as a whole, not the myth, the perpetual return of the same thing; not that which certainly moved Blake to write it; but when I had understood the double cones, I understood it also. The woman and man are two competing gyres growing at one another's expense, but with Blake it is not enough to say that one is beauty and one is wisdom, for he conceives this conflict as that in all love—whether between the elements as in Parmenides, "the wanton love" of Aristotle, or between man and woman—which compels each to be slave and tyrant by turn. In our system also it is a cardinal principle that anything separated from its opposite—and victory is separation— "consumes itself away." The existence of the one depends upon the existence of the other.[69]

In the 1938 *Vision*, Yeats showed that his symbolism of the Mask and the Body of Fate was similar to Blake's symbolism in the poem: "When my instructors see woman as man's goal and limit, rather than as mother, they symbolize her as *Mask* and *Body of Fate*, object of desire and object of thought, the one a perpetual rediscovery of what the other destroys." [70] Yeats was convinced that the student of *A Vision* would understand "The Mental Traveller" at once.

Before Yeats and Ellis had pondered the meaning of Blake's poem only W. M. Rossetti had grasped it as a whole. In his book on Blake, S. Foster Damon writes:

W. M. Rossetti came fairly near the fundamental idea of the poem, which, he said, "indicates an explorer of mental phænomena. The great phænomena here symbolized seems [*sic*] to be the career of any great idea, or intellectual movement—as, for instance, Christianity, chivalry, art, etc.—represented as going through the stages of (1) birth, (2) adversity and persecution, (3) triumph and (4) maturity, (5) decadence through over-ripeness, (6) gradual transformation, under new conditions, into another renovated Idea, which again has to pass through the same stages." [71]

Rossetti saw that the dominant form of this movement was organic. He saw that Blake applied the analogy of organism not only to growth of ideas but also to all movement in time, the central form of which is called history. In Blake's fallen world, space and time form into the Mundane Shell and the Circle of Destiny. Although the world of imagination is best symbolized as flat, the delusory space world seems to be a globe and time seems to be a cycle. "The Mental Traveller" is an exploration, as Rossetti says, of "mental phænomena" because the form of all things —history, space, and time—is mental.

The first-born babe of Blake's poem is an Orc spirit caught and held by an old woman or nature goddess. As the Orc grows older the old woman grows younger and eventually becomes Orc's mistress. Then Orc, gyring away toward Urizenic impotency, loses the control he has held over nature at the moment of sexual intercourse (Michael Robartes' "symbol of the solved antinomy"). After equilibrium the female moves backward to childhood and rebukes the hoary Orc, now become Urizen, and leaves him for another. At this point the flat earth of imagination becomes the globe of restriction. Then again Urizen is reborn as Orc, the now aged female principle nails him down, "and all is done as I have told." Here we have seen the birth, generation, new seed, and conflict which is the central form of history.

Strangely enough, "The Mental Traveller" presents only a picture of the Orc-Urizen cycle. There is apparently no linear teleology, no spiraling progress. The first stanza gives us the reason for its omission:

I travel'd thro' a Land of Men,
A Land of Men & Women too,
And heard & saw such dreadful things
As cold earth wanderers never knew.[72]

The Traveller is a visionary who has returned to eternity from the horrors of our own enclosed circle, where men are divided from women and are unable even to recognize that things are "dreadful." The delusion of determinism is all-powerful and the idea of spiritual progress is in decadence. "The Mental Traveller" pictures a fallen world, "a globe rolling through voidness."

When Yeats spoke of this poem in the first version of *A Vision*, he spoke of "the myth," the single pattern the poem displays; and he called the myth "the perpetual return of the same thing." [73] Yet the myth of the poem must include the Traveller himself, the visionary who comprehends delusion. The Mental Traveller finds his way out of the circle and affirms that man may discover something more than the "perpetual return of the same thing."

A purely cyclical theory of history dominated by the organic imagery of birth, growth, death, and birth seems to stand in direct opposition to the principle of Christian historical interpretation which has traditionally preached belief in a straight-line movement toward apocalypse—history as eschatology. In a recent study of the cyclic historian Oswald Spengler, H. Stuart Hughes finds the roots of the cyclic view of history far in the past, and he sees Spengler's adoption of the image of organism in his theory as the culmination of a rapid development in historical thought since the Middle Ages. Such a development marks a half-return to classical, secular thought:

By the time that Voltaire and Gibbon came to write their elegant attempts at a rationalistic interpretation of the past, the consciously Christian . . . structure remained. The outlook was still eschatological: the eighteenth-century historians sought out the purpose of man—and found it in his advance toward reason.[74]

But Blake's theory is not purely or literally cyclical, nor does progress either move toward or come about by means of reason. Blake thought that the modern age had maintained vestiges of Christian optimism without its substance, and he wished to re-affirm the substance in visionary form. He thought of himself as a reinterpreter of Christianity, asserting that the cycle whirls to a vortex instead of rolling endlessly in space. That is, one proceeds toward vision if one rejects the idea of history as a simple straight line for the idea of history as a cycle. But one *attains* to vision only when one sees time as a point.

The cyclic view was by no means a new idea; Blake thought it the oldest in the world, for he had come to believe that all mythologies told the cyclic story superimposed upon progression and climax. Even the medieval historian, Joachim de Flora (1145–1202)—the same monk discovered by Owen Aherne—had developed a system of perpetual correspondences between the Old and New Testaments, and he saw those similar acts being renewed in our own cycle of history. Joachim was a kind of model for modern cyclical theorists, and Spengler speaks of him with reverence.[75] Yet Spengler saw no progress, no vortex, no apocalypse.

It is not surprising to discover that Yeats mentions Spengler in *A Vision:*

When in 1926 the English translation of Spengler's book came out, some weeks after *A Vision* [1925], I found that not only were dates that I had been given the same as his but whole metaphors and symbols that had seemed my work alone.[76]

And of the instructors Yeats wrote:

They drew their first symbolical map of that history, and marked upon it the principal years of crisis, early in July 1918, some days before the publication of the first German edition of Spengler's *Decline of the West,* which, though founded upon a different philosophy, gives the same years of crisis and draws the same general conclusions.[77]

Like Yeats, Spengler vehemently attacked the idea of progress, proposed a cyclic view without the paradoxical spiritual evolution. His world was totally deterministic:

> It will no doubt be objected that such a world-outlook, which in giving this certainty as to the outlines and the tendency of the future cuts off all far-reaching hopes, would be unhealthy for all and fatal for many, once it ceased to be a mere theory and was adopted as a practical scheme of life by the group of personalities effectively moulding the future.
>
> Such is not my opinion. We are civilized, not Gothic or Rococo, people; we have to reckon with the hard cold facts of a *late* life, to which the parallel is to be found not in Pericles's Athens but in Caesar's Rome. Of great painting or great music there can no longer be, for Western people, any question. Their architectural possibilities have been exhausted these hundred years. Only *extensive* possibilities are left to them. Yet, for a sound and vigorous generation that is filled with unlimited hopes, I fail to see that it is any disadvantage to discover betimes that some of these hopes must come to nothing. And if the hopes thus doomed should be those most dear, well, a man who is worth anything will not be dismayed. It is true that the issue may be a tragic one for some individuals who in their decisive years are overpowered by the conviction that in the spheres of architecture, drama, painting there is nothing left for *them* to conquer. What matter if they do go under! [78]

In spite of its Yeatsian pattern, Spengler's melodramatic, pessimistic theory militates against important Yeatsian assertions of mystery and becomes the dreaded positivism Yeats so hated. In Yeats's system, if there is apparently no progress in history, there is at least the impingement of mystery which moves beyond antinomy and cries occasionally to time-borne man. These flashes of insight allow man to synthesize the many reflections of mystery into a nondiscursive vision, which paradoxically by a kind of denial affirms spirituality and eternity. Unlike Spengler, Yeats recognized that the future remains a mystery susceptible to God's Chance. It is true that Yeats sometimes suggested that his system would make predictions of events possible, but as he grew older these propositions became a mask for an attitude in direct opposition to them. The poet tried to be not a prognosticator but a seer, not what Blake called an "arbitrary dictator" of future events but a prophet. But among poets there are finally two kinds of prophets, the prophet of resolution and the prophet of irresolution, for poets may choose (if it is their choice) between two points of view. The negative prophet may make what appears to be a denial of prophecy, if one thinks of prophecy as apocalyptic vision. Nevertheless this negative statement is extremely valuable as an intuition of human life, for it may dramatize in its own poignant fashion man's own dilemma and his striving. Therefore, though Yeats's Ribh, for example, seems never to achieve Blake's prophetic clarity of vision, as a character in a poem he acts out man's striving and tells us what that striving means. Because Yeats's poetry is often negative prophecy (but still prophecy) the positive prophets of his poems are madmen or fools. Because Blake was a positive prophet the positive prophets of his poems are not madmen or fools. To call Blake a madman, as some have done, would not, however, assure the accuser of a place among negative prophets. It would probably place him entirely outside the realm of prophets. To call a man a madman in prose is far different from calling him one in poetry.

In Yeats's later poetry and in the 1938 *Vision*, prediction gives way to negative prophecy. In the 1925 *Vision*, Yeats had included a short prediction, not of particular events but of their pattern, based on the pattern of the past. But again the pattern moves beyond human comprehension: "This much can be thought because it is the reversal of what we know, but those kindreds once formed must obey irrational force and so create hitherto unknown experience, or that which is incredible."

In another discarded climax for the history section of *A Vision*, Michael Robartes admits that for the future all must be deduced from "our cones and symbols." [79] In the final edition of *A Vision*, all prediction was deleted and a new climax written. If the old predictions even obliquely suggested that the system gave Yeats the ability to predict pseudoscientifically and dogmatically, the final edition finally wiped away all such suggestion. In the introduction Yeats wrote:

Some will ask whether I believe in the actual existence of my circuits of sun and moon. Those that include, now all recorded time in one circuit, now what Blake called the "pulsaters [*sic*] of an artery," are plainly symbolical, but what of those that fixed, like a butterfly upon a pin, to our central date, the first day of our Era, divide actual history into periods of equal length? To such a question I can but answer that if sometimes, overwhelmed by miracle as all men must be when in the midst of it, I have taken such periods literally, my reason has soon recovered; and now that the system stands out clearly in my imagination I regard them as stylistic arrangements of experience comparable to the cubes in the drawings of Wyndham Lewis and to the ovoids in the sculpture of Brancusi. They have helped me to hold in a single thought reality and justice.[80]

Again Yeats has dramatized his own conflict between hopes for knowledge and understanding of the existence of mystery. When hopes are high he may muse on possibility: "What if there is an arithmetic that can exactly measure the balance, the dip of the scale?" Again, "Will some mathematician some day question and understand, as I cannot, and confirm all, or have I also dealt in myth?"

In the final edition of *A Vision*, the discussion of history ends on an abrupt note:

I am filled with excitement. I think of recent mathematical research; even the ignorant can compare it with that of Newton—so plainly of the 19th Phase—with its objective world intelligible to the intellect; I can recognise that the limit itself has become a new dimension, that this ever-hidden thing which makes us fold our hands has begun to press down upon the multitudes. Having bruised their hands upon that limit, men, for the first time since the seventeenth century, see the world as an object of contemplation, not as something to be remade, and some few, meeting the limit in their special study, even doubt the possibility of science.[81]

Yeats finally rejected prediction. The story of the incredible
appearance of the instructors with their words of wisdom is the
story of the vacillation of Yeats's hopes and his own understanding of the meaning of the knowledge given to him. When we
read the last page of *A Vision*, we know that Yeats's own hands
have been bruised upon the limits of Blake's Mundane Shell. The
note is one of pathos. It ends, the counterpart of Yeats's farce
"The Herne's Egg":

> All that trouble and nothing to show for it,
> Nothing but just another donkey.[82]

These lines from the play are strange self-satire. In *A Vision*,
Yeats is again alone, the thinker in the lonely tower:

Day after day I have sat in my chair turning a symbol over in my
mind, exploring all its details, defining and again defining its elements, testing my convictions and those of others by its unity, attempting to substitute particulars for an abstraction like that of
algebra. I have felt the convictions of a lifetime melt though at an
age when the mind should be rigid, and others take their place, and
these in turn give way to others. . . . Then I draw myself up into
the symbol and it seems as if I should know all if I could but banish
such memories and find everything in the symbol.

II

But nothing comes—though this moment was to reward me for all
my toil. Perhaps I am too old. Surely something would have come
when I meditated under the direction of the Cabalists. What dis-
cords will drive Europe to that artificial unity—only dry or drying
sticks can be tied into a bundle—which is the decadence of every
civilisation? How work out upon the phases the gradual coming and
increase of the counter movement, the *antithetical* multiform influx:

> Should Jupiter and Saturn meet,
> O what a crop of mummy wheat!

Then I understand. I have already said all that can be said. The particulars are the work of the *thirteenth sphere* or cycle which is in
every man and called by every man his freedom. Doubtless, for it
can do all things and knows all things, it knows what it will do with
its own freedom but it has kept the secret.[83]

In the climax of Yeats's play "The Hour Glass," the Wise Man speaks before he dies:

> The stream of the world has changed its course,
> And with the stream my thoughts have run
> Into some cloudy thunderous spring
> That is its mountain source—
> Aye, to some frenzy of the mind,
> For all that we have done's undone,
> Our speculation but as the wind.[84]

And as he dies, the fool who holds the secret and has kept it from him tells him he will disclose it for a penny. But it is too late:

Wise Man—Wise Man, wake up and I will tell you everything for a penny. It is I, poor Teigue the Fool. Why don't you wake up, and say, "There is a penny for you, Teigue"? No, No, you will say nothing. You and I, we are the two fools, we know everything but we will not speak.[85]

Ironically, in tragedy, in apparent hopelessness, in the frustration of continual beating against the wall, Yeats and the Wise Man have gained a kind of knowledge. It is a knowledge arrived at through wonder, a knowledge both enriched and limited by sudden realization.

That which Yeats calls "man's freedom," the work of the "thirteenth sphere" is purposely obscure. It will be discussed in Chapter IX. For the present it is enough to say that the sphere symbolizes a freedom harboring complete possibility:

> There all the barrel-hoops are knit,
> There all the serpent-tails are bit,
> There all the gyres converge in one,
> There all the planets drop in the Sun.[86]

CHAPTER IX

Personality

I must lie down where all the ladders start,
In the foul rag-and-bone shop of the heart.
—W. B. YEATS [1]

IN THE face of the rise and fall of civilizations and of men, even of his own friends, Yeats sought to express his concept of heroic personality, ravaged by old age, led on and yet frustrated by momentary visions, terrorized by world-shaking or soul-shaking events. In "The Hour Glass," Yeats's Wise Man says that truth itself is the product of violence; the appearance of truth to the single man is a figurative ascension of Christ from the broken sepulcher, a renewal of the phoenix, an apocalyptic shattering of Blake's great egg:

> Only in spiritual terror can the Truth
> Come through the broken mind—as the pease burst
> Out of a broken pease-cod. [2]

Over and over again the images of Yeats's poems suggest such mysterious moments of intense passion. These moments Yeats characterizes as the completion of "a partial mind." [3] The man we see is only the partial man. Man striving for knowledge is man striving for completion of self in a communal unity of all men:

Before the mind's eye whether in sleep or waking came images that one was to discover presently in some book one had never read, and after looking in vain for an explanation to the current theory of forgotten personal memory, I came to believe in a great memory passing on from generation to generation. But that was not enough, for these images showed intention and choice. They had a relation to what one knew and yet were an extension of one's knowledge. If no mind was there, why should I suddenly come upon salt and antimony upon the liquefaction of gold, as they were understood by the alchemists, or upon some detail of cabalistic symbolism verified at last by a learned scholar from his never published manuscripts, and who can have put together so ingeniously, working by some law of association and yet with clear intention and personal application, certain mythological images. They had shown themselves to several minds, a fragment at a time, and had only shown their meaning when the puzzle picture had been put together. The thought was again and again before me that this study had created a contact or mingling with minds who had followed a like study in some other age, and that these minds still saw and thought and chose. Our daily thought was certainly but the line of foam at the shallow edge of a vast luminous sea.[4]

Yeats sees such a unity symbolized, in the temporal world, in many images which are central to his symbolic structure and correspond to certain Blakean images.

MASK AND DAIMON

Two important Yeatsian images are the Mask and the Daimon. The Mask is really more than one image. It is the self man discloses to others, a social weapon. For the writer, style itself is a mask: "Style, personality—deliberately adopted and therefore a mask—is the only escape from the hot-faced bargainers and the money changers."[5] Poetry embodies the Mask in another way too: "If a man is to write lyric poetry he must be shaped by nature and art to some one out of half a dozen traditional poses, and be lover or saint, sage or sensualist, or mere mocker of all life." [6] The poet speaks through characters like Ribh, Robartes, and Aherne or identifies himself with one of his characters, as Blake identified himself with Los. Usually the poet mixes these two techniques and achieves a dramatic tension:

If we cannot imagine ourselves as different from what we are and assume the second self, we cannot impose a discipline upon ourselves, though we may accept one from others. Active virtue as distinguished from the passive acceptance of a current code is therefore theatrical, consciously dramatic, the wearing of a mask. It is the condition of arduous full life. [7]

By wearing the Mask, the poet achieves an equilibrium of style and a passion of expression.

Beyond the practical meaning of the Mask there is a more complex but related meaning. In *A Vision* the Mask is the object of Will, the "ought" of things, the idea of the good, the object of desire. It is thus related to those concepts which flicker far back in the "vast luminous sea" of the mind. Yeats's instructors symbolize woman as man's Mask when she is the object of desire. [8] Thus the physical and mental worlds are by analogy interchangeable, the one symbolizing the other.

The image which Yeats calls the Daimon (sometimes Daemon or Demon) is related to the Mask.* In *Per Amica Silentia Lunae* he characterizes the Daimon as the opposite of each man. "Man and Daimon feed the hunger of one another's hearts." [9] In *A Vision* he suggests that the Daimons of all men are related to one another. Perhaps they are ultimately one.

Memory is a series of judgments and such judgments imply a reference to something that is not memory, that something is the *Daimon*, which contains within it, co-existing in its eternal moment, all the events of our life, all that we have known of other lives, or that it can discover within itself of other *Daimons*. [10]

* In his published prose Yeats spelled the word "Daimon." In many typescripts he spelled it "Daemon" or "Demon." In the poems it is spelled "Demon." The Daimon of the prose is a less concrete visualization than the Demon of the poems. Perhaps the spellings are supposed to accentuate this difference.

The Daimon is a peculiar Yeatsian *élan vital*, which out of time inhabits the deep sea of images man seeks to fathom again and again when he is released into sleep; and the Mask is a partial adoption in time of the Daimon, an imperfect completion of self by means of style, personality, and the social weapons:

I think that all happiness depends upon the energy to assume the mask of some other self; that all joyous or creative life is a re-birth as something not oneself, something which has no memory and is created in a moment and perpetually renewed.[11]

The instructors of *A Vision* acted as Yeats's Daimons. They were continually reminding Yeats that their thoughts came with a speed incomprehensible to the time-borne human:

All things are present as an eternal instant to our *Daimon* (or *Ghostly Self* as it is called, when it inhabits the sphere), but that instant is unintelligible to all bound to the antinomies. My instructors have therefore followed the tradition by substituting for it a *Record* where the images of all past events remain for ever "thinking the thought and doing the deed." They are in popular mysticism called "the pictures in the astral light," a term that became current in the middle of the nineteenth century, and what Blake called "the bright sculptures of Los's Halls." [12]

The eternal instant is Blake's vortex, the caught motion of the "bright sculptures." Those who struggle in antinomy symbolize it as the "needle's eye" or the point of the gyre. To experience such a moment is to achieve the whirling not-whirl of mental or bodily perfection symbolized by the dancer. These symbols are in themselves, from Yeats's point of view, somewhat imperfect:

The soul cannot have much knowledge till it has shaken off the habit of time and place, but till that hour it must fix attention upon what is near, thinking of objects one after another as we run the eye or finger over them. Its intellectual power cannot but increase and alter as its perceptions grow simultaneous. Yet even now we seem at moments to escape from time in what we call prevision and from place when we see distant things in a dream and in concurrent dreams.[13]

Yeats vacillates in his attitude toward the reality of all images, both of thought and perception. He is not always sure that reality is capable of symbolization at all and that all of his thought is not the product of Daimonic frustration. He does think, however, that there is some kind of immanent reality which is experiential—the unintelligible instant:

> For certain moments at the least
> That crafty demon and that loud beast
> That plague me day and night
> Ran out of my sight;
> Though I had long perned in the gyre,
> Between my hatred and desire,
> I saw my freedom won
> And all laugh in the sun.[14]

He achieves a gyre vortex long enough to rid himself of his inner conflict and to become one with his Ghostly Self. But he cannot hold to the moment:

> Yet I am certain as can be
> That every natural victory
> Belongs to beast or demon,
> That never had freeman
> Right mastery of natural things,
> And that mere growing old, that brings
> Chilled blood, this sweetness brought.

When it is over, he is caught in the web of rationalization and must define and kill the subjective experience: "I begin to study the only self that I can know, myself, and to wind the thread upon the perne again." [15] All through life man stands between Demon and Beast, soul and body, Mask and Will.

In *A Vision*, Yeats symbolizes this personal war of opposites by dividing the life of man into twenty-eight moon phases. Each man, to begin with, is of a certain type, symbolized by one of the phases; but he moves through all phases during his lifetime, his type in perpetual conflict with time, his soul in perpetual conflict with his temporal self. He also finds himself in conflict with the phase of history into which he has been born. An example is Maud Gonne, the Irish patriot with whom Yeats was for many years in love:

> What could have made her peaceful with a mind
> That nobleness made simple as a fire,
> With beauty like a tightened bow, a kind
> That is not natural in an age like this,
> Being high and solitary and most stern?
> Why, what could she have done, being what she is?
> Was there another Troy for her to burn? [16]

Led naturally by her Daimon, she is frustrated by the conflict between her own personality and the world about her. Yeats thinks that every man and woman has a myth ("an activity of the Daimon"), "which, if we but knew it, would make us understand all that he did or thought." [17] For Yeats the myth of Maud Gonne is the myth of Leda and Helen:

> Why should I blame her that she filled my days
> With misery, or that she would of late
> Have taught to ignorant men most violent ways,
> Or hurled the little streets upon the great.

She is driven by Daimon to act the myth in a historical period antithetical to her own nature.

Other Yeatsian types are the saint and the fool. The saint and fool phases come at the very close of life. Of all people, the saints and the fools are closest to joining self and Mask, Beast and Demon. Yeatsian fools such as Crazy Jane and Old Tom are strangely sage, but they speak in an obscure symbolism:

> Things out of perfection sail,
> And all their swelling canvas wear,
> Nor shall the self-begotten fail
> Though fantastic men suppose
> Building-yard and stormy shore,
> Winding-sheet and swaddling-clothes.[18]

In the light of the symbolism of Blake, whose madness had its method, the fool's words have meaning. "Swaddling-clothes" and "stormy shore" are images of the material and natural world. The "winding-sheet," an image from Gray's "Bard," which fascinated Blake, represents the death image that all material suggests. The "fantastic men" are "Bacon, Newton, Locke." The self-begotten are the fools themselves who have joined with Daimons come "out of perfection."

Yeats's fools have attained to Mask; the only Mask left for them to achieve is oblivion itself. This state has a certain terrible beauty to those outside of it.

Aherne: You speak constantly of beauty. I do not understand your definition.

Robartes: Only the symbolism is considered authoritative by the Arabs but various communicators have made definitions. To Kusta ben Luka it is Energy in its greatest extension, while a commentary of the 16th century says that entire beauty is the form or image of any life, or condition of soul which has attained to entire solitude.[19]

The Yeatsian "terrible beauty" is "complete energy" consumed in the vortex whirl of entire solitude.

> What matter that you understood no word!
> Doubtless I spoke or sang what I had heard
> In broken sentences. My soul had found
> All happiness in its own cause or ground.[20]

It is the third stage of mystical annihilation called *Shushupti:* "a complete disappearance of all but this identity. Nothing exists but . . . that beauty; the man has disappeared as the sculptor in his statue, the musician in his music." [21] Of the fool phase Yeats wrote:

At his worst his hands and feet and eyes, his will and his feelings, obey obscure subconscious fantasies, while at his best he would know all wisdom if he could know anything. The physical world suggests to his mind pictures that have no relation to his needs or even to his desires.[22]

This is the real innocence, the attainment to equilibrium and visionary rapture. It is no wonder that the word "innocent" means also "fool" and that the real wisemen of our poetry are so often the fools, that man returns to a new Blakean innocence in its visionary form after he has traveled through the realm of experience.

BIRD

When I came home: on the abyss of the five senses, where a flat sided steep frowns over the present world, I saw a mighty Devil folded in black clouds, hovering on the sides of the rock: with corroding fires he wrote the following sentence now perceived by the minds of men, & read by them on earth:

How do you know but ev'ry Bird that cuts the airy way,
Is an immense world of delight, clos'd by your senses five? [23]

So writes Blake in *The Marriage of Heaven and Hell*, predicting the meaning of the bird symbol which appears over and over again in Yeats's poetry. If man's soul, as Yeats says, "has not thrown off the habit of time and space," he must keep his attention on what is near and perceptible, for his only links with reality are those things he sees or thinks.[24] For Blake, if one looks correctly, the bird seen is immediately the world of delight. For Yeats, locked in the preposterous natural world, the bird is a symbol of mystery. It also symbolizes the strange subjectivity and solitude to which fools and mystics attain.

Certain birds, especially as I see things, such lonely birds as the heron, hawk, eagle, and swan, are the natural symbols of subjectivity, especially when floating upon the wind alone. Or alighting upon some pool or river, while the beasts that run upon the ground, especially those that run in parks, are the natural symbols of objective man.[25]

The Yeatsian bird, the bird cry, and related images lead us to the very center of Yeats's symbolic structure and recall other images previously mentioned. As symbol of subjectivity the Yeatsian bird plays many parts. It may be a symbol of something in the mind; it may symbolize something which the mind cannot fully grasp. It may trouble the mind; it may act as the anti-self, Mask, or Daimon; it often half suggests the part of being toward which man strives. As a white gull it may be a death symbol. As a swan it may represent the supernatural or God.

Yeats's early bird symbols are not intentionally complex. In "The White Birds" his gull represents death and rebirth. In "The Indian to His Love" the raging parrot is a symbol of self-entrancement foreshadowing conflicting search for Mask and Daimon; its cry breaks the tranquillity of the tropic island. In the later poetry, however, the bird symbol has greater nondiscursive significance. Professor Donald Stauffer called the bird cry in Yeats's poems "an emblem of instinctive passionate unthinking life that breaks the trance of eternity," but this is not a fully accurate description.[26] The raging parrot, for instance, breaks "the trance of eternity," but represents the thinking life; more often the bird cry represents a "passionate unthinking" moment which, rather than breaking "the trance of eternity," breaks into time *from* eternity as a symbol of momentary vision, a natural image of Daimonic power.

An excellent example, from "The Hour Glass," is the frenzied vision of the Wise Man just before his death.

Wise Man: Twice have I dreamed it in a morning dream,
Now nothing serves my pupils but to come
With a like thought. Reason is growing dim;
A moment more and Frenzy will beat his drum
And laugh aloud and scream;
And I must dance in the dream.
No, no, but it is like a hawk, a hawk of the air,
It has swooped down—and this swoop makes the third—
And what can I, but tremble like a bird.[27]

As the Wise Man dances into vision, Daimon comes to him in the guise of a hawk, and the man himself becomes by simile a bird.

In each poem the bird image has a unique quality. Here is the image again in "A Memory of Youth":

> We sat as silent as a stone,
> We knew, though she'd not said a word,
> That even the best of love must die,
> And had been savagely undone
> Were it not that Love upon the cry
> Of a most ridiculous little bird
> Tore from the clouds his marvellous moon.[28]

Here the cry suddenly averts, on the very brink, a climax of psychological and social disaster; it preserves a precarious balance between happiness and despair, changing the pace of the whole poem. The cry is something hard and cold within the Will that saves the actors of the poem from a mawkish mental death. Since Yeats himself is one of the actors, the bird cry gives Yeats, as poet, an opportunity to castigate Yeats, as actor in the poem, for a cloying sentimentality.

The bird may act as Yeats's desires, or as some lost desire which impinges upon the present moment, the appearance of an image from the subconscious, something within the mind which, forming a dramatic tension, may flow between two minds:

> He: Never until this night have I been stirred.
> The elaborate starlight throws a reflection
> On the dark stream,
> Till all the eddies gleam;
> And thereupon there comes that scream
> From terrified, invisible beast or bird:
> Image of poignant recollection.
>
> She: An image of my heart that is smitten through.[29]

The idea, emerging from "Spiritus Mundi," takes form in this world as an image from another life.

In the short poem "Paudeen" the cry of a curlew and the answer of another high in the wind symbolizes for Yeats the perfect joining of the two selves, the momentary wonder of complete harmony:

> . . . and suddenly thereupon I thought
> That on the lonely height where all are in God's eye,
> There cannot be, confusion of our sound forgot,
> A single soul that lacks a sweet crystalline cry.[30]

The bird cry or the "sweet crystalline cry" is a microcosmic apocalyptic trumpet note, but it is always "an unintelligible instant" charged with mystery, like that of "Stream and Sun at Glendalough":

> What motion of the sun or stream
> Or eyelid shot the gleam
> That pierced my body through?
> What made me live like these that seem
> Self-born, born anew? [31]

There are other moments, too, when the bird becomes that same strange hawk which swooped on the Wise Man of "The Hour Glass":

> "What tumbling cloud did you cleave,
> Yellow-eyed hawk of the mind,
> Last evening? that I, who had sat
> Dumbfounded before a knave,
> Should give to my friend
> A pretence of wit." [32]

The hawk is something within the mind, but it is only half understood, not consciously controlled. It may be that it represents the "freedom" of which Yeats speaks in the conclusion to *A Vision* or an "uncontrollable mystery." Man in the face of this troubling aspect of self (his Mask) seems but a pawn, just as Cuchulain is a pawn of the hawk woman in "At the Hawk's Well." This bird-woman-deity as an image of physical desire symbolizes also intellectual search. As a supernatural incarnation the Morrigu is the antinomy solved in death, the object of quest. It is she who remains when Cuchulain is beheaded in the last play of the Cuchulain series. Before his death Cuchulain visualizes his own future form, a shape which would make possible the fulfillment of his desire for the hawk woman:

> . . . There floats out there
> The shape that I shall take when I am dead,
> My soul's first shape, a soft feathery shape,
> And is not that a strange shape for the soul
> Of a great fighting-man? [33]

Emer, Cuchulain's wife, who appears after his death to perform the traditional Yeatsian Salome dance previous to the new cycle, rages against the killers of Cuchulain. To her and to the audience the bird notes from offstage, heard in silence, are momentary deities with nondiscursive meaning. The concluding stage direction:

She then moves towards the head of Cuchulain; it may, if need be, be raised above others on a pedestal. She moves as if in adoration or triumph. She is about to prostrate herself before it, perhaps does so, then rises, looking up as if listening; she seems to hesitate between the head and what she hears. Then she stands motionless. There is silence, and in the silence a few faint bird notes.[34]

This, for Emer, is the moment of tension, when she is led to the brink of comprehension. Here the bird cry may be the sound of troubling frustrators like those of *A Vision,* or it may be the voice of Cuchulain himself, freed from antinomy.

The bird image with its related meanings is suggested by the short poem "An Irish Airman Foresees His Death." Something beyond or deep within the mind, which embodies the characteristic perfect solitude of the bird, takes the hero to the sky and to death:

> A lonely impulse of delight
> Drove to this tumult in the clouds.[35]

The strange, indescribable urge is the Daimon driving man to bird flight. The flight itself—man attained to dancelike equilibrium—is a vision of solved antinomies and death:

> I balanced all, brought all to mind,
> The years to come seemed waste of breath,
> A waste of breath the years behind
> In balance with this life, this death.

The airman achieves a vortex of timeless vision between past and future where present is really eternity.

Other images of sound and sight have significance similar to the bird images. "In Memory of Major Robert Gregory" contains an image of sound:

> Lionel Johnson comes the first to mind,
> That loved his learning better than mankind,
> Though courteous to the worst; much falling he
> Brooded upon sanctity
> Till all his Greek and Latin learning seemed
> A long blast upon the horn that brought
> A little nearer to his thought
> A measureless consummation that he dreamed.[36]

Like the notes from Wagnerian opera, the horn device performs a simple magical incantation just as it does in Yeats's early poem "The Ballad of the Foxhunter," where the dying hunter asks a friend to blow one final blast:

> "Huntsman Rody, blow the horn,
> Make the hills reply."
> The huntsman loosens on the morn
> A gay wandering cry.[37]

Here, in the early poem, the image suggests little more than vague nostalgia, while in the later elegy it symbolizes the momentary vision. Such visions, or Daimons, are the real causes of heroic actions. Along with the Irish Airman, the martyrs of the Easter Rebellion exemplify men moved to action by Daimon. Their Daimon—the myth which every man has could we but know it—is Cuchulain, the legendary Irish hero. They join with him to achieve, in the words of "Easter 1916," a "terrible beauty," born of some nameless "impulse of delight." Here are lines from "The Death of Cuchulain":

> Are those things that men adore and loathe
> Their sole reality?
> What stood in the Post Office
> With Pearse and Connolly?
> What comes out of the mountain
> Where men first shed their blood?
> Who thought Cuchulain till it seemed
> He stood where they had stood? [38]

Yeats refers here to the Dublin General Post Office, garrison of the patriots. A statue of Cuchulain, erected in memory of these rebels, now stands in the lobby. Cuchulain is strapped to a tree and about to die, and on his shoulder a black bird has come to rest. Just as the myth of Helen and Leda is the myth of Maud Gonne, so is the myth of Cuchulain the myth of the Easter heroes.

But if for each man there is a true myth, a true Daimon, and a true Mask, there is also a false myth, Daimon, and Mask. Blake, whom Yeats classified in phase 16 of his system, is characterized as follows:

Will—The Positive Man.
Mask (from Phase 2). *True*—Illusion. *False*—Delusion.
Creative Mind (from Phase 14). *True*—Vehemence. *False*—Opinionated will.
Body of Fate (from Phase 28)—Enforced Illusion. [39]

Yeats tells us that a man of phase 16 has a Body of Fate from the phase of the fool (phase 28) and a Mask from "what might have been called the phase of the Child," phase 2.

Phase 16 . . . finds within itself an aimless excitement. This excitement, and this dream, are both illusions, so that the *Will*, which is itself a violent scattering energy, has to use its intellect (*Creative*

Mind) to discriminate between illusions. They are both illusions, because, so small is the *primary* nature, sense of fact is an impossibility. If it use its intellect, which is the most narrow, the most unflinching, even the most cruel possible to man, to disengage the aimless child (*i.e.* to find *Mask* and Image in the child's toy), it finds the soul's most radiant expression and surrounds itself with some fairyland, some mythology of wisdom or laughter. . . .

If, however, it subordinate its intellect to the *Body of Fate*, all the cruelty and narrowness of that intellect are displayed in service of preposterous purpose after purpose till there is nothing left but the fixed idea and some hysterical hatred.[40]

Any assumption of a false Mask by Blake would have amounted to an abdication of visionary power and a setting out after delusion. Blake's true Mask is Los, his false Mask, Orc.

[Men of phase 16] produce the comedy of Aretino and of Rabelais or the mythology of Blake, and discover symbolism to express the overflowing and bursting of the mind. There is always an element of frenzy, and almost always a delight in certain glowing or shining images of concentrated force: in the smith's forge; in the heart; in the human form in its most vigorous development; in the solar disc; in some symbolical representation of the sexual organs; for the being must brag of its triumph over its own incoherence.[41]

Yeats's description of men of phase 16 accurately weighs what logically seem the two possible directions in which a personality such as Blake's must move—toward a "mythology of wisdom" or a "preposterous purpose." But, ironically, Yeats's system fails to give the rationalist any means of determining from the evidence which way the personality in question did, in fact, move. To the rationalist a "mythology of wisdom" *is* the creation of "preposterous purpose." An answer to the important question cannot be formulated rationalistically.

Yeats classified himself in phase 17:

[The intellect of a man of phase 17] finds, not the impassioned myth that Phase 16 found, but a *Mask* of simplicity that is also intensity. This *Mask* may represent intellectual or sexual passion. . . .[42]

Yeats's Mask and Daimon are, it is true, images of intellectual or sexual desire particularized in beasts, birds, "instructors," and women. This group of images corresponds to Blake's spectres and emanations, which are particularized by his divided mythical figures. An example is Urthona, divided in the fallen world into the intellectual Los and the female form, Enitharmon, who in turn is capable of distortion and appearance to Los in the spectral forms of Rahab and Vala, or the image of visionary desire, Jerusalem. The difference in handling this archetypal cluster of imagery lies in point of view. Yeats's spectral figures are always powerful and often apparently benevolent, if capricious. They are always mysterious because (as Blake would see Yeats's poetry) they are being viewed by their opposite spectral half, with no full realization on the viewer's part that this is the case. Blake's images of division are viewed from a position in which unity is accepted as the reality and division as the delusion. Yeats's attitude, though intellectually with Blake, is emotionally ambivalent, caught in the tension between spectre and emanation.

Since for Yeats there are true and false Masks, there are also true and false birds. In "On a Picture of a Black Centaur by Edmund Dulac" the "horrible green birds" represent the delusory dangers of a life of imagination once it is released from the elemental world of things. Such a release is but another flying off into the dark world of abstraction and the mill of the mind. The centaur of the poem, which can be taken to represent Yeats's art (being a combination of the elemental and fabulous worlds) can act as guard against the assumption of a false Mask. The "indignant desert birds" of "The Second Coming" are the false Masks of a dying civilization.

The final and perhaps most important of Yeats's bird symbols is, of course, the swan, symbolizing, as we have seen, sometimes Godhead, sometimes the human soul. The most beautiful and solitary of birds, it can evoke the most intense reaction:

At sudden thunder of the mounting swan
I turned about and looked where branches break
The glittering reaches of the flooded lake.

Another emblem there! That stormy white
But seems a concentration of the sky;
And, like the soul, it sails into the sight
And in the morning's gone, no man knows why;
And is so lovely that it sets to right
What knowledge or its lack had set awry,
So arrogantly pure, a child might think
It can be murdered with a spot of ink.[43]

The beautiful swan in the air is a symbol of unity between man's soul and his work. It possesses the solitary coldness Yeats sought in his own art; it suggests the heroic personality in the face of change.

All strange human revelation is thus figuratively the bird or the cry of a bird, symbol from some great unknown "clos'd by [our] senses five." Even the great vortexes of history, like the swan's annunciation to Leda, take the bird as symbol.

A civilization is a struggle to keep self-control, and in this it is like some great tragic person, some Niobe who must display an almost superhuman will or the cry will not touch our sympathy. The loss of control over thought comes towards the end; first a sinking in upon the moral being, then the last surrender, the irrational cry, revelation—the scream of Juno's peacock.[44]

On September 6, 1921, Yeats wrote to Sturge Moore in regard to a cover design the latter was doing for one of his books:

My dear Moore:
I am sorry for it would make a fine design but don't nail the hawk on the board. The hawk is one of my symbols and you might rather crudely upset the subconsciousness. It might mean nightmare or something of the kind for some of us here. Life when one does my kind of work is rather strange.[45]

If one myth is necessary to every man, perhaps Yeats's myth is that of the bird.

ARTIFICE

The heroes of the Easter Rebellion have joined figuratively with their Daimon; in a sense they have become their own myth, they have created the old Irish legend anew. Yeats thinks of them now as statues; and in "The Statues" he asks:

> When Pearse summoned Cuchulain to his side,
> What stalked through the Post Office? What intellect,
> What calculation, number, measurement, replied? [46]

Pearse, Connolly, and the others have become Cuchulain, whom Yeats associates with the statue standing in the Post Office. But more than that they have become legendary symbols; they have taken their places among Blake's "bright sculptures of Los's halls." Yet how all of this happened is still a mystery. The lines above are again the typical Yeatsian question. The stalking statue-figure creates an impression of "terrible beauty." How did Pearse summon up such a Daimon? Was it his choice at all? What causes man to attain to the heroic foolhood of these lines?

> "But where can we draw water,"
> Said Pearse to Connolly,
> "When all the wells are parched away?
> O plain as plain can be
> There's nothing but our own red blood
> Can make a right Rose Tree." [47]

The apparent simplicity and logic of Connolly's answer (the rose tree symbolizes Ireland) provides the cover for a strange mockery of the consequences, a voluntary sacrifice. "Enchanted to a stone," these heroes attain to a strange new eternal status.

Yeats himself seeks to achieve that "lonely impulse of delight" and to hold it in time, and he seeks also to conjure up in his mind and to create out of himself an artificial mental form for his own eternal existence—his own chosen Daimon. In the strangely moving poem, "All Souls' Night," which served as the epilogue of *A Vision*, Yeats dramatizes his striving to achieve that mental equilibrium which the dancer symbolizes. In the poem he attempts to articulate some "marvellous thing" or hidden truth, presumably the prediction which will never come from *A Vision* itself. In order to do this he must maintain a difficult mental balance, that same balance which occurs at the first phase of every historical wheel:

> I need some mind that, if the cannon sound
> From every quarter of the world, can stay
> Wound in mind's pondering
> As mummies in the mummy-cloth are wound;
> Because I have a certain marvellous thing to say,
> A certain marvellous thing.[48]

Perhaps a ghost may come, he thinks; but it does not come, and the tremendous mental exertion is for nothing. He fails to escape the wheel of time and space by the exertion of sheer will. Yet till the end he holds out hope for victory of the intellect. The poem ends:

> Such thought—such thought have I that hold it tight
> Till meditation master all its parts,
> Nothing can stay my glance
> Until that glance run in the world's despite
> To where the damned have howled away their hearts,
> And where the blessed dance;
> Such thought, that in it bound
> I need no other thing,
> Wound in mind's wandering
> As mummies in the mummy-cloth are wound.

Writing on this poem, R. P. Blackmur has, mistakenly I think, complained because it fails in its promise to achieve revelation through magical incantation.[49] But the point of the poem is that it dramatizes a failure, just as *A Vision*, of which it is a part, dramatizes a failure. It conveys the tension of violent exertion and striving, and thus it restates an archetypal tragic theme which is also Yeats's major theme.

In the Byzantium poems the same imagery and the same theme are present, elaborated by description of the world Yeats would forsake and the eternity he would seek. "Sailing to Byzantium" is a poem written by an old man who realizes that his old age excludes him from all sensual joys. In fact, he says, an old man is really hardly a man at all any more—he is more like a scarecrow—except that he has an advantage over youth, the advantage of maturity. But maturity is itself a paradoxical advantage; it brings with it concern over the problem of death and the nature of the soul. In old age man may celebrate life, but it must be a new kind of life glorifying imagination over the animal nature. He has thus sought to forsake the world of generation, for it is the fallen cyclic world. He has attempted to address his intellect to images of a timeless reality. The environment of this contemplative act he calls "Byzantium," the city of artifice. Like Blake he sees an identity between the work of art and eternity. In the statue or painting movement becomes not-movement. The great symbols of art are the archetypal figures of Los's Halls, pounded and shaped on the anvil of imagination and fixed permanently in that changeless metal which symbolizes the Great Memory of mankind.

As an old man Yeats prays that "once out of nature" his soul may achieve this state of artifice, attain to this purity and divest itself of the corporeal form. Such an attainment is the joining of self and Daimon. He invokes in his prayer the great sages now dead, whom he sees standing in the holy purifying flames of God, where what Blake calls "vegetal lusts" are consumed, where nothing but an imaginative quintessence remains. Standing in this fire they seem to stand in artifice—"the gold mosaic of a wall"— and Yeats asks them to "perne in a gyre," consuming his heart away and whirling him into the complete equilibrium of eternity.

The symbol for what he will become in eternity must be an unchanging representation of the complete soul, and Yeats chooses to become a golden bird, a form of the many mysterious visionary experiences of his poems, hardened into bright sculpture:

> Once out of nature I shall never take
> My bodily form from any natural thing,
> But such a form as Grecian goldsmiths make
> Of hammered gold and gold enamelling
> To keep a drowsy Emperor awake;
> Or set upon a golden bough to sing
> To lords and ladies of Byzantium
> Of what is past, or passing, or to come.[50]

The cycle of generation with its "blood-dimmed tide" and "rough beast" is rejected. Artifice is glorified; nature is disdained. Only what man has created out of his own imagination is of value.

In the second poem on the Byzantine theme, Yeats invokes the contemplative quiet of "All Souls' Night." In the resonant Byzantine stillness the "mere complexity" of human nature, at least as we know it on earth and in the body, seems inconsequential. The whole atmosphere of thought disdains it:

> The unpurged images of day recede;
> The Emperor's drunken soldiery are abed;
> Night resonance recedes, night-walkers' song
> After great cathedral gong;
> A starlit or a moonlit dome disdains
> All that man is,
> All mere complexities,
> The fury and the mire of human veins.[51]

Yeats begins to imagine a strange image floating before his mind's eye:

> Before me floats an image, man or shade,
> Shade more than man, more image than a shade;
> For Hades' bobbin bound in mummy-cloth

May unwind the winding path;
A mouth that has no moisture and no breath
Breathless mouths may summon;
I hail the superhuman;
I call it death-in-life and life-in-death.

The image fails to take form immediately, but Yeats asserts that it "may" communicate itself to him if only he can maintain the tightly wound, taut mental trance symbolized by Hades' bobbin; bound in mummy-cloth, it is an image out of death, artifice, and eternity, the gyre tightened to a vortex opening out into reality, temporal images of which are the point of the cone, the whirling dancer of Michael Robartes' vision, and the balance achieved by the Irish Airman.

He holds the trance, or thinks he does, and the image materializes into the golden bird:

Miracle, bird or golden handiwork,
More miracle than bird or handiwork,
Planted on the star-lit golden bough,
Can like the cocks of Hades crow,
Or, by the moon embittered, scorn aloud
In glory of changeless metal
Common bird or petal
And all complexities of mire or blood.

This vision symbolizing to him his own eternal state leads him to other visions: spirits from the world of generation whirling into dance and flames of purification:

Where blood-begotten spirits come
And all complexities of fury leave,
Dying into a dance,
An agony of trance,
An agony of flame that cannot singe a sleeve.

The Byzantine mosaics come into his mind, their dolphins carrying these souls over the sea to the place of purgation; the artificers of these great works have symbolized in caught motion all the stages of attainment to "artifice of eternity." Again, as in the first Byzantium poem, Yeats returns to the work of art as a symbol for the timeless reality.

Byzantine artifice supposedly "breaks the flood" of time, yet both poems end by returning to an image from the world of generation. In "Sailing to Byzantium" the golden bird sings of "what is past, or passing, or to come"; and in "Byzantium" the last line returns us to:

> That dolphin-torn, that gong-tormented sea.

The Byzantium poems are prayers said in the natural world, in which Yeats seeks to make his major symbol of momentary vision a symbol of timeless reality by creating it in artificial form. But the bird itself is a symbol out of the very same material world which Yeats disparages in the poems, and since Yeats never clearly tells us, as Blake does, just what nature is, whether or not it is delusory, whether or not our images are our reality, it is difficult to accept the Byzantium poems as positive prophecies in the way that we accept Blake's "The Tyger" as positive. Yet the poems are truly great poems for the reason that they dramatize their own failure as truly visionary documents. They are tragic evocations of great momentary images, of great strivings, and of tortured faith. The poems are songs of experience. The innocence of the saint and the fool seems to be bestowed upon men by God's mysterious Chance.

GAIETY

Facing a world of violent conflict and forced tension, the Urizenic traveler fails to achieve faith and is driven to seek some rational explanation for the movement of things, relegating the great mystery of God's Chance to the dull explainable. Such a philosophy for Yeats as well as for Donne and Blake "calls all in doubt." In his 1930 diary Yeats wrote:

I would found literature on the three things which Kant thought we must postulate to make life livable—Freedom, God, Immortality. The fading of these three before "Bacon, Newton, Locke" has made literature decadent. Because Freedom is gone we have Stendhal's "mirror dawdling down a lane"; because God has gone we have realism, the accidental; because Immortality is gone we can no longer write those tragedies which have always seemed to me alone legitimate—those that are a joy to the man who dies.[52]

Yeats rebelled against that limited rationalism which eliminates from thought all musing not only on God's Chance but also on man's. Affirming mystery, he affirmed the "perhaps" of things:

There is perhaps no final happy state except in so far as man may gradually grow better; escape may be for individuals alone who know how to exhaust their possible lives, to set, as it were, the hands of the clock racing. Perhaps we shall learn to accept even innumerable lives with happy humility—"I have been always an insect in the roots of the grass"—and putting aside calculating scruples be ever ready to wager all upon the dice.[53]

This is a tragic view but it is also comic. In "The Green Helmet," a mysterious deity called the "Red Man" lauds the Irish hero Cuchulain:

. . . And I choose the laughing lip
That shall not turn from laughing, whatever rise or fall;
The heart that grows no bitterer although betrayed by all;
The hand that loves to scatter; the life like a gambler's throw.[54]

Cuchulain is the willing gambler. Yeats, commenting upon a performance of one of his plays, wrote to Dorothy Wellesley in 1938: "There was a fine performance of my 'Baile's Strand.' 'Cuchulain' seemed to me a heroic figure because he was creative joy separated from fear." [55] In another letter he wrote, "To me the supreme aim is an act of faith and reason to make one rejoice in the midst of tragedy." [56] Such rejoicing Yeats called "tragic ecstasy," [57] and elsewhere he referred to it as, "heroic, ecstatic passion, prolonged through years, through many vicissitudes." [58]

The proper conclusion of tragedy is thus a strangely simple attitude. It is symbolized by the heroic disdain of Cuchulain, the solitary innocence of the fool, and the gay acceptance of paradox:

> But Love has pitched his mansion in
> The place of excrement;
> For nothing can be sole or whole
> That has not been rent.[59]

The one heroic sanction is that of the last battle of the Norse Gods, of a gay struggle without hope. Long ago I used to puzzle Maud Gonne by always avowing ultimate defeat as a test.[60]

One short line of Yeats's late poem "Lapis Lazuli" epitomizes Yeats's conception of the proper personality: "Gaiety transfiguring all that dread." Surely, it might be answered, such a transfiguration is precarious indeed and even perhaps a false, forced gaiety. Yeats would undoubtedly agree. Gaiety is really a mask to be striven for; yet even a gaiety sought or forced does symbolize a proper striving. Furthermore, the striving affirms the existence of that pervasive conflict which is the breath of life itself. The dilemma of how to achieve the final purified balance of fools, dancers, and birds is perhaps never fully solved; but awareness of a kind of goal eliminates the hysteria which is the unacceptable alternative. Yeats illustrates that alternative in "Lapis Lazuli":

> I have heard that hysterical women say
> They are sick of the palette and fiddle-bow,
> Of poets that are always gay,
> For everybody knows or else should know
> That if nothing drastic is done
> Aeroplane and Zeppelin will come out,
> Pitch like King Billy bomb-balls in
> Until the town lie beaten flat.[61]

Changing the pace of the poem, Yeats then answers this hysteria:

All perform their tragic play,
There struts Hamlet, there is Lear,
That's Ophelia, that Cordelia;
Yet they, should the last scene be there,
The great stage curtain about to drop,
If worthy their prominent part in the play,
Do not break up their lines to weep.
They know that Hamlet and Lear are gay;
Gaiety transfiguring all that dread.

Men attain to gaiety by seeking out the completed self in Daimon just as Yeats himself in the Byzantium poems casts derision on the world of generation and seeks his own Mask or Daimonic form. Forcing gaiety, man dons the Mask of social and psychological armor—the practical Mask. He is searching, as he does this, for the more complex Mask representing the completion of his "partial mind." In Yeats's eye, all the world really is a stage. Forms of art—drama, dance, and sculpture—are truly timeless images of attainment. Those who achieve oneness with Mask become one with the archetypal heroic figure symbolized by artifice—a "bright sculpture of Los's halls." In the world of generation, the world of history, things rise and fall—civilization, even the work of Callimachus:

On their own feet they came, or on shipboard,
Camel-back, horse-back, ass-back, mule-back,
Old civilisations put to the sword.
Then they and their wisdom went to rack:
No handiwork of Callimachus,
Who handled marble as if it were bronze,
Made draperies that seemed to rise
When sea-wind swept the corner, stands;
His long lamp-chimney shaped like the stem
Of a slender palm, stood but a day;
All things fall and are built again,
And those that build them again are gay.

In spite of birth and death, the archetypal hero returns as if never dead to rebuild from the ruins; Blake, for example, is the

Poetic Genius born in his age "to record and eternize its acts"
and to find the eternal pattern in them.

The piece of lapis lazuli which Yeats studies symbolizes, itself,
a heroic vision:

Someone has sent me a present of a great piece carved by some
Chinese sculptor into the semblance of a mountain with temple,
trees, paths, and an ascetic and pupil about to climb the mountain.
Ascetic, pupil, hard stone, eternal theme of the sensual east. The
heroic cry in the midst of despair. But no, I am wrong, the east has
its solutions always and therefore knows nothing of tragedy. It is
we, not the east, that must raise the heroic cry.[62]

The eastern art suggests to Yeats the achievement of Mask, some
strange Daimonic unity. The piece of lapis lazuli, like the Noh
drama which so fascinated him, represents this unity:

> Every discoloration of the stone,
> Every accidental crack or dent,
> Seems a water-course or an avalanche,
> Or lofty slope where it still snows
> Though doubtless plum or cherry-branch
> Sweetens the little half-way house
> Those Chinamen climb towards, and I
> Delight to imagine them seated there;
> There, on the mountain and the sky,
> On all the tragic scene they stare.
> One asks for mournful melodies;
> Accomplished fingers begin to play.
> Their eyes mid many wrinkles, their eyes,
> Their ancient, glittering eyes, are gay.

The eyes of the wisemen are themselves Mask symbols, the Mask
having become the reality, the corporeal body the real falsehood—things correctly transvaluated at last.

In this poem Yeats himself is an actor, musing on the strange
quality of the work of art and the mysterious attainments of
those ancient eyes. As such, Yeats looks at things from a point of
vantage directly opposite to that of the Mental Traveller, Blake.

Yeats stands in the fallen world staring backward at the sources of truth, but halted at the eyes of the wisemen through which he is, of course, unable to see the infinite expressed as symbols. The Mental Traveller begins his journey in the real or eternal world behind those eyes, comes down into the fallen world, and returns with description of its degradation. Yeats, smitten by the unseen, affirms mystery; Blake unravels the knots, rolls the thread back into apprehensible unity.

Yeats's dramatic achievement is a strife of forced balance, a controlled recklessness, a "laughing lip," a Cuchulain offering his head:

There is in the creative joy an acceptance of what life brings, because we have understood the beauty of what it brings, or a hatred of death for what it takes away, which arouses within us, through some sympathy perhaps with all other men, an energy so noble, so powerful, that we laugh aloud and mock, in the terror or the sweetness of our exultation, at death and oblivion.[63]

Yeats's half love of his "brazen winged beast," his exultation over the vision he called "The Second Coming," his fascination with the horrific image, and his "ecstasy at the contemplation of ruin" were rooted in his revolt against Victorian positivism and progressivism; but these roots gave life to something more complex, a code of attitude restating the requirements for human dignity. Yeats once commented to Dorothy Wellesley on some poems: "Those little poems of yours are nonchalant, & nonchalance is declared by Castiglione essential to all true courtiers." [64] The courtier symbolizes the heroic mood of balanced discipline and solitary control:

I think that the true poetic movement of our time is toward some heroic discipline. People much occupied with morality always lose heroic ecstasy. Those who have it most often are those Dowson has described (I cannot find the poem but the lines run like this or something like this)

> Wine women and song
> To us they belong
> To us the bitter and gay.

"Bitter and gay," that is the heroic mood. When there is despair, public or private, when settled order seems lost, people look for strength within or without. Auden, Spender, all that seem the new movement *look* for strength in Marxian socialism or in Major Douglas; they want marching feet. The lasting expression of our time is not this obvious choice but in a sense of something steel like and cold within the will, something passionate and cold.[65]

Yeats himself consciously sought to attain to such balance in his own poems, through a chiseled hard coldness like Los's sculptures, an unadorned spare style. A last poem "The Gyres" illustrates through rhythm, language, and total image Yeats's success. The theme of the poem is the violent death of an old civilization crumbling everywhere.

> The gyres! The gyres! Old Rocky Face, look forth;
> Things thought too long can be no longer thought,
> For beauty dies of beauty, worth of worth,
> And ancient lineaments are blotted out.
> Irrational streams of blood are staining earth;
> Empedocles has thrown all things about;
> Hector is dead and there's a light in Troy;
> We that look on but laugh in tragic joy.[66]

"Old Rocky Face" is Yeats himself in old age, addressed by that voice out of mystery, his Daimon, who instead of acting the part of instructor for a whole system of symbolical thought now gives new advice about proper attitude. Yeats has already been told about the gyres by his Daimon instructors; now he must learn personality. In the face of the conflicting rise and fall, the proper attitude is "tragic joy," heroic disdain in spite of the loss of the years of one's own life, the remembrance of a more gracious past time:

> What matter though numb nightmare ride on top,
> And blood and mire the sensitive body stain?

What matter? Heave no sigh, let no tear drop,
A greater, a more gracious time has gone;
For painted forms or boxes of make-up
In ancient tombs I sighed, but not again;
What matter? Out of cavern come a voice,
And all it knows is that one word "Rejoice!"

The nostalgia for what has been built and must be destroyed is itself transfigured by an active acceptance of the cyclic turn of things from birth to death and back to rebirth. There is no progress, but there is the cyclic attainment to spiritual heroism—the rebirth of a kind of truth emerging in every age from that Great Memory which Yeats calls "Spiritus Mundi" or "Anima Mundi," the timeless reality known to all poets:

All things acted on Earth are seen in the bright Sculptures of Los's Halls, & every Age renews its power from these Works.[67]

Spenser, for example, sang its nature:

The substance is not changed nor altered
But th' only forme and outward fashion.[68]

Yeats sees the substance of things unchangingly renewed in the Circle of Destiny, reborn like the Poetic Genius itself:

Conduct and work grow coarse and coarse the soul,
What matter? Those that Rocky Face holds dear,
Lovers of horses and of women, shall,
From marble of a broken sepulchre,
Or dark betwixt the polecat and the owl,
Or any rich, dark nothing disinter
The workman, noble and saint, and all things run
On that unfashionable gyre again.

Three images suggest the sources of new birth. Between polecat (beast) and owl (bird) there is, according to the system of *A Vision*, the equilibrium of revelation and new birth. The "broken sepulchre," suggesting Christ's ascension, symbolizes the breaking forth of new life from old degradation. The "rich, dark nothing" is the mysterious "Anima Mundi" itself, a strange image of truth. The gyre image is "unfashionable" first because it is part of an eccentric personal system of symbolism subject to derision, and second because it implies that the fashionable idea of progress is really an untruth. "Lovers of horses and women" symbolize aristocracy, which in turn symbolizes for Yeats solitude, disdain, and, most important, tradition. It is tradition and memory which get nearest to the source of "that rich, dark nothing." Tradition and ceremony preserve the timeless and therefore valuable elements through all manner of adversity. The poet as a celebrator of "traditional sanctity and loveliness" is an aristocratic figure whether in rags or riches. He may be a beggarman, a fool, or a noble—Old Tom, Crazy Jane, Cuchulain, or Robert Gregory.

In another late poem, "The Man and the Echo," Yeats speaks with himself or with his Mask. The echo which answers for his Mask tells him to "lie down and die," and Yeats, questioning what can be gained by that, asks:

> . . . O Rocky Voice,
> Shall we in that great night rejoice?
> What do we know but that we face
> One another in this place?
> But hush, for I have lost the theme,
> Its joy or night seem but a dream;
> Up there some hawk or owl has struck,
> Dropping out of sky or rock,
> A stricken rabbit is crying out,
> And its cry distracts my thought.[69]

Here, instead of a bird, an animal cries out, and Yeats is distracted back into the swim of life, where in the last analysis all men, like Los, must do their work. The incantatory cry may represent in the final stages of its manipulation fiercely gay acceptance and celebration of life, the last battle of Yeats's Norse gods. He who celebrates life must accept the antinomies.

Yet the cry of the bird and the cry of the beast are really the

same image, representing paradoxically man's subconscious freedom, his Daimon driving him on to heroic action. As Yeats says
in *A Vision:* "Only one symbol exists, though the reflecting
mirrors make many appear and all different." [70] This is true of
Yeats's own symbols. The cry of bird and beast, the gyres, the
top, the wheel, and the dancer are all related images which are
in turn related to the mysterious final image called the "thirteenth
gyre" of *A Vision.*

In one rejected typescript for *A Vision,* Yeats approached an
explanation of it:

Every *Daimon* differs from every other and each is perfect, and it is
because of this that we can talk of a perfect man, or horse or tree. I
asked my instructor if there was not one *Daimon* of *Daimons* that
lived in all and made all one, and when he said "yes" asked how each
Daimon could be perfect seeing that it was less than the whole,
thereupon he became angry and said that each is perfect. I did not
care to ask why if each is perfect man should come into existence;
I did not want another scene, and besides one cannot know everything. I accept his thought, and say, to introduce the chief person
of my drama, that nothing can be taken from or added to the
Daimon, and being a symbolist and dramatist and not a dialectician
declare that this is its shape.* [Below this quotation is a rough pen
drawing which is evidently a sphere.] [71]

A final, published statement about the thirteenth gyre suggests
that it is an image of unity:

The ultimate reality because neither one nor many, concord nor
discord, is symbolized as a phaseless sphere, but as all things fall into
a series of antinomies in human experience it becomes, the moment
it is thought of, what I shall presently describe as the thirteenth
cone.[72]

Yeats says that Blake called this sphere, "which can be symbolized but cannot be known," [73] the "bright sculptures of Los's

* The comedy here is, as I have already attempted to show, a most important
part of the gesture Yeats makes in *A Vision*, and it is consistent with his
vision of gaiety.

halls." Yeats's instructors called it "a Record where the images of all past events remain forever." It is the opposite toward which we strive and from which mystery emerges:

That month of the other cone which corresponds to ours is always called by my instructors the Thirteenth Cycle or *Thirteenth Cone* for every month is a cone. It is that cycle which may deliver us from the twelve cycles of time and space. The cone which intersects ours is a cone in so far as we think of it as the antithesis of our thesis, but if the time has come for our deliverance it is the phaseless sphere, sometimes called the Thirteenth Sphere.[74]

The Blakean vortex image is related to Yeats's sphere image, for the true reality is our mock reality turned inside out:

A system symbolizing the phenomenal world as irrational because a series of unresolved antinomies, must find its representation in a perpetual return to the starting-point. The resolved antinomy appears not in a lofty source but in the whirlpool's motionless centre, or beyond its edge.[75]

The whirlpool center is the ultimate movement, where movement and not-movement appear to coincide. Related symbols are the mind wound in pondering, in mummy-cloth, the whirling holy sages of Byzantium, who "perne in a gyre," and the dancer.

The *Thirteenth Cone* is a sphere because sufficient to itself; but as seen by Man it is a cone. It becomes even conscious of itself as so seen, like some great dancer, the perfect flower of modern culture, dancing some primitive dance and conscious of his or her own life and of the dance.[76]

The dancer whirling into a vortex, consumed in equilibrium, is the image of momentary vision, the image of truth. The dancer has during the moments of the dance all the attributes of the fool, perfect aristocratic solitude.

> The girl goes dancing there
> On the leaf-sown, new-mown, smooth
> Grass plot of the garden;
> Escaped from bitter youth,

Escaped out of her crowd,
Or out of her black cloud.
Ah, dancer, ah, sweet dancer!

If strange men come from the house
To lead her away, do not say
That she is happy being crazy;
Lead them gently astray;
Let her finish her dance,
Let her finish her dance.
Ah, dancer, ah sweet dancer! [77]

In another poem, "A Crazed Girl," the same image appears:

That crazed girl improvising her music,
Her poetry, dancing upon the shore,
Her soul in division from itself
Climbing, falling she knew not where,
Hiding amid the cargo of a steamship,
Her knee-cap broken, that girl I declare
A beautiful lofty thing, or a thing
Heroically lost, heroically found.

No matter what disaster occurred
She stood in desperate music wound
Wound, wound, and she made in her triumph
Where the bales and the baskets lay
No common intelligible sound
But sang, "O sea-starved, hungry sea." [78]

The symbology reaches extreme coherence and complexity, for the dance itself is the "wound" mind; it is a symbol of the fool's aimless, active joy, the hero's "lonely impulse of delight"; and with Salome as dancer it represents the moment before revelation, the dark of the moon, a supernatural incarnation, the sudden disappearance of time. As characterized in "Rosa Alchemica," it symbolizes the rhythm of the universe itself. It is a form of art, a perfect act, a symbol of freedom, cone in sphere, symbol in symbol. It proclaims the solidarity of life transcending appearances:

O body swayed to music, O brightening glance,
How can we know the dancer from the dance? [79]

A Vision helps to expound the significance of the all-impor-
tant "thirteenth gyre." As it does this, it is, in addition to other
things that have been mentioned, Yeats's own book of literary
theory, for it comments upon the symbology of his poetry. It
brilliantly expresses the working of the poetic mind in the following words:

I have now described many symbols which seem mechanical because united in a single structure, and of which the greater number,
precisely because they tell always the same story, may seem unnecessary. Yet every symbol, except where it lies in vast periods of
time and so beyond our experience, has evoked for me some form
of human destiny, and that form, once evoked, has appeared everywhere, as if there were but one destiny, as my own form might
appear in a room full of mirrors.[80]

In Yeats's poetry the thirteenth gyre appears in various disguises. One important appearance links it with the sexual act
in the short poem "Chosen," in which the marriage bed appears
for one instant to be (in the words of the Michael Robartes of
A Vision) "the symbol of the solved antinomy." The second
and last stanza of the poem follows:

. . . If questioned on
My utmost pleasure with a man
By some new-married bride, I take
That stillness for a theme
Where his heart my heart did seem
And both adrift on the miraculous stream
Where—wrote a learned astrologer—
The Zodiac is changed into a sphere.[81]

The reference is to Kusta ben Luka, philosopher of *A Vision*'s
system, the simile developed is that of perfect freedom and
balance achieved in the sphere. The poem itself, however, characteristically dramatizes the fleeting nature in time of the ex-

perience as much as the significance of the simile. This is also true of an earlier poem "Solomon and the Witch," in which the marriage bed is the scene of a dialogue-drama. Here, it seems, Chance and Choice are one at last. The microcosmic sexual apocalypse is identified with the moon's phase:

> Yet the world ends when these two things,
> Though several, are a single light,
> When oil and wick are burned in one;
> Therefore a blessed moon last night
> Gave Sheba to her Solomon.[82]

However, the dramatic twist appears. One of the participants must declare:

> Yet the world stays.

There is no sudden stoppage of time, no trumpet blast; this ironically proves the movement of the wheel, the existence of antinomy, and finally human striving and desire:

> The night has fallen; not a sound
> In the forbidden sacred grove
> Unless a petal hit the ground,
> Nor any human sight within it
> But the crushed grass where we have lain;
> And the moon is wilder every minute.
> O! Solomon! let us try again.

The antinomies joined in the sexual act, symbolizing attainment to the sphere, form a major image of Yeats's last poems. "News for the Delphic Oracle" seeks to describe the geography of the mysterious sphere, reality, and ends with complete abandonment as:

> . . . nymphs and satyrs
> Copulate in the foam.[83]

But like the crystalline cry of the bird the sexual act as symbol is only a momentary release. The thirteenth gyre stands inviolable. Man's freedom itself joins in the human conflict and plays the part of the frustrator, barring the door to the future.

Of the new age, Yeats wrote in *A Vision:* "Something of what I have said it must be, the myth declares, for it must reverse our era and resume past eras in itself; what else it must be no man can say, for always at the critical moment the *Thirteenth Cone,* the sphere, the unique intervenes." [84] One who is "wound in mind's wandering" may muse on possibility, and he may reaffirm mystery: "Perhaps now that the abstract intellect has split the mind into categories, the body into cubes, we may be about to turn back towards the unconscious, the whole, the miraculous." [85]

There is always the twist of irony, self-satire, and gaiety in the Yeatsian musings. He has purposely dealt in myth; but with a semantic change, he may exclaim as Owen Aherne might: "Will some mathematician someday question and understand, as I cannot, and confirm all, or have I also dealt in myth?" [86] Conflict exists at every turn in the dance of the gyres. This is most evident to the poet himself, who deals in the immediate experience of conflict. In *Per Amica Silentia Lunae,* written before *A Vision,* the poet had recognized conflict in his own experience:

I think that we who are poets and artists, not being permitted to shoot beyond the tangible, must go from desire to weariness and so to desire again, and live but for the moment when vision comes to our weariness like terrible lightning, in the humility of the brutes. I do not doubt those heaving circles, those winding arcs, whether in one man's life or in that of an age, are mathematical, and that some in the world, or beyond the world, have foreknown the event and pricked upon the calendar the life-span of a Christ, a Buddha, a Napoleon: that every movement in feeling or in thought, prepares in the dark by its own increasing clarity and confidence its own executioner. We seek reality with the slow toil of our weakness and are smitten from the boundless and the unforeseen.[87]

In response the poet strives to assume the heroic mask. That is why Seanchan in "The King's Threshold" speaks boldly before his own death:

> . . . I would have all know that when all falls
> In ruin, poetry calls out in joy,

Being the scattering hand, the bursting pod,
The victim's joy among the holy flame,
God's laughter at the shattering of the world.[88]

Late in life Yeats wrote down in "Seven Propositions" what he called his "private philosophy":

I. Reality is a timeless and spaceless community of Spirits which perceive each other. Each Spirit is determined by and determines those it perceives, and each Spirit is unique.

II. When these Spirits reflect themselves in time and space they still determine each other, and each Spirit sees the others as thoughts, images, objects of sense. Time and space are unreal.[89]

One suspects the immediate influence of McTaggart's denial of time and space in these propositions, as well as the denial which lies at the foundation of Blake's whole mythology. Proposition I provides us with the same interacting system as that of the Zoas in their perfect harmony. Proposition II may be illustrated by the whole Orc-Urizen relationship. Without Orc there is not Urizen, and vice versa. The proposition also expresses in other terms what Blake was attempting to get at in the concept of the "minute particular" as an image of the eternal.

III. This reflection into time and space is only complete at certain moments of birth, or passivity, which recur many times in each destiny. At these moments the destiny receives its character until the next such moment from those Spirits who constitute the external universe. The horoscope is a set of geometrical relations between the Spirit's reflection and the principle masses in the universe and defines that character.

The elaborate system of *A Vision* is related to the horoscope, in which the relation of each spirit to its Body of Fate is defined.

IV. The emotional character of a timeless and spaceless spirit reflects itself as its position in time, its intellectual character as its position in space. The position of a Spirit in space and time therefore defines character.

This, very likely, is purely Blakean. Blake conceived of time as
a man, space as a woman. He associated his Los spirit with time,
which though delusory does move spirally toward its self-denial.
Space, or matter, is Los's emanation, Enitharmon, the earth
mother. But in reality time and space are not entities in themselves, Los without Enitharmon being a spectre of himself. Thus
to call Los time is to comment simultaneously upon both his
apocalyptic force and his fallen position. In reality Los and
Enitharmon (time and space, spirit and intellect) disappear into
the community of spirits described in Proposition I.

V. Human life is either the struggle of a destiny against all other
destinies, or a transformation of the character defined in the horoscope into timeless and spaceless existence. The whole passage from
birth to birth should be an epitome of the whole passage of the
universe through time and back into its timeless and spaceless condition.

This proposition repeats the theory of contraries and of macrocosm and microcosm held by Blake, and it recalls Yeats's comments in the Quaritch edition on Blake's symbolic system.

VI. The acts and nature of a Spirit during any one life are a section
or abstraction of reality and are unhappy because incomplete. They
are a gyre or part of a gyre, whereas reality is a sphere.

Sub specie aeternitatis, this proposition repeats the important
image of *A Vision*, meant to transcend the discouraging vision
of gyres.

VII. Though the Spirits are determined by each other they cannot
completely lose their freedom. Every possible statement or perception contains both terms—the self and that which it perceives
or states.

Although in substance these propositions tell us little more than
we find elsewhere in Yeats, they are stated in a somewhat different manner. There is no logical argument, as there is in McTaggart, to back them up; nor is there a specific poem to enforce

their truth. Instead they appear to be arrived at as the result of much pondering, as a distillation or logical reduction of what had come to Yeats over the years from his instructors and his reading. One suspects that in writing down these propositions Yeats was arguing for what his experiences had told him *must be*, rather than what he knew *is*. Whether or not these propositions represent the adoption of the point of view of a higher, aged innocence probably must be left up to the reader. I submit that Yeats stands nearer the vortex of vision in his last poem than in his last philosophy:

> Though grave-diggers' toil is long,
> Sharp their spades, their muscles strong,
> They but thrust their buried men
> Back in the human mind again.[90]

CHAPTER X

At the Vortex

> Learn about the egg and cut it with a flaming sword.
> In our world, there is a bird more sublime than all
> others. To search for his egg be thy only concern.
> —MICHAEL MAJER (1568–1622) [1]

BLAKE'S brief epigram in *The Marriage of Heaven and Hell*—
"Without contraries is no progression"—clearly states a metaphysics of paradox which emerges from his myth. In many ways
the world is paradoxical, especially if it is judged, as modern man
seems to judge it, from within the Circle of Destiny. It is from
this position that Yeats judged it and declared that "the antinomy
is there and can be represented only by a myth," [2] the paradox
symbolized if not broken. "Of late I have tried to understand in
its practical details the falsehood that is in all knowledge, science
more false than philosophy, but that too false." [3]

Both the Blakean and Yeatsian worlds accept the existence of
dimensions beyond those which our reason apprehends. Urizen
whirling on the edge of the great circle lacks the necessary
spiritual dimension—the dimension which Yeats, perhaps remembering Blake's phrase, "Passion & Expression is Beauty Itself," calls "passion":

I am trying to understand why certain metaphysicians whom I have
spent years trying to master repel me, why those invisible beings I

have learned to trust would turn me from all that is not conflict, that is not from sword in hand. Is it not like this? I cannot discover truth by logic unless that logic serve passion, and only then if the logic be ready to cut its own throat. . . . I must not talk to myself about "the truth" nor call myself "teacher" nor another "pupil"—these things are abstract—but see myself set in a drama where I struggle to exalt and overcome concrete realities perceived not with the mind only but as with the roots of my hair. The passionless reasoners are pariah dogs and devour the dead symbols.[4]

An example of the strange paradox of reasoned truth may be taken from the writing of a scientist on science. J. W. N. Sullivan in *The Limitations of Science* attempts to explain to the layman the paradox of unbounded, finite space. He tells us that the total volume of space is finite but that space itself does not stop short anywhere. Nor is it not unlimited:

This is a very singular idea, but fortunately we can illustrate it by an example drawn from ordinary experience. Everybody knows that a volume has three dimensions, length, breadth, and thickness, whereas a surface has only two, length and breadth. Now it is quite possible, for the purposes of argument, to imagine creatures who live only in two dimensions. They never look up or down; they know nothing of up or down. They are conscious only of length and breadth. Now, if these creatures lived on a flat surface, like the surface of a table, they would find that their space (the surface of the table) could not be unbounded unless it was also infinite. They could only go on in a straight line forever provided the table went on for ever. Unless the table was actually infinite in length and breadth, they would sooner or later reach its edges and find that it had boundaries. They could not continue to go on without leaving the surface of the table altogether. Now consider the surface of a sphere. Here the creatures could crawl about indefinitely, sticking to the surface of the sphere, crawling in any direction.[5]

Sullivan tells us that, according to the Reimannian geometry, our three-dimensional space can have the same odd properties as two dimensional space, that we can go in any direction indef-initely, but that in an infinite length of time we shall return to our starting point. "Space is finite but unbounded." But note that this whole conception of boundlessness is possible only from the limited perceptual view of the two-dimensional or, in our case, three-dimensional creature.

Now, according to Blake, Urizen is locked in the circle of spatial dimensions. He thinks that his world is infinite and unbounded whereas it is really finite and circular. He sees everything inside out. He thinks he stands on the egg called the world, but actually he revolves inside it. He looks to the stars for guidance when he should look into himself—back into what Eliot in "Burnt Norton" calls "the still point of the turning world." Urizen arranges things in a hierarchy or chain of being, one on top of another with God high in the heavens, hell somewhere down in the depths of rock. But such an arrangement is itself a grave error, for hell is not below him; it is where he is.

Blake, of course, calls hell "Ulro" and heaven "Eden" or "Eternity." There are two other states of existence called "Generation" and "Beulah." But the states are not subject to hierarchical arrangement. They may, however, though somewhat falsely, be symbolized as concentric circles (as in the drawing). The diagram below is really inside out. It represents the way Urizen would see things if he knew a little more than he now does. If he knew quite a bit more, he would recognize that, inside the circles below, all things are paradoxical and that all true expansion is an inward rather than outward motion; and since the greatest expansion is eternity, eternity must be the central point of the concentric circles rather than the outward circumference. Because of the perpetual conflict which every paradox reflects, eternity should be symbolized as a "centre." In *The Kaballah Unveiled*, Yeats's friend Macgregor Mathers quotes from the Book of Concealed Mystery:

"The Book of Concealed Mystery is the book of the equilibrium of balance." What is here meant by the terms "equilibrium of balance"? Equilibrium is that harmony which results from the analogy

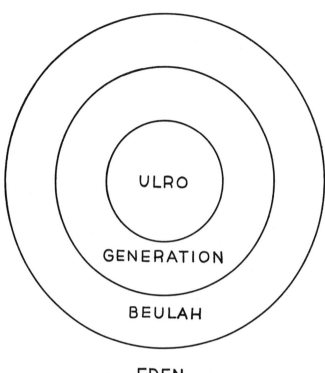

EDEN

of contraries, it is the dead centre, where the opposition of opposing forces being equal in strength, rest succeeds motion. It is the central point. It is the "point within the circle" of ancient symbolism. It is "the living synthesis of counterbalanced powers." [6]

The equilibrium of balance is apocalypse, Orc and Urizen proved one, man joined to Daimon. Blake's Circle of Destiny, Yeats's Great Wheel are enclosures. From another point of view they are gyres, whirling from circumference to a point and back. They are, as Michael Robartes says, a great egg continually turning itself inside out without breaking its shell. This strange circle begins with birth into the world of generation—Yeats's world of beasts, birds, flesh, and mackerel; Blake's childhood world of innocence. But soon man must face up to the dark journey of his maturity—Albion's dream, "the forests of the night," Yeats's moon phases. It is here that he comes to crises in Yeats's symbolical full moon, and if successful he is reborn to a higher innocence—a sainthood, or a Cuchulain-like foolhood. He routs his tiger from the forests and "disdains all that man is." Some men complete the delusory circle (delusory because completion of it means not coming back to the beginning but bringing things to a timeless "centre") in their life on earth. These men are mystics, capable as Yeats says of setting the hands of the clock running. They are more than saints, more than fools, and have in the eyes of the mass something of the terrible about them.

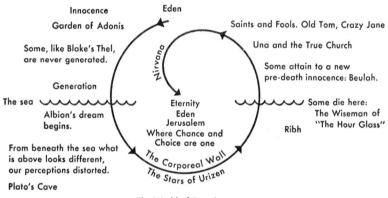

The Journey of Man and History

In the eyes of Yeats (although Yeats uses the term "mystic" vaguely) Blake is perhaps such a man. From Blake's point of view Yeats is trapped in the circle. It is not too much to say that Yeats's self-enclosure is the scene not only for serious self-analysis but also for the creation of a dramatic situation. Yet to place Blake and Yeats in direct opposition is, as I hope I have shown, to exaggerate their differences. It is first of all questionable whether a poet, who must really choose the beast, bird, and fish of this world for his contemplation, can ever really be a mystic. Blake seems to have understood this, and he never used the term "mystic." It might even be said that his whole system, including the denial of materiality, makes the mystic-nonmystic dichotomy meaningless. Nevertheless, he chose to battle delusion in behalf of fallen man rather than to leave delusion totally behind in behalf of himself.

As for Yeats, if he was trapped, he at least recognized his dilemma. As Blake so ably preached, such recognition is the first and most important step toward new freedom. Even Urizen comes to some similar knowledge in the course of his whirling travels. Yeats had in common with Blake a deep suspicion of the divisive, analytical mind; to both poets "corporeal" logic was not the only logic. Yeats thought that he saw in his own time the scientists beginning to bruise their hands on the limits of objective reality, forced to re-examine all positivist premises, and finally perhaps doubting "the possibility of science," as that possibility was once conceived.[7] "I want to make my readers understand that explanations of the world lie one inside another, each complete in itself," Yeats wrote.[8] Yet he knew that such concentric circles, or explanations, are themselves enclosures and that all explanations are in a sense failures. We ourselves are those two-dimensional creatures placed on the globe. Our rationality ceases to be rationality enough; our explanations of reality fail for they allow no paradox. With "corporeal" logic as our only tool, without "sword in hand," "the antinomies cannot be solved." [9]

Yet with the contrary vision of poetry as a tool, the antinomies can be unclothed and shown to be part of the limited circle of things, if instead of being *explained* they are dramatically *presented*. Here Blake and Yeats took two different roads to similar ends. They developed individual points of view, focuses for the narration of their stories. In an age of science more advanced than that of Blake's age, Yeats dramatized the human conflict with himself as the scapegoat—a creature trapped in the shell of time, space, and matter, aware of his plight but incapable of totally transcending it: "For Heraclitus was in the right. Opposites are everywhere face to face, dying each other's life, living each other's death." [10] On the other hand, Blake dramatized himself as the artist who sees beyond the walls of the cavern hollowed out by our fallen perceptual faculties.

Some see Nature all Ridicule & Deformity, & by these I shall not regulate my proportions; & some scarce see Nature at all. But to the Eyes of the Man of Imagination, Nature is Imagination itself. As a man is, so he sees. As the Eye is formed, such are its Powers. You certainly Mistake, when you say that the Visions of Fancy are not to be found in This World. To Me This World is all One continued Vision of Fancy or Imagination.[11]

In a sense, therefore, Blake and Yeats stand contrary—Daimon or Spectre to one another. But both work in our sunken world, asserting that the strange light glimmering down fathoms through fish, flesh, and heavy atmosphere comes from a reality of added dimensions, a sphere instead of a wheel—"a centre"—the perfect marriage of energy and form. Within their conflict they join to perpetuate the great myth of the Poetic Genius.

APPENDIX A

The Last Few Pages of "Dove or Swan" as They Appeared in the *1925 Edition of* A Vision*

[211] I find at this 23rd Phase which is it is said the first where there is hatred of the abstract, where the intellect turns upon itself, Mr. Ezra Pound, Mr. Eliot, Mr. Joyce, Signor Pirandello, who either eliminate from metaphor the poet's phantasy and substitute a strangeness discovered by historical or contemporary research or who break up the logical processes of thought by flooding them with associated ideas or words that seem to drift into the mind by chance; or who set side by side as in "Henry IV," "The Waste Land," "Ulysses," the *physical primary*—a lunatic among his keepers, a man fishing behind a gas works, the vulgarity of a single [212] Dublin day prolonged through 700 pages—and the *spiritual primary*, delirium, the Fisher King, Ulysses' wandering. It is as though myth and fact, united until the exhaustion of the Renaissance, have now fallen so far apart that man understands for the first time the rigidity of fact, and calls up, by that very recognition, myth—the *Mask*— which now but gropes its way out of the mind's dark but will shortly pursue and terrify. In practical life one expects the same technical inspiration, the doing of this or that not because one would, or should, but because one can, consequent licence, and with those "out of phase" anarchic violence with no sanction in general prin-

* These pages from the privately printed edition of 1925 were deleted in the 1938 version. Original page numbers appear in brackets.

ciples. If there is violent revolution, and it is the last phase where political revolution is possible, the dish will be made from what is found in the pantry and the cook will not open her book. There may be greater ability than hitherto for men will be set free from old restraints, but the old intellectual hierarchy gone they will thwart and jostle one another. One tries to discover the nature of the 24th Phase which will offer peace—perhaps by some generally accepted political or religious action, perhaps by some more profound generalisation—calling up before the mind those who speak its thoughts in the language of our earlier time. Peguy in his Joan of Arc trilogy displays the national and religious tradition of the French poor, as he, a man perhaps of the 24th Phase, would have it, and Claudel in his "L'Otage" the religious and secular hierarchies perceived as history. I foresee a time when the majority of men will so accept an historical tradition that they will quarrel, not as to who can impose his personality upon others but as to who can best embody the common aim, when all personality will seem an impurity—"sentimentality," "sullenness," "egotism"—something that revolts not morals alone but good taste. There will be no longer great intellect for a ceaseless [213] activity will be required of all; and where rights are swallowed up in duties, and solitude is difficult, creation except among avowedly archaistic and unpopular groups will grow impossible. Phase 25 may arise, as the code wears out from repetition, to give new motives for obedience, or out of some scientific discovery which seems to contrast, a merely historical acquiescence, with an enthusiastic acceptance of the general will conceived of as a present energy—"Sibyll what would you?" "I would die." Then with the last gyre must come a desire to be ruled or rather, seeing that desire is all but dead, an adoration of force spiritual or physical, and society as mechanical force be complete at last.

> Constrained, arraigned, baffled, bent and unbent
>> By those wire-jointed jaws and limbs of wood
> Themselves obedient,
>> Knowing not evil or good.

A decadence will descend, by perpetual moral improvement, upon a community which may seem like some woman of New York or Paris who has renounced her rouge pot to lose her figure and grow coarse of skin and dull of brain, feeding her calves and babies somewhere upon the edge of the wilderness. The decadence of the Greco-

Roman world with its violent soldiers and its mahogany dark young athletes was as great, but that suggested the bubbles of life turned into marbles, whereas what awaits us, being democratic and *primary*, may suggest bubbles in a frozen pond—mathematical Babylonian starlight.

When the new era comes bringing its stream of irrational force it will, as did Christianity, find its philosophy already impressed upon the minority who have, true to phase, turned away at the last gyre from the *Physical Primary*. And it must awake into life, not Durer's, nor Blake's, nor Milton's human form divine—nor yet [214] Nietzsche's superman, nor Patmore's catholic, boasting "a tongue that's dead"—the brood of the Sistine Chapel—but organic groups, *covens* of physical or intellectual kin melted out of the frozen mass. I imagine new races, as it were, seeking domination, a world resembling but for its immensity that of the Greek tribes—each with its own Daimon or ancestral hero—the brood of Leda, War and Love; history grown symbolic, the biography changed into a myth. Above all I imagine everywhere the opposites, no mere alternation between nothing and something like the Christian brute and ascetic, but true opposites, each living the other's death, dying the other's life.

It is said that the *primary* impulse "creates the event" but that the *antithetical* "follows it" and by this I understand that the Second Fountain will arise after a long preparation and as it were out of the very heart of human knowledge, and seem when it comes no interruption but a climax. It is possible that the ever increasing separation from the community as a whole of the cultivated classes, their increasing certainty, and that falling in two of the human mind which I have seen in certain works of art is preparation. During the period said to commence in 1927, with the 11th gyre, must arise a form of philosophy, which will become religious and ethical in the 12th gyre and be in all things opposite of that vast plaster Herculean image, final *primary* thought. It will be concrete in expression, establish itself by immediate experience, seek no general agreement, make little of God or any exterior unity, and it will call that good which a man can contemplate himself as doing always and no other doing at all. It will make a cardinal truth of man's immortality that its virtue may not lack sanction, and of the soul's re-embodiment that it may restore to virtue that long preparation none can give and hold death an interruption. [215] The supreme experience, Plotinus's ecstasy, ecstasy of the Saint, will recede, for men—finding it difficult —substituted dogma and idol, abstractions of all sorts, things beyond experience; and men may be long content with those more trivial supernatural benedictions as when Athena took Achilles by his yellow hair. Men will no longer separate the idea of God from that of human genius, human productivity in all its forms.

Unlike Christianity which had for its first Roman teachers cobblers and weavers, this thought must find expression among those that are most subtle, most rich in memory; that Gainsborough face floats up; among the learned—every sort of learning—among the rich—every sort of riches—among men of rank—every sort of rank —and the best of those that express it will be given power, less because of that they promise than of that they seem and are. This much can be thought because it is the reversal of what we know, but those kindreds once formed must obey irrational force and so create hitherto unknown experience, or that which is incredible.

Though it cannot interrupt the intellectual stream—being born from it and moving within it—it may grow a fanaticism and a terror, and at its first outsetting oppress the ignorant—even the innocent— as Christianity oppressed the wise, seeing that the day is far off when the two halves of man can define each its own unity in the other as in a mirror, Sun in Moon, Moon in Sun, and so escape out of the Wheel.

"Finished at Capri, February, 1925."

APPENDIX B

"*Michael Robartes Foretells*"—
Unpublished Typescript Written for
A Vision *and Rejected**

[1] Daniel O'Leary was sitting by a window at Thoor Ballylea [*sic*], watching a yellow flooded river, when Hudden, Dudden and Denice walked in unannounced.

"We heard you were here," said the first, "and have come from London to ask you a question."

"Yeats sent me the key" said L'Leary [*sic*]. "Somebody told him that I wanted to spend a week or two within reach of Coole House that I might look into the empty rooms, walk the woods and grass-grown gardens, where a great Irish social order climaxed and passed away."

"Have you the prophecy" said Dudden, "that Michael Robartes made at Albert Road? You wrote it out at the time. In London there are young men fresh from the Universities who perplex us. It is seven years since Michael Robartes disappeared into Arabia. Perhaps we are growing old."

"Yes, that is it." said Denice, smiling at Dudden, [2] "Even I am faithful to the past."

"One night I brought in some London Journalist," Dudden went on, "You began a Communistic argument; I said that the Proletariat was an abstraction and must disappear before the German and

* Original page numbers of typescript, in possession of Mrs. W. B. Yeats, appear in brackets.

Italian conception of the State moulded by History yet transparent to reason and at last completely intelligible; then the Journalist derided the State, argued that nothing mattered but internationalism, democracy and disarmament."

"Oh, yes, I remember." said O'Leary. "Robartes talked of the next Cycle, forgetting that the Journalist was ignorant of our terms, of the influx at the second, third and fourth Phases, said that some Asiatic Nation would base its whole civilisation upon War, that its governing class would take care of the common people as our governing class could not or would not, that they might obey in War and be loyal in defeat. [3] That its Schools and Universities would combine some Asiatic philosophy with the latest results of that psychical research founded by William Crookes, preparing all to face death without flinching, perhaps even with joy. As according to their philosophy the dead will not pass to a remote Heaven, but return to the Earth, it will seem as though the soldier's dead body manured the fields he himself would till. Furthermore, that they would subordinate class to class, that certain virtues created in leisure might descend to all; whatever music, dancings, painting, literature best served the perpetuation or perfection of the race or man's ultimate deliverance. Yet the State would be but little in men's minds, for the State as an idea, whatever definition we make of it, is but a degree less abstract than that of the Proletariat. Men's minds will dwell upon some company of governing men whom, though they seem every man's, even every base man's very self, it is natural to call noble."

"You are speaking from memory, I thought you had notes," said Hudden.

"No, not of those words. When you had shown the Journalist out and gone to your beds, I asked Robartes if I might [4] put them down. He said, no, he made them up while talking and didn't know whether they were true or not; he knew nothing of the next cycle except that it would be the reverse of ours. I begged him to say what we who took the gyres and cones as the framework of our thought might safely prophesy, and on that night and the two following, we sat late. I made notes and a few days later I wrote what I could remember. Here it is."

II

"We know that our own life, or the year, or the civilisation must pass through certain changes, that we, or it, approach the prime, or have passed it, that this or that character must increase or decrease, but we cannot know the particulars. When we speak of the past, we can say that in *Divina Comedia*, or the Russian Revolution, expressed such and such a phase, but are misled the moment we try to imagine some future work of art or historical event. [5]

"I will re-examine the Wheel. Every triad of phases is a separate Wheel. Whatever existence we think of, a Civilisation's or an individual's, it arises from the general mass, wins its victory and returns. All our morality is heroic, this falling back or falling asleep brings its gains with it though conventializes [*sic*], formalises, mechanizes. I reject Hegel's all-containing, all sustaining, all satisfying, fresh wakefulness. I reject Marxian Socialism, in so far as it is derived from him.

"The general mass, call it Nature, God, the Matrix, the Unconscious, what you will, becomes a unity when interlocked with some separating or subsiding existence; nor is it greater than that existence; the Will and Creative Mind of the one, the Mask and Body of Fate of the other, each dying, the others life, living the others death.

"The 22nd. phase of our civilisation has just passed, the Russian violence and the art and thought of our time, where even logic has compelled the isolation and exaggeration of a single element, represent the 23rd. phase, the first phase of the first Primary Triad; the Dictatorships in various parts of the world, including the Russian, are the approach of the 24th. Phase. So much we deduce from our general knowledge and from our Cones and symbols. [6] But after that we have nothing but our cones and symbols. From Phase 22. the *Creative Mind* and the *Body of Fate* cease to be *enforced*, man more and more accepts, more and more thinks his Fate. The *Creative Mind* from the twelfth century has been like stretched elastic, like a swaying pot, now the elastic is released, the pot recovers equilibrium.

"The antithetical is creative, painful—personal—the Primary imitative, happy, general. It is this imitativeness in which there is always happiness, that makes the Movements of our time attract the young. The art and politics of the antithetical age expressed a long maturing tradition and were best practised by old men. That age has ended in the old political juglers of liberal Democracy. I insist upon the paradox, that the old age of our civilisation begins with young men marching in step, with the shirts and songs that give our politics an air of sport. Phase 24. will perform the taks [task?] of Augustus, but the end of our civilisation will differ from that of an antithetical civilisation; the imitation of those who seem to express most completely the mass mind, the [7] discovery of the mass mind in ourselves, will create a political system, more pre-occupied with the common good, more derived from the common people than that of Rome and later Greece. Yet as Phase 25 draws near, in thirty or sixty years—we have no means of fixing the date, nor will it be the same date everywhere—men will turn from the leadership of men who offer nothing reason cannot understand. They will return to women, horses, dogs, prefer to the political meeting, the football field or whatever thirty or sixty years hence may have taken its place. Some equivalent preference will overtake occupations that have no part in politics; for all thought, under the pressure of some practical necessity will seek unity but weary of all reasoned expressions of that unity. I do not say reason will die as the pot ceases to sway, the return to the normal requires reason. An Achilles will be no longer possible, but some Virgil at Phase 24 may celebrate whatever popularisation our civilisation permits for the perfect official, carrying out the plan of an Olympian Board of Works amid many perils, amid much self-conquest; may he not gaze from his boat's deck on Dido's Pyre; some Ovid of the films, at Phase 25. surpass even his [8] popularity by celebrating our common casual pleasures. Every event will compel man's free acceptance of the external mask, objective man, life lived in common. Fate is multiple, particular, has as it were personality, but the Mask is always one.

"Merely personal distinction, as past times used the word, will be out of date, will no longer exist except in archaic studious circles, or as a pretension of the vulgar; the ugly will sting man to life because it rids him of the desire and hope he can no longer employ.

"I cannot say these things without hatred, I am an antithetical man, born in a still antithetical age, yet the men of that day, lacking our inequality, lacerations, artificialities, judged by any accepted standard will be happier than we are.

"Phases 24. and 25 must see the completion of a public ideal, its assimilation in the common civilisation, where all, whatever degree or rank and station remain, will live and think in much the same way. But at Phase 26. [9] will come, enforced by some intellectual necessity or change of circumstances impossible to foreknow, the knowledge of a form of existence, of a private aim opposite to any our civilisation has pursued. This knowledge affecting minorities, and organising their disgust, will create a turbulence, like that we see about us to-day, but moral and spiritual; the knowledge enforced upon Primary Minds of antithetical civilisation.*

* Note: In finding concrete events for the dates given me by my instructors, I considered that the historical chart was that of the Christian Era and what led to it. I considered this Era as a distinct cycle, different from those of Greece and Rome, but have the authority of my instructors for making it arise from that of Greece. We must consider the Roman cycle as two or three centuries later than that of Greece. I accept Schneider's identification of Virgil, Ovid, Nero, Epictetus with certain logical developments of Roman thought and I name those developments Phases. 24. 25. 26. 27. The personal exaggeration of Nero and his Court may be described as an antithetical vision of a Primary Ideal. In Epictetus that ideal is clearly seen, a Universal Being present in every particular person. A Primary Vision of an antithetical ideal might at Phase 26. be a moral and spiritual Nationalism, antinomean differences, personal in their final form, but first seen as differing ways of life.

NOTES

The following abbreviations have been employed in the notes:

J	*Jerusalem*
M	*Milton*
MHH	*The Marriage of Heaven and Hell*
4Z	*The Four Zoas*
Auto.	*The Autobiography of William Butler Yeats.* New York, 1953.
CL	*The Letters of W. B. Yeats.* Ed. Allan Wade. New York, 1955.
CP	*The Collected Poems of W. B. Yeats.* New York, 1952.
C Plays	*The Collected Plays of W. B. Yeats.* London, 1952.
CW	*The Collected Works in Verse and Prose of William Butler Yeats.* 8 vols. Stratford-on-Avon, 1908.
E-Y	*The Works of William Blake.* Eds. Edwin John Ellis and William Butler Yeats. 3 vols. London, 1893.
IGE	W. B. Yeats. *Ideas of Good and Evil.* London and Stratford, 1914.
K	*The Writings of William Blake.* Ed. Geoffrey Keynes. 3 vols. London, 1925.
PASL	W. B. Yeats. *Per Amica Silentia Lunae.* New York, 1918.
A Vision "A"	[W. B. Yeats.] *A Vision: An Explanation of Life Founded upon the Writings of Giraldus and upon Certain Doctrines Attributed to Kusta Ben Luka.* London, 1925.
A Vision "B"	W. B. Yeats. *A Vision.* New York, 1938.
Y-M	*W. B. Yeats and T. Sturge Moore, Their Correspondence, 1901–1937.* Ed. Ursula Bridge. London, 1953.

CHAPTER ONE

1. *CP*, 168.

2. *A Vision "B,"* 8.

3. *Ibid.*, 11.

4. *Feeling and Form* (New York, 1953), x.

5. *Ibid.*, xi.

6. *Philosophy in a New Key* (New York, 1948), 72.

7. *Essay on Man* (New Haven, 1944), 24–26.

8. "On the Philosophical Anthropology of Ernst Cassirer and Its Relation to the History of Anthropological Thought," in *The Philosophy of Ernst Cassirer*, ed. P. A. Schilpp (Evanston, 1949), 497.

9. *Feeling and Form*, 379 n.

10. "The Laocoon Group," *K*, III, 357.

11. Quoted by Vivienne Koch, *W. B. Yeats, the Tragic Phase* (London, 1951), 24.

12. "Blake's Treatment of the Archetype," *English Institute Essays, 1950*, ed. Allen S. Downer (New York, 1951), 185.

13. *A Vision "A,"* 133.

14. Intro. to "The Resurrection," *Wheels and Butterflies* (New York, 1935), 101.

15. *A Vision "B,"* 67.

16. *CL*, 917.

17. *CL*, 631.

18. *CP*, 169.

19. *CP*, 185.

20. *CP*, 229.

21. "A Prayer for My Daughter," *CP*, 187.

22. Intro. to *The Poems of William Blake* (New York: Modern Library, n.d.), xxiii.

23. *CP*, 191.

24. "Remorse for Intemperate Speech," *CP*, 249.

25. *CL*, 873.

26. "To a Poet, Who Would Have Me Praise Certain Bad Poets, Imitators of His and Mine," *CP*, 92.

27. "Rossetti MS," *K*, III, 67.

28. *CP*, 309.

29. *CP*, 205.

30. *K*, I, 287.

31. *CP*, 316.

32. *K*, I, 191–192.

33. "An Acre of Grass," *CP*, 299.

34. *MHH*, *K*, I, 186.

35. *CL*, 823–824.
36. *CL*, 825.
37. Aug. 7, 1934, *CL*, 826.
38. "Rossetti MS," *K*, I, 247.
39. "A Drinking Song," *CP*, 92.
40. "Meditations in Time of Civil War," *CP*, 202.
41. *Songs of Experience, K*, I, 288.
42. "Fragments," *CP*, 211.
43. *Ibid.*
44. *CP*, 258.
45. Oct. 27, 1927, *CL*, 730–731.
46. "Yeats and the Language of Symbolism," *University of Toronto Quarterly*, XVII (Oct. 1947), 1.

CHAPTER TWO

1. "The Laocoon Group," *K*, III, 358.
2. Letter to Thomas Butts, July 6, 1803, *K*, II, 246.
3. "A Vision of the Last Judgment," *K*, III, 145.
4. *Ibid.*, 162.
5. *K*, I, 107.
6. Annotations to Reynolds' *Discourses, K*, III, 25.
7. Annotations to Wordsworth's *Excursion, K*, III, 379.
8. Annotations to Wordsworth's *Poems, K*, III, 377.
9. *Ibid.*, 376.
10. *Fearful Symmetry* (Princeton, 1947), 19.
11. Annotations to Reynolds' *Discourses, K*, III, 13.
12. *Ibid.*, 25.
13. "A Public Address," *K*, III, 134.
14. *Feeling and Form*, 50–51.
15. Annotations to Lavater's *Aphorisms, K*, I, 116–117.
16. *Fearful Symmetry*, 21–22.
17. *K*, I, 187–188.
18. "A Public Address," *K*, III, 130.
19. *J, K*, III, 284.
20. *MHH, K*, I, 189.
21. Annotations to Swedenborg's *Divine Love, K*, I, 120.
22. "A Descriptive Catalogue," *K*, III, 108.
23. *MHH, K*, I, 187.
24. "A Descriptive Catalogue," *K*, III, 111.
25. "A Vision of the Last Judgment," *K*, III, 147.
26. Annotations to Reynolds' *Discourses, K*, III, 41.
27. "A Vision of the Last Judgment," *K*, III, 146.
28. *K*, I, 187.

29. *Ibid.,* 186.
30. "A Vision of the Last Judgment," *K,* III, 145.
31. Annotations to Reynolds' *Discourses, K,* III, 10–11.
32. Annotations to Wordsworth's *Poems, K,* III, 377.
33. *MHH, K,* I, 183.
34. "A Public Address," *K,* III, 133–134.
35. *K,* I, 195.
36. Letter to Thomas Butts, Jan. 10, 1802, *K,* II, 201.
37. "A Vision of the Last Judgment," *K,* III, 159.
38. D. J. Sloss and J. P. R. Wallis, *The Prophetic Writings of William Blake* (Oxford, 1926), II, 227.
39. *K,* I, 170.
40. "Rossetti MS," *K,* II, 218.
41. Annotations to Reynolds' *Discourses, K,* III, 44.
42. *M,* II, *K,* II, 218.
43. "A Public Address," *K,* III, 135.
44. "Edmund Spenser," *The Cutting of an Agate* (London, 1919), 220.
45. "All Religions Are One," *K,* I, 132.
46. *E-Y,* I, viii.
47. *E-Y,* II, 300.
48. *E-Y,* I, 337–338.
49. *William Blake: A Critical Study* (London, 1906; first pub. 1866), vii–viii.
50. Marginal annotation, Yeats's personal copy, *E-Y,* II, 2.
51. Letter in possession of Mrs. Yeats.
52. Letter in the Yeats collection of the National Library of Ireland.
53. Quoted by Joseph Hone, *W. B. Yeats, 1865–1939* (New York, 1941), 80.
54. Note on flyleaf of Yeats's personal copy of *E-Y.*
55. Marginal annotation, Yeats's personal copy, *E-Y,* I, 265.
56. "Yeats and the Language of Symbolism," *University of Toronto Quarterly,* XVII (Oct. 1947), 12.
57. *E-Y,* I, 238.
58. May 7, 1889, *CL,* 125.
59. *E-Y,* I, xii.
60. *Ibid.,* xiii.
61. *Ibid.,* 242.
62. *Ibid.,* 239.
63. *Ibid.,* xii.
64. *Ibid.,* 246ff.
65. *Ibid.,* 239.
66. *Ibid.,* 382–383.
67. *Ibid.,* 244.

68. *Ibid.*, 328.
69. *Ibid.*, 404.
70. *Ibid.*, 293.
71. *Ibid.*, 287.
72. "William Blake and the Imagination," *IGE*, 117.
73. "William Blake and His Illustrations," *IGE*, 123.
74. *Ibid.*
75. "William Blake and the Imagination," *IGE*, 117.
76. *Ibid.*, 120.
77. *E-Y*, I, 240.
78. *Ibid.*, 96.
79. *The Symbolist Movement in Literature* (London, 1899), 146.
80. *CL*, 211.

CHAPTER THREE

1. "There Is No Natural Religion," *K*, I, 130.
2. *The White Goddess* (New York, 1948), 378.
3. *K*, III, 111.
4. *Ibid.*, 109.
5. *Songs of Experience*, *K*, I, 287.
6. "A Descriptive Catalogue," *K*, III, 109.
7. *Ibid.*, 110.
8. *Ibid.*
9. "A Vision of the Last Judgment," *K*, III, 152
10. *K*, III, 221.
11. "Pickering MS," *K*, II, 232.
12. *Songs of Experience*, *K*, I, 286.
13. "A Vision of the Last Judgment," *K*, III, 151.
14. *MHH*, *K*, I, 182.
15. *K*, III, 145.
16. New York, 1953, 28.
17. "A Vision of the Last Judgment," *K*, III, 162.
18. Annotations to Reynolds' *Discourses*, *K*, III, 22.
19. Annotations to Watson's *Apology*, *K*, II, 164.
20. *Collected Poems* (New York, 1933), 178.
21. *The Poetic Image* (London, 1947), *passim*.
22. "Poetry and Design in William Blake," *Journal of Aesthetics and Art Criticism*, X (Sept. 1951), 41.
23. *K*, I, 304–305.
24. *Ibid.*, 304.
25. Hans L. Martenson, *Jacob Boehme*, trans. T. Rhys Evans (New York, 1949), 50.
26. "A Vision of the Last Judgment," *K*, III, 158.

27. "Urizen," *K*, I, 305.
28. *Ibid.*, 306.
29. *Ibid.*, 307.
30. *Ibid.*, 308.
31. *Ibid.*
32. Annotations to Reynolds' *Discourses*, *K*, III, 32.
33. "Urizen," *K*, I, 310.
34. *Ibid.*, 312.
35. "A Vision of the Last Judgment," *K*, III, 159.
36. "Urizen," *K*, I, 315.
37. *K*, I, 323.
38. *Life Symbols* (New York, 1928), 75.
39. "Urizen," *K*, I, 306.
40. "Ahania," *K*, I, 327.
41. *Ibid.*, 324.
42. "Europe," *K*, I, 298.
43. *Ibid.*
44. *Ibid.*
45. *Ibid.*, 299.
46. *Ibid.*, 303.
47. *Ibid.*, 301.
48 *K*, II, 273.

CHAPTER FOUR

1. *4Z*, I, *K*, II, 2.
2. *Ibid.*, 13.
3. *Ibid.*, 2.
4. *Ibid.*,'21.
5. *4Z*, II, *K*, II, 27.
6. *Ibid.*, 30–31.
7. *4Z*, VI, *K*, II, 67.
8. *Ibid.*, 69–70.
9. "Rossetti MS," *K*, III, 83.
10. *K*, I, 191.
11. *K*, II, 40.
12. Harold Bayley, *The Lost Language of Symbolism* (New York, 1951), I, 88.
13. *CP*, 337.
14. *CP*, 191.
15. "The Delphic Oracle upon Plotinus," *CP*, 264.
16. *4Z*, II, *K*, II, 30.
17. *4Z*, IV, *K*, II, 45.
18. *Ibid.*, 49.

19. *4Z*, I, *K*, II, 9.
20. *Ibid.*, 12.
21. *Ibid.*, 20.
22. *4Z*, VIII, *K*, II, 112–113.
23. *4Z*, IV, *K*, II, 53.
24. *4Z*, VIII, *K*, II, 102.
25. *Ibid.*, 103.
26. *Ibid.*, 104.
27. *Ibid.*, 109.
28. *Ibid.*, 111.
29. *Ibid.*, 119.
30. *Ibid.*, 113.
31. *Ibid.*
32. *4Z*, IX, *K*, II, 125–126.
33. *4Z*, VIII, *K*, II, 119.
34. *J*, IV, *K*, III, 310.
35. *4Z*, IX, *K*, II, 147.

CHAPTER FIVE

1. *J*, I, *K*, III, 174.
2. Letter to the Rev'd Dr. Trusler, Aug. 23, 1799, *K*, II, 174–176.
3. Mona Wilson, *The Life of William Blake* (London, 1948), 234.
4. *M*, I, *K*, II, 325–326.
5. *Ibid.*, 349–350.
6. "Crabb Robinson's Diary, &c.," in Arthur Symons, *William Blake* (New York, 1907), 291.
7. "The Trembling of the Veil," *Auto.*, 107.
8. *4Z*, VIII, *K*, II, 101.
9. *J*, I, *K*, III, 168.
10. *Ibid.*, 169–170.
11. *Ibid.*, 185.
12. *J*, *K*, III, 242.
13. *J*, II, *K*, III, 233.
14. *J*, I, *K*, III, 169.
15. *4Z*, VIIa, *K*, II, 85–86.
16. *J*, I, *K*, III, 173.
17. *Ibid.*, 183.
18. *Ibid.*
19. "An Acre of Grass," *CP*, 299.
20. "Rossetti MS," *K*, II, 214.
21. *J*, II, *K*, III, 225–226.
22. *J*, I, *K*, III, 183.
23. *Ibid.*, 188.

24. *Ibid.,* 185.
25. *Songs of Experience, K,* I, 278.
26. *A Vision "B,"* 279–280.
27. *J,* I, *K,* III, 191.
28. *4Z,* III, *K,* II, 40.
29. *J,* III, *K,* III, 274.
30. "A Descriptive Catalogue," *K,* III, 99.
31. *J,* II, *K,* III, 237.
32. *J,* IV, *K,* III, 292.
33. *Ibid.,* 314.
34. "A Descriptive Catalogue," *K,* III, 96.
35. *J,* II, *K,* III, 207.
36. *J,* III, *K,* III, 248.
37. *Ibid.,* 276.
38. *Blake and Modern Thought* (London, 1929), 82.
39. *Ibid.,* 85.
40. W. B. Yeats's annotation, *ibid.,* 63.
41. *Ibid.,* 85.
42. "A Vision of the Last Judgment," *K,* III, 145.
43. *Ibid.,* 146.
44. *J, K,* III, 177.
45. "Seven Propositions," among Yeats MS.
46. *Attitudes toward History* (New York, 1937), I, 71.
47. *Ibid.,* 218.
48. "A Descriptive Catalogue," *K,* III, 101.
49. *Ibid.,* 98.
50. *M,* preface, *K,* II, 305.

CHAPTER SIX

1. "The Trembling of the Veil," *Auto.,* 210.
2. Reproduced in Arthur Symons, *William Blake,* 348.
3. *Ibid.,* 349.
4. *William Blake: A Critical Study* (London, 1866).
5. "The Trembling of the Veil," *Auto.,* 70.
6. See letter to Ernest Boyd, *CL,* 592.
7. Page v.
8. Paul Berger, *William Blake: Mysticisme et Poésie* (Paris, 1907).
9. See A. N. Whitehead, *Science and the Modern World* (New York, 1941), chs. iii–v.
10. *Axël's Castle* (New York, 1932), 4–5.
11. *The Works of Dante Gabriel Rossetti,* ed. W. M. Rossetti (London, 1911), 92.
12. *Moby Dick* (New York, 1946), 532.

13. *Language and Myth,* 9–10.

14. *Ibid.,* 56.

15. *Ibid.,* 91–92.

16. *Works,* 596.

17. *Ibid.,* 597.

18. *The Letters of William Michael Rossetti* (Durham, 1934), 4.

19. See S. Foster Damon, *William Blake: His Philosophy and Symbols* (Boston, 1924), 131.

20. *William Blake: A Critical Study,* 99–100.

21. *Ibid.,* 212.

22. Quoted by Louis MacNeice, *The Poetry of W. B. Yeats* (New York, 1941), 52–53.

23. Quoted by Louis Untermeyer, *Modern British Poetry* (New York, 1950), 7.

24. *The Renaissance* (New York: Modern Library, n.d.), 196.

25. *The Symbolist Movement in Literature,* 132.

26. *CP,* 7.

27. *Science and the Modern World,* 80.

28. *CP,* 8–9.

29. *CP,* 14.

30. *CP,* 19.

31. *CP,* 70.

32. *CP,* 67.

33. "The Trembling of the Veil," *Auto.,* 196.

34. *Pages from a Diary Written in 1930* (Dublin, 1944), 50.

35. "Reveries over Childhood and Youth," *Auto.,* 45.

36. "Synge and the Ireland of his Time," *The Cutting of an Agate,* 172.

37. "The Trembling of the Veil," *Auto.,* 165.

38. "Reveries over Childhood and Youth," *Auto.,* 17.

39. *Further Letters of John Butler Yeats,* ed. Lennox Robinson (Dundrum, 1920), 22–23.

40. *Ibid.,* 25.

41. *CW, IV,* 117.

42. *Ibid.,* 124, 148.

43. *Ibid.,* 153.

44. *Ibid.,* 155.

45. "Reveries over Childhood and Youth," *Auto.,* 49–50.

46. *On the Boiler* (Dublin, 1938), 15.

47. "The Trembling of the Veil," *Auto.,* 70–71.

48. *The Symbolist Movement in Literature,* 5.

49. "Reveries over Childhood and Youth," *Auto.,* 55.

50. *Ibid.,* 48.

51. "Magic," *IGE*, 21.
52. *Ibid.*, 30.
53. *Ibid.*, 42–43.
54. "The Philosophy of Shelley's Poetry," *IGE*, 75.
55. "Dramatis Personae," *Auto.*, 300.
56. Quoted by Richard Ellmann, *Yeats: The Man and the Masks* (New York, 1948), 55.
57. "The Trembling of the Veil," *Auto.*, 93.
58. "The Philosophy of Shelley's Poetry," *IGE*, 89–90.
59. "Magic," *IGE*, 46–47.
60. "The Trembling of the Veil," *Auto.*, 164.
61. "Magic," *IGE*, 45.
62. *Y-M*, 59.
63. *Ibid.*, 63–64.
64. *Ibid.*, 67–68.
65. *Ibid.*, 70.
66. *Ibid.*, 81.
67. *Ibid.*, 92.
68. *Ibid.*, 106.
69. "William Blake and His Illustrations," *IGE*, 123.
70. "Edmund Spenser," *The Cutting of an Agate*, 200.
71. *Ibid.*, 202.
72. "The Symbolism of Poetry," *IGE*, 176–177.
73. *Ibid.*, 173.

CHAPTER SEVEN

1. *A Vision "B,"* 8.
2. "To Ezra Pound," *ibid.*, 27.
3. Quoted by A. N. Jeffares, *W. B. Yeats: Man and Poet* (New Haven, 1949), 267.
4. *Y-M*, 131.
5. *Pages from a Diary Written in 1930*, 18–19.
6. *CW*, VII, 105–106.
7. "Reveries over Childhood and Youth," *Auto.*, 48.
8. *CW*, VII, 110.
9. *Ibid.*, 113.
10. *Ibid.*, 114–115.
11. *Ibid.*, 116.
12. See Appendix "B."
13. *CW*, VII, 130–131.
14. *Ibid.*, 135.
15. *Ibid.*, 144–145.
16. *Ibid.*, 147.

17. *Ibid.*, 153.
18. *Ibid.*, 160.
19. "The Speckled Bird," *The Bell*, I (March 1941), 23ff.
20. "Swedenborg, Mediums, and the Desolate Places," *If I Were Four and Twenty* (Dublin, 1940), 24.
21. "J. M. Synge and the Ireland of his Time," *The Cutting of an Agate*, 145–146.
22. *A Vision "A,"* xi–xii.
23. Introduction to "The Resurrection," *Wheels and Butterflies*, 93, and *A Vision "B,"* 11.
24. Introduction to "The Resurrection," *Wheels and Butterflies*, 95.
25. Introduction to "The Cat and the Moon," *ibid.*, 124–125.
26. Unpublished typescript for *A Vision*.
27. *Y-M*, 117.
28. Unpublished typescript for *A Vision*.
29. *A Vision "B,"* 246.
30. Preface to "The Holy Mountain," *Essays 1931–1936* (Dublin, 1937). 114.
31. *Ibid.*, 114–115.
32. *A Vision "B,"* 248.
33. *4Z*, II, *K*, II, 30–31.
34. *A Vision "B,"* 249.
35. Unpublished typescript for *A Vision*. Further discussion of the sphere in Chapter IX.
36. *A Vision "B,"* 248–249.
37. *Ibid.*, 69.
38. *Ibid.*, 72.
39. *Four Plays for Dancers* (New York, 1921), 434.
40. *Wheels and Butterflies*, 109.
41. *A Vision "B,"* 262.
42. "Estrangement," *Auto.*, 298.
43. *CP*, 135.
44. Introduction to "The Cat and the Moon," *Wheels and Butterflies*, 124.
45. *CP*, 164–165.
46. *A Vision "B,"* 248.
47. *Ibid.*, 54–55.
48. *Ibid.*, 38.
49. *A Vision "A,"* xviii.
50. *A Vision "B,"* 41.
51. *A Vision "A,"* xix.
52. *Ibid.*, xxi.
53. *A Vision "B,"* 55.

54. *CP*, 161, and *A Vision "B,"* 60.
55. *CP*, 164.
56. *A Vision "A,"* xxiii.
57. "The Scholars," *CP*, 139.
58. *A Vision "A,"* 9–11.
59. Unpublished typescript for *A Vision.*
60. "The Trembling of the Veil," *Auto.*, 159.
61. *A Vision "B,"* 22–23.
62. Unpublished typescript for *A Vision.*
63. *A Vision "B,"* 8.
64. *Ibid.*, 8–9.
65. *Pages from a Diary Written in 1930*, 58.
66. *A Vision "B,"* 11.
67. *Ibid.*, 10.
68. *Ibid.*, 13.
69. *Ibid.*
70. *Ibid.*, 5.
71. *Ibid.*, 13–14.
72. *Ibid.*, 14.
73. *Ibid.*, 21.
74. *Ibid.*, 19.
75. *Ibid.*, 33.
76. *Ibid.*, 51.
77. *Ibid.*, 22.

CHAPTER EIGHT

1. "A Needle's Eye," *CP*, 287.
2. Unpublished typescript for *A Vision.*
3. *A Vision "B,"* 268.
4. Introduction to *The Ten Principal Upanishads* (New York, 1937), 8.
5. *CP*, 211–212.
6. "Fragments," *CP*, 211.
7. "Whence Had They Come," *CP*, 286.
8. "Tom at Cruachan," *CP*, 264.
9. "The Trembling of the Veil," *Auto.*, 119–120.
10. *CP*, 283.
11. *A Vision "B,"* 52.
12. Quoted by A. N. Jeffares, *W. B. Yeats: Man and Poet*, 266.
13. *CP*, 240.
14. *CP*, 282–283.
15. "Nineteen Hundred and Nineteen," *CP*, 206.
16. "Rossetti MS," *K*, II, 210.
17. "Demon and Beast," *CP*, 183.

18. "Death," *CP*, 230.
19. *CP*, 260.
20. *CP*, 210.
21. "Two Songs from a Play," *CP*, 211.
22. *A Vision "B,"* 11.
23. See Yeats's discussion of these terms in *A Vision "B,"* 73ff.
24. *Ibid.*, 89.
25. *E-Y*, I, 308.
26. *Four Plays for Dancers*, 137–138.
27. *On the Boiler*, 25.
28. *A Vision "B,"* 272–273.
29. "The Mother of God," *CP*, 244.
30. *A Vision "B,"* 273.
31. *Ibid.*
32. *A Vision "B,"* 183–184.
33. Preface to *The Herne's Egg and Other Plays* (New York, 1938), vi.
34. *The White Goddess*, 10.
35. *Ibid.*, 10, 319–320.
36. *C Plays*, 624.
37. *Ibid.*
38. *Ibid.*, 626.
39. *Pages from a Diary Written in 1930*, 8.
40. *CP*, 237.
41. *CP*, 218ff.
42. *Ibid.*, 219–220.
43. *CP*, 144–145.
44. *A Vision "B,"* 270.
45. *Ibid.*, 261–262.
46. *Wheels and Butterflies*, 101.
47. *Ibid.*, 102.
48. *A Vision "B,"* 285.
49. *Wheels and Butterflies*, 22.
50. *CP*, 211.
51. *A Vision "B,"* 50.
52. *CP*, 167.
53. *Ibid.*
54. *A Vision "A,"* 213.
55. *CP*, 185.
56. "Easter 1916," *CP*, 178.
57. *J*, I, *K*, III, 183.
58. *CP*, 214.
59. *CP*, 184.
60. *A Vision "B,"* 280.

61. *Ibid.*, 214.
62. *K*, I, 303.
63. *Songs of Experience, K*, I, 284.
64. *J*, III, *K*, III, 248.
65. Letter to Thomas Butts, Nov. 22, 1802, *K*, II, 205.
66. *Essays 1931–1936*, 62.
67. *A Vision "B,"* 203.
68. *Ibid.*, 211–212.
69. *A Vision "A,"* 133–134.
70. *A Vision "B,"* 213.
71. *William Blake: His Philosophy and Symbols*, 131.
72. "Pickering MS," *K*, II, 223.
73. *A Vision "A,"* 133–134.
74. *Oswald Spengler, A Critical Estimate* (New York and London, 1952), 29–30.
75. *The Decline of the West*, tr. C. F. Atkinson (New York, 1926), I, 19–20.
76. *A Vision "B,"* 18.
77. *Ibid.*, 11.
78. *The Decline of the West*, 40.
79. See Appendix "B."
80. *A Vision "B,"* 24–25.
81. *Ibid.*, 300.
82. *C Plays*, 678.
83. *A Vision "B,"* 301–302.
84. *C Plays*, 323.
85. *Ibid.*
86. "There," *CP*, 284.

CHAPTER NINE

1. "The Circus Animals' Desertion," *CP*, 336.
2. *C Plays*, 318.
3. "Under Ben Bulben," *CP*, 342.
4. *PASL*, 50–51.
5. "Estrangement," *Auto.*, 279.
6. "The Trembling of the Veil," *Auto.*, 53.
7. "Estrangement," *Auto.*, 285.
8. *A Vision "B,"* 213.
9. *PASL*, 29.
10. *A Vision "B,"* 192.
11. "The Death of Synge," *Auto.*, 306.
12. *A Vision "B,"* 193.

13. *PASL*, 72–73.
14. "Demon and Beast," *CP*, 183.
15. *PASL*, 85.
16. "No Second Troy," *CP*, 89.
17. "At Stratford-on-Avon," *IGE*, 112.
18. "Old Tom Again," *CP*, 264.
19. Unpublished typescript for *A Vision*.
20. "Ribh in Ecstasy," *CP*, 283.
21. *Essays 1931–1936*, 113.
22. *A Vision "B,"* 182.
23. *MHH, K*, I, 184.
24. *PASL*, 72–73.
25. *Four Plays for Dancers*, 136.
26. *The Golden Nightingale* (New York, 1949), 77.
27. *C Plays*, 303.
28. *CP*, 121.
29. "An Image from Past Life," *CP*, 176.
30. *CP*, 107.
31. *CP*, 250.
32. "The Hawk," *CP*, 147.
33. *C Plays*, 702.
34. *Ibid.*, 704.
35. *CP*, 133.
36. *CP*, 130.
37. *CP*, 25.
38. *C Plays*, 704–705.
39. *A Vision "B,"* 137.
40. *Ibid.*, 137–138.
41. *Ibid.*, 138–139.
42. *Ibid.*, 141.
43. "Coole Park and Ballylee," *CP*, 239.
44. *A Vision "B,"* 268.
45. *Y-M*, 38.
46. *CP*, 323.
47. "The Rose Tree," *CP*, 181.
48. *CP*, 224.
49. "The Later Poetry of W. B. Yeats," *The Permanence of Yeats*, eds. James Hall, and Martin Steinmann (New York, 1950), 55.
50. *CP*, 192.
51. *CP*, 243.
52. *Pages from a Diary Written in 1930*, 49–50.
53. *Wheels and Butterflies*, 108.
54. *C Plays*, 243.

55. *Letters on Poetry from W. B. Yeats to Dorothy Wellesley* (New York, 1949), 202.
56. *Ibid.,* 13.
57. *On the Boiler,* 35.
58. Introduction to "The Indian Monk," *Essays 1931–1936,* 86.
59. "Crazy Jane Talks with the Bishop," *CP,* 255.
60. *Y-M,* 154.
61. *CP,* 291.
62. *Letters on Poetry,* 8–9.
63. "J. M. Synge and the Ireland of His Time," *The Cutting of an Agate,* 147.
64. *Letters on Poetry,* 69–70.
65. *Ibid.,* 8.
66. *CP,* 291.
67. *J, I, K,* III, 188.
68. Quoted by Yeats in *PASL,* 68.
69. *CP,* 338–339.
70. *A Vision "B,"* 240.
71. Unpublished typescript for *A Vision.*
72. *A Vision "B,"* 193.
73. *Ibid.*
74. *Ibid.,* 210.
75. *Ibid.,* 194–195.
76. *Ibid.,* 240.
77. "Sweet Dancer," *CP,* 293–294.
78. *CP,* 301.
79. "Among School Children," *CP,* 214.
80. *A Vision "B,"* 213–214.
81. *CP,* 268.
82. *CP,* 175.
83. *CP,* 324.
84. *A Vision "B,"* 263.
85. Introduction to "The Cat and the Moon," *Wheels and Butterflies,* 140.
86. *A Vision "B,"* 213.
87. *PASL,* 38.
88. *C Plays,* 114.
89. Yeats's MS.
90. "Under Ben Bulben," *CP,* 341.

CHAPTER TEN

1. Quoted by Kurt Seligmann, *The Mirror of Magic* (New York, 1948), 159.

2. Quoted by A. N. Jeffares, *W. B. Yeats: Man and Poet*, 267.

3. *On the Boiler*, 36.

4. *Pages from a Diary Written in 1930*, 15.

5. *The Limitations of Science* (New York, 1949), 19.

6. *The Kaballah Unveiled* (London, 1887), 15–16.

7. *A Vision "B,"* 300.

8. *On the Boiler*, 25.

9. Quoted by Jeffares, *W. B. Yeats: Man and Poet*, 351.

10. *On the Boiler*, 21.

11. Letter to the Rev'd Dr. Trusler, Aug. 23, 1799, *K*, II, 175.

Index